THE COLLINS GUIDE TO DOG NUTRITION

The COLLINS GUIDE to
DOG NUTRITION

by
Donald R. Collins, DVM

ILLUSTRATED

Sixth Printing–1982

HOWELL BOOK HOUSE INC.
230 Park Avenue
New York, N.Y. 10169

Copyright © 1972 by Donald R. Collins, DVM
Library of Congress Catalog Card No. 79-182241
ISBN 0-87605-418-1   Printed in U.S.A.

Contents

Part V—Fact and Fancy

Foreword

It was good news to learn that Dr. Donald Collins has written this book on dog nutrition. It was badly needed. Many technical publications are available for veterinarians but THE COLLINS GUIDE TO DOG NUTRITION fills a long felt want by owners of dogs of all breeds whether kept as pets or whole kennelsful.

Dog feeding has come a long way since the days of hush puppies, table scraps or mixtures of boiled cornmeal and lard. Dr. Collins has taken much of the confusion out of the problem facing the dog owner who is confronted with the vast display of dog foods offered by supermarkets.

In 20 helpful chapters the author has answered the why, what and how questions of dog dietetics for all breeds under all environmental conditions and for all purposes.

The author, Dr. Donald R. Collins, is the ideal authority to present this valuable knowledge to the lay leader. His qualifications include years in the field as a practicing veterinarian and seven years as the Director of Professional Education for Mark Morris Associates, nationally recognized nutritional consultants in research, development and education of small animal practitioners. To his professional competence he adds the happy faculty of being able to communicate with the general public, including young people. Among his credits are highly acclaimed articles in *Sports Afield*, *The Rotarian*, and *Scholastic* magazines. His work has given him inside knowledge of the pet food industry and deep appreciation for the real, day to day problems encountered by dog owners as they attempt to feed their pets properly. The many letters he receives from owners seeking answers to feeding problems have enabled him to accumulate much practical and valuable material for inclusion in this book. He knows what dog owners want to know on practical dog feeding.

7

Dr. Collins tells the reader the essential facts about commercial and non-commercial dog foods of all kinds and how to evaluate them in terms of a balanced diet. He describes equipment, feeding methods and how much to feed. He gives feeding programs for the growing dog, the pregnant bitch, the house pet, show dogs, sporting dogs and working dogs. His chapter on feeding the sick dog can be most helpful in accelerating convalescence and recovery. For owners who wish to "do it themselves," he gives instructions for formulating a well-balanced homemade diet using common household items at low cost.

As a breeder of over 12,000 dogs in the past 50 years, I can attest to the soundness of Dr. Collins' information. And as a writer of more than 50 books on pets, I heartily commend this fascinating, educational work to dog lovers everywhere.

Leon F. Whitney, D.V.M.

Preface

THE wild forefathers of our modern dog were forced to hunt their own food. They spent most of their time and energy in search of enough food to last them from one meal to the next. When man brought modern dog's ancestor into the cave with him, he assumed the responsibility for replacing the foods the dog left behind him, outside the cave. This responsibility has proven to be no easy task!

The most important thing any dog owner does for his dog is feeding it. He only needs to housetrain it once in a lifetime. He only vaccinates it once a year. He bathes it when it is dirty or grooms it before a show, but he feeds it every day of every year of the dog's life.

Some people feed their dogs today the same way dog books recommended they be fed in 1900. That's because some dog books haven't changed their section on "Dog Nutrition" since that time. This book is written for *today's* dog feeders. It is not really about dog nutrition, it is about dog feeding. It does not emphasize nutritional deficiencies, but instead nutritional adequacies. It does not spend unnecessary time telling the dog feeder about what happens when he feeds his dog the wrong way, but rather it tells him how best to feed his dog the right way. It is not a book designed to make the reader a dog-feeding expert, only to enable him to begin a successful feeding program—a feeding program that adequately nourishes his dog.

This book is divided into five sections—Why a Dog is Fed, What a Dog is Fed, How a Dog is Fed, Feeding Programs, and Feeding Fact and Fancy.

There is only one reason *why* a dog owner becomes a dog feeder —to provide his dog with adequate nourishment. If his feeding program fails to do this, the dog feeder might just as well stop feeding

9

altogether. By not feeding he will accomplish the same results as improper feeding, and for a great deal less trouble and expense.

Faced with the daily task of properly feeding his dog, the modern dog feeder's most common question is, "What food should I feed?" Those who have tried to answer that question know there is no simple answer. With over 1,500 manufacturers of pet foods marketing foods, under 10,000 brand labels, the job of choosing a food to feed a dog can be a staggering task. Staggering, that is, unless one has an expert to eliminate the inadequate foods and choose between the adequate ones. And, every dog feeder has just such an expert. In fact, he is the *only* expert when it comes to what to feed a dog. That expert is the dog, itself. Dog feeders only can become expert in understanding what their dog tells them about the food it is eating.

All research remains useless, both for those for whom it was done and for those who did it, until it has been put to some useful application. One of the applications that is most useful is that of showing us how to do something correctly. A lot of research has been completed in dog nutrition since 1900. Most of it has been incorporated into this book in some form or fashion. What could not be worked directly into one of the three sections was compiled into related groupings and appended as a ready reference for those dog feeders who wish to explore the science of nutrition and its application to the art of feeding at a greater length.

No book is the work of one man, particularly a book like this one. Its contents reflect the accumulated efforts of mankind, from the first one who shared his cave with a wild dog to the typesetter and printer who converted this paper into a printed page. To each of them, and to every man in between, the reader of this book owes a little debt of gratitude. But, to a few of them in particular, the author owes a large debt of gratitude and publicly acknowledges that debt at this time.

To Dr. Mark Morris, Sr. for inspiring me, Dr. Mark Morris, Jr. for instructing me, and Mr. Claude Ramsey who opened the first door, I am grateful for your help. To Mr. E.S. Howell for encouraging me I am grateful for your trust. To my wife Elise and daughters Camille, Cathy and Cindy, for not forgetting who that guy at the typewriter in the basement was, I am grateful for your patience.

And, most of all, to Him whom I have yet to meet, I am grateful for the mind and body that made all of this possible in the first place.

Donald R. Collins, D.V.M.

10

PART I

WHY THE DOG IS FED

Chapter 1

To Feed 100-million Tiny Fires

THE dog is a living creature. It lives because it burns—not in one great big fire, but in 100-million tiny fires throughout its body. If these fires go out, the dog dies.

The tiny fires burn in the cells of the dog's body. Except for a flame, the fires are similar in many ways to those burning in a furnace or in a fireplace. They both require fuel, they both require oxygen, and they both convert the fuel into heat and energy.

The fires burning in the dog's cells use the food that the dog eats as fuel. Within each cell tiny particles of food become the central figure in a chain of chemical reactions. At the end of the chain the food particle has been changed into carbon dioxide, water and a molecule of *adenosine triphosphate*, called ATP, for short. ATP is the main source of energy in the dog's body.

As food is converted into ATP energy, heat is also produced. This heat helps to maintain the dog's body temperature around 101.5°F. The chemical reactions—the tiny fires of the body—will not occur except at the proper temperature, and in a dog that temperature is ideal at 101.5°F. If the body's temperature drops too low the fires go out and the dog dies.

Every dog, then, must produce a certain amount of ATP and heat if it is to live. The quantity of energy and heat production a dog needs just to stay alive has been obtained by measuring the amount of heat produced by a fasting, resting animal. This quantity of energy and heat is called the *basal metabolic rate*, or BMR. The

13

BMR of a dog varies with its size. An active dog's metabolic rate may fluctuate considerably above this basal rate depending on how hard the dog works, the environmental temperature, emotional and physiological stress, etc.

The ability to convert fuel into energy (food into ATP) is one of the characteristics of life. The other characteristics—the ability to react to stimuli and transmit impulses, the ability to grow and reproduce, and the ability to move—all require that energy if they are to occur and the dog is to live.

Most dogs do more than simply live, however. They walk and run, they hunt and play, they grow and repair, and they periodically overcome disease. All of these things, as well as everything else the dog does, requires energy from ATP. How well a dog is able to produce energy to perform the activities of life, play and work is directly related to the quality and quantity of food it eats. The quality and quantity of food a dog eats is determined by the nutrients within that food.

The production of energy is the first priority for which all nutrients are used. Without energy the vital functions of the body grind to a halt. Every day of its life a dog must produce enough heat to maintain its body temperature and enough energy to support its heart-beat, breathing, urine production, nerve irritability, and all the other basal metabolic functions necessary to keep a dog alive. The activities of basal metabolism have top priority for every bit of energy available. Once the energy requirements of basal metabolism have been met any remaining energy will be used according to other priorities, such as wound repair, infection fighting, growth, work, play or other activities.

The ability of a nutrient to produce energy is measured in terms of *calories*. Calories actually measure the nutrients' ability to produce heat. But, the ability of a nutrient to produce heat parallels its ability to produce ATP, so calories are also an accurate measure of the energy a nutrient produces. For each gram of fat the dog eats it produces about nine calories. For each gram of protein and carbohydrate about four calories are produced.

The number of calories in a food can be determined several ways. The most accurate way, and the one used by nutritionists, is to actually burn the food and measure the amount of heat it produces. Another way, and one convenient for dog feeders, is to calculate how many calories are in the food by multiplying the number of cal-

14

ories each type of nutrient produces by the amount of that nutrient present in the food. The amount of a nutrient in a food can be obtained either by actually analyzing a sample of the food or by calculating the amount from the ingredients in the food.

Because energy is the top priority for which all food is used, *a dog eats to meet its needs for calories.* This is one of the most important and fundamental principles of dog feeding. If a dog requires 1500 calories each day, and it is fed a food containing 1500 calories in every pound, it will eat a pound of that food every day. If it is fed a food containing 750 calories in every pound that dog will eat two pounds each day. If the food being fed contains only 500 calories per pound then the dog will eat three pounds each day. This can be continued until a point is reached where no dog could consume the quantity needed to provide it with the calories it must have. Since all dogs eat to meet their caloric needs, the number of calories in a pound of dog food is among the most important bits of information a dog feeder must know about the food that he feeds.

Proteins, fats and carbohydrates all produce energy. The most efficient source of energy the dog can eat is fat. Fat supplies the dog with more than twice as much ATP and heat as similar amounts of carbohydrates and proteins would supply. The major role of fat in

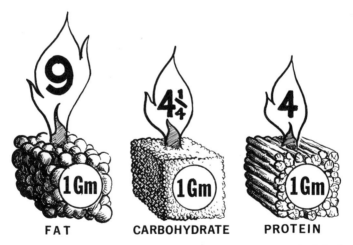

Figure 1. All nutrients are fuel for the 100-million tiny fires in a dog's body. Fat is the most efficient fuel and furnishes twice as much energy as carbohydrates and proteins furnish.

15

any dog's diet is that of furnishing energy. In fact, without at least some fat, no diet can supply the dog with enough energy to meet its caloric needs and still spare other nutrients for their essential roles elsewhere. This fact has significance to dog feeders because it means that if a food is marginal in energy the essential nutrients for growth, enzyme production, blood formation, or combating infections may be diverted into energy. When sufficient fat is present, and enough energy is available in the diet, the nutrients needed for such purposes are likewise available.

The chemical reactions that convert food to ATP occur in a stepwise manner, each step in the proper sequence. This sequence is maintained by substances called enzymes. A particular enzyme appears, triggers a reaction when its turn comes, then disappears after the reaction has gone far enough and another enzyme appears to trigger the next reaction. The chemicals that a cell utilizes to make these enzymes come from the food the dog eats. Without food the dog cannot produce enzymes, the tiny fires will not burn, and the dog dies.

Some of the most important enzymes cannot perform their role of regulating chemical reactions without the presence of a metal, such as zinc or copper. It may require only a minute amount of the metal, but without it the enzyme remains functionless. Other enzymes require the assistance of substances called co-enzymes. Co-enzymes are frequently vitamins, or else vitamins form an integral part of the co-enzyme molecule. Since the dog's cells are unable to manufacture either the metals or the vitamins, the food a dog eats must contain them, as well as fuel, if it is to supply energy. Without minerals and vitamins from its food, the dog's fires will go out and the dog will die.

A dog's food supplies more than just energy. When a food has adequate calories to meet the dog's energy needs that food will also supply the raw materials with which the dog builds the house in which it lives, its body.

16

Chapter 2

To Build a House

THE first reason every dog must be fed is to supply it with fuel to keep the 100-million tiny energy-producing fires in its body from going out. The second reason a dog must be fed is to furnish the dog with the raw materials needed to build and maintain the house within which it lives, its body.

Growing dogs are like houses under construction—complex structures made from many different materials put together in a definite order and arrangement.

During growth the body actively produces virtually every structural element (e.g. bone, tendon, nervous tissue, organs, glands, muscles, blood etc.), every chemical (e.g. proteins, hormones, enzymes, co-enzymes etc.) and every metabolic waste product that it will produce during all the phases of its life cycle except for lactation. At each stage of growth the puppy's body will demand the proper raw materials, balanced and in adequate amounts, in order to maintain a uniform and successful growth to maturity. If you do not use the best materials and workmanship when you build a house it is much more difficult, and sometimes impossible, to remake or replace the defective parts after the house has been completed. If you provide second-rate materials to your growing dog it can build only a second-rate body. If you provide a puppy with the best raw materials available, in the proper order and amounts, the puppy will reward you with the best body its genetic makeup will allow it to produce.

17

Without such materials a puppy will build an inferior body, whatever its heritage.

A dog must be fed from the time it is nothing more than a pair of cells. As the two cells become four, the four—eight, the eight—sixteen, and so on, until the unborn puppy is within minutes of being born, it is fed directly and without choice by its mother. Once born, a puppy continues to be fed by its mother, but by a less obligatory and somewhat more indirect method. Finally, about 6 or 7 weeks later, the mother dog tires completely of the sharp little teeth and the confinements of constant maternal care, and discards her feeding role entirely. From that day onward the job of properly providing a dog with a nourishing diet rests solely with you, the dog feeder.

During the first six months of its life, when growth is most rapid, a healthy, properly fed puppy will enjoy a constant, uniform growth rate, Figure 2. The average puppy will increase its birthweight 15 to 40 times (depending on breed) during this period. By the time it is a year old, a puppy will have increased its birth weight by 30 to 60 times! Figure 3 illustrates the growth rate of a human being compared to several breeds of dogs during the same period of growth. The slope of these curves dramatically illustrates that the nutritional needs of a puppy are far more critical than those of children. A mother can allow several days to escape without becoming concerned about an adequate meal or the balanced nutrition of her child and the infant suffers little. For the dog feeder to allow the same few days to elapse before becoming alarmed about improperly feeding a puppy may be waiting until it is too late.

As the puppy reaches maturity, its need for increased energy and raw materials slowly decreases. The puppy's behavior frequently reflects this change. To the dog owner unfamiliar with this occurrence this behavior often is mistaken for some illness because it consists of reduced activity, a loss of curiosity and a lowered food intake. The change is a perfectly natural and expected happening, however, and heralds the end of a puppy's growth phase. It also serves as an excellent signal to dog feeders that the time has come to change the dog's diet from one designed to support growth to one designed to support maintenance.

The raw materials a dog uses for body-building and maintenance are called *nutrients*. Like energy, the dog must have nutrients to live. Like energy, the dog obtains nutrients from the food it eats. The growing dog needs about twice as much energy and nutrients as

18

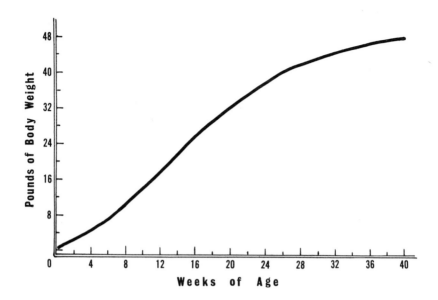

Figure 2. A puppy should grow at a steady, uniform rate. This is an average body weight curve for healthy, growing, hunting-dog-type pups, from birth to 40 weeks of age.

Figure 3. A human baby grows for 20 years before reaching maturity. A puppy grows for only about 20 months. This means that things happen to a growing dog about 12 times faster than to a baby, and feeding a pup improperly for only one month is like feeding a baby improperly for a whole year!

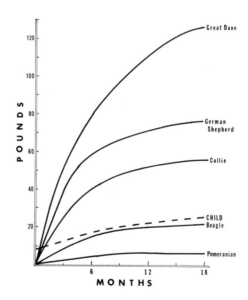

19

the adult dog needs. Evidence is beginning to accumulate to show that some nutrients may even be needed in amounts up to 10 times the adult maintenance requirements during certain critical periods of growth.

There are six kinds of nutrients required by every dog to build a strong body and to maintain it in a healthy condition. These are, water, protein, fats, carbohydrates, vitamins and minerals. The least amount of a nutrient that will sustain a dog in a healthy condition for a 24-hour period is called the *minimum daily requirement* (MDR) of that nutrient. A nutrient's MDR changes for each phase of a dog's life cycle. These phases are growth, maintenance, work, pregnancy and lactation.

Water

The dog's body can lose all of its fat and half of its protein and still live, but if its body loses only one-tenth of its water, the dog dies. An adult dog needs at least two milliliters (mls) of water for every pound it weighs every day if it is to live. There are 30 mls of water in one ounce. The two mls are used by the dog for urine production. Without the ability to produce urine any dog will die.

When offered an unrestricted amount of water, dogs will drink considerably more than these essential two mls. The additional water will be used to aid in the digestion and absorption of nutrients, the burning of fuel for energy, the maintenance of the body's temperature, and the replacement of water lost in body secretions. Water forms the great mixing medium into which the many chemicals of the body are dissolved, and within which chemical reactions (the body's tiny fires) can occur. Water is necessary for the transportation of nutrients to the cells and the transfer of toxic waste products from the cells to the organs of elimination. Without water these organs are unable to eliminate toxic substances from the body. Water is also a must for the regulation of the blood's acid level. Indeed, almost any function that occurs within a dog's body has some dependency on water.

Because of the variety of its functions and the magnitude of its requirements, water is the most essential nutrient required by any dog. When water becomes deficient the functions of the body will be eliminated in a definite order, following a set of priorities that eliminate the least essential functions first. One of the first to go is eating—and with it the need for the large quantities of water needed

20

for the digestion and absorption of food. Another early casualty is energy production for almost all activities except those necessary to maintain basal metabolism. The last function to be eliminated is urine production. Urine production stops when less than 1/15th of an ounce of water for every pound of body weight is drunk during a twenty-four-hour period.

Protein

The role of protein in a dog is similar to the role of the strings of beads in a beadwork picture of a dog. Each protein is like a different string of beads. Just as the different strings are put together, in the proper order, to produce a picture of the dog, different proteins go together to produce the real dog. Each string consists of a varying number of different colored beads, arranged in a definite pattern, to make up some part of the nose, ear or foot of the picture. These colored beads are similar to *amino acids*, the substances that are attached, one to another in a string, to make up different proteins.

By imagining we are making a beadwork picture of a dog, we can have a model for understanding what happens when Nature makes a real dog.

We will have a possibility of 23 different colors of beads from which to choose to make each string in our picture because there are 23 different amino acids. We already have more than enough beads in 13 different colors, but none of the other 10 colors. Since it takes all 23 colors of beads to make our picture, those 10 colors of beads become essential to our project. We will need to purchase these 10 colors of beads from the hobby shop. If the hobby shop is closed, or does not have the colors we need, we cannot make a complete picture of a dog.

In a dog, only 13 amino acids can be made inside its body. The remaining 10 amino acids must come from some source outside the body. If the growing pup cannot obtain these 10 essential amino acids it will not grow. It will die. If the adult dog is deprived of these 10 essential amino acids it, too, will eventually die. Just as our beadwork picture of a dog will be incomplete without the 10 essential colors of beads, the real dog will be incomplete without all 10 essential amino acids.

Let's suppose, however, that we can also obtain the 10 colors of beads we need from some other beadwork pictures of animals and plants we already have. Since these 10 colors are the colors critical to completing our dog picture, then those strings of beads in the other pictures that contain the greatest number of essential colored beads will be of the greatest value to us as we put our dog picture together.

The essential amino acids can be obtained from the proteins of real animals and plants just as essential beads can be obtained from the strings of plant and animal pictures. Furthermore, just as with the strings of beads, those proteins containing the largest number of essential amino acids will be of the greatest biological value to the real dog.

By choosing only those strings containing the greatest number of essential beads and unstringing them into a bowl already containing the 13 colors of beads we have plenty of, we can begin to put our beadwork dog together. From the bowl of beads we can choose each color, as we need it, to string into the proper order for our picture. If we come to a position on the string where we don't have the right color bead the rest of the string cannot be strung and the picture of our dog will be incomplete. If too many beads are missing, the picture of a dog never takes shape at all. When we have ample supplies of all 23 beads we can easily and quickly put together a complete dog's picture.

The bowl containing the colored beads serves the same purpose as the body's amino acid pool from which the cells choose the right amino acids. If the dog's amino acid pool has an ample number of all 23 amino acids when the dog's cells look for them, then the dog's cells can easily put together and maintain a complete dog.

The dog, therefore, has an MDR for amino acids, not proteins. How much protein a dog will need every day will depend on how well that protein can supply the dog's MDR for amino acids. The ability of a protein to supply the dog's MDR for amino acids is called its *biological value*. The higher a protein's biological value, the smaller the quantity of that protein is needed to provide the dog's MDR for amino acids, Figure 4.

Proteins are often described as the building blocks of the body. In reality, they serve far more important functions than merely as structural elements of muscles, bones and organs. Proteins make up most of the molecules of enzymes which keep the body's chemical fires burning. They are essential parts of most hormones which regulate the body's functions and activities. Finally, the antibodies that protect the body against infection are almost entirely proteins. All of these proteins are made by the dog's cells from the bits and pieces

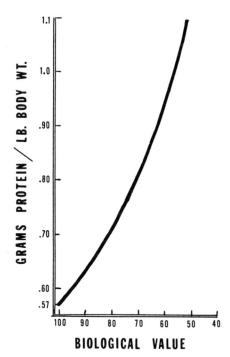

Figure 4. The lower the biological value (BV) of a protein, the more of it is required to meet a dog's needs. When a protein's biological value falls below 60 it cannot meet a dog's needs for raw materials, no matter how much of it is fed.

of the proteins the dog eats. These bits and pieces are the amino acids and they are the true building blocks of the body.

All 23 amino acids have a common chemical—nitrogen. Amino acids (hence proteins) are the *sole* sources of nitrogen to the dog. A dog's body cannot use nitrogen to build its own body protein unless the nitrogen is in the ready-made form of amino acids. For this reason proteins containing adequate amounts of the essential amino acids must be included in every dog's diet.

Fats

The major role of fats in any dog's diet is not building, but furnishing the energy to do the building.

Much has been written about a dog's need for essential fatty acids. Like essential amino acids, essential fatty acids cannot be made by the dog. Unlike amino acids, however, fatty acids do not constitute the key elements in many vital structural components of the dog's body. About the only place fats become building blocks is in a few

23

enzymes and vitamin structures. The real essential nature of these fatty acids is their role in the proper metabolism of the other fatty acids taken into the body. In diets that supply adequate amounts of energy from fat, it is unlikely that a fatty acid deficiency will ever develop.

The only time fat becomes a major part of the building elements in a dog's body is when the dog eats too much fat. Or, for that matter, too much fuel of any kind. Excess energy, regardless of its source, is converted by a dog into fat and stored within its body. A certain amount of stored fat is useful. It serves to cushion the body, insulate it against the cold, and fill in around organs that need a protective covering. A dog is particularly adapted to making good use of its fat stores since it has the ability to quickly and easily reconvert its fat to energy, any time it needs a little extra.

When too much fat is stored in the body it leads to obesity. The amount of fat needed for cushioning, insulating, protecting and extra energy is limited. Once the optimum amount of fat storage has been reached, however, the dog does not stop depositing fat. Instead, it continues to do so at a rate equal to the excess energy intake. For every 3000 to 3500 calories a dog eats in excess of its body's needs it will deposit a pound of fat within its body.

This fact is important to dog feeders because it is the *only* way a dog can get too fat . . . consuming more calories than it can use. Likewise, there is *only* one way a dog can lose fat, by consuming less energy (hence, less calories) than it needs.

Carbohydrates

Carbohydrates come from plant sources almost exclusively. The only carbohydrate from an animal tissue is called *glycogen*, and it is found in only tiny amounts in the muscles and liver. If carbohydrates are not supplied in the diet, the liver must perform extra labor to produce glucose from dietary proteins. When there is adequate carbohydrate in a diet, proteins are "spared" the fate of being converted to glucose and they can be used for the more vital things for which they are needed.

Vitamins

Vitamins neither supply energy nor form structural components, yet many of them are quickly missed if they become deficient in a diet. The role of vitamins may be described as the "activators"

24

because they trigger many of the body's chemical reactions. Without entering into the actual reaction, vitamins play a vital role in assisting two or more chemicals to react with one another.

Minerals

Minerals are used by the body in a wider variety of functions than any other group of nutrients. Some serve as structural elements, others as activators, still others as regulators. Some minerals control the movements of other nutrients through cellular walls. Others may, when paired with another mineral, serve to help maintain the body's acid-base balance.

This extremely diverse role leads to numerous occasions where one mineral's function is dependent upon another. Such dependency produces a complex, often quite delicate, inter-relationship between the various minerals. Iron, for example, is needed to make hemoglobin in red blood cells. It forms an essential structural part of the hemoglobin molecule. Copper is equally essential to hemoglobin formation, but makes up no part of the molecule, whatsoever. Without copper, however, iron cannot become a part of the hemoglobin molecule. Figure 5 is a graphic diagram of the known inter-relation-

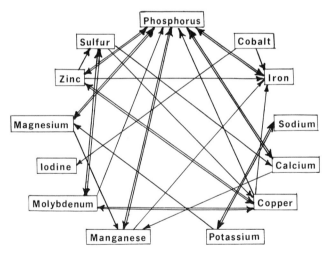

Figure 5. There are numerous inter-relations between the nutrients in a dog's diet. One of the most complex groups of inter-relationships is the one illustrated here, between the minerals. A single arrow indicates that the first mineral is dependent on the other. A double arrow indicates that they are dependent on each other.

25

ships between minerals that are used to build the house the dog lives in.

Once its house is built, life does not stop for a dog. The house must be continuously repaired, and damaged parts replaced. In addition, it must be moved from place to place; warmed and cooled, according to the environmental temperature; and ready for whatever happens next. Food continues to serve a dog by helping that dog to meet its changing needs.

Chapter 3

To Meet a Changing Need

E VERY dog lives in a world that is constantly changing. Some of these changes are subtle or may occur over an extended period of time. Others may be drastic changes or may occur very rapidly. Constant environmental change produces a continuously changing need for the kind and amount of fuel a dog needs to feed its 100-million tiny fires and for the raw materials to maintain its body's activities. The third and final reason a dog is fed, therefore, is to provide it with the proper fuel and raw materials to meet its changing needs.

The Growing Puppy

From conception to weaning, the growing puppy is undergoing tremendous changes. So great are some of these changes, in fact, they can be detected from one day to the next. During the same period the nature of the food the puppy receives is changing to keep pace with the changing needs of a rapidly growing puppy.

First, the fetal puppy is nourished with pre-digested, pre-absorbed nutrients circulating through the bitch's blood. These nutrients are transferred to the puppy's blood without any active effort on the puppy's part. Following birth, the puppy's inexperienced digestive tract can absorb only easily digested nutrients so the bitch places into her milk some of the most easily digested and absorbed nutrients known. The bitch's milk changes in content during the weeks of nursing. The initial 24 hours of milk contain large amounts of a substance known as *colostrum*. Colostrum is rich in those proteins that protect a newborn pup from the world of infections into which it is born. The early milk also has lots of energy in it to help the newborn puppy over the critical first few hours of its life. Once the life-preserving proteins are in the pup's blood the colostrum disappears from the milk. As the puppy matures the milk becomes more concentrated, increasing the nutrients in the milk to meet the puppy's rapidly changing needs. As weaning approaches, the milk becomes dilute again as the puppies eat increasing amounts of solid foods.

The most critical period in the natural history of a dog's life occurs during the first two to five days following birth. The second most critical period commences at weaning and continues during the two to three weeks while the puppy's digestive tract learns to make the transition from the easily digested nutrients in the bitch's milk to the more difficult-to-digest nutrients in the solid foods eaten by adult dogs.

The more abruptly the change is made from milk to solid foods during the weaning process, the more stressing the procedure becomes. By gradually increasing the number and amount of solid foods, a puppy's digestive tract and metabolic system can be trained to properly handle each new solid food as it is added. Such precautions may seem a waste of time to some dog feeders, but will certainly be appreciated by the weanling puppy. Its appreciation will be evidenced by the healthy digestive system and strong, sound body the puppy builds when the extra care is given.

Maintenance

A dog reaches its full growth at an optimum body weight. If a fully grown dog is fed a diet containing a constant level of calories and is kept in an environment that remains unchanged, its weight should theoretically remain constant. Most dogs, however, live in a world that is constantly changing. One of the major objectives of a successful feeding program for adult dogs is to maintain them at their optimum body weight in spite of the constant change they are experiencing.

The effort made to feed the correct amount of food to maintain a dog's optimum weight is called maintenance. To successfully maintain a dog's body weight the dog's energy intake must balance the energy output. It is not necessary however, for a dog to balance its energy on a day to day basis. If a dog expends more energy than it

28

obtains from its food on one day, it will make it up on succeeding days by eating more food. If the dog eats more energy than it expends then it will balance it with a lowered intake later. This is done without any conscious attempt on the part of the dog, but is controlled by an appetite center within its brain. It is because of this built-in energy balance center that the dog is able to eat only enough to meet its energy needs and no more.

Simple maintenance exists when a dog is living under conditions of reasonable shelter and its only exercise is that necessary to eat food, eliminate wastes, and move about within the restrictions imposed by a limited environment.

It should be readily apparent that maintenance situations may vary widely from dog to dog. Consider, for example, the contrast between a 25-pound Beagle living in a dog house and confined to a 10' x 20' fenced run, a 25-pound Whippet housed in an indoor-outdoor kennel and exercised in a small, outdoor training run twice weekly and a 25-pound Poodle living in a heated, air-conditioned apartment and seeing sunshine about once a week during a Saturday afternoon stroll in the park.

Such variations in environment are not the only things that alter maintenance needs. Maintenance needs vary between dogs of the same age and breed being kept under identical circumstances. Every dog has its own individual ability to utilize calories. Some do so with more efficiency than others. These are the dogs referred to as "easy keepers" and must have their food intake closely regulated to prevent them from becoming too fat. Others, the "hard keepers", will always seem to be on the verge of starvation, requiring special handling to prevent any weight loss. The great majority of dogs fit somewhere in between.

Another thing that may cause a variation in maintenance needs is a dog's temperament. Nervous, high-strung dogs will eat more and gain less than quiet, easy-going dogs of the same breed and weight. Occasionally a dog may not only be a hard keeper, but will be a poor eater as well. These dogs pose particularly exasperating problems for owners who are unaware of the reasons for their dog's condition or who don't know how to cope with it.

The most accurate way to determine if a dog is being fed a proper maintenance diet is to weigh the dog at frequent, regular intervals. The dog itself is the only completely accurate indicator of what its needs are. If its diet is not meeting its needs, a dog will lose weight.

29

If a dog is eating in excess of its maintenance needs it will gain weight. The principle of maintenance is that simple.

Anytime a dog's situation changes from a simple maintenance situation to one requiring more energy and nutrients the dog's diet must be altered to meet the increased need or the dog will lose weight. Whether the added requirement for energy and nutrients is the result of reproduction, hard work, emotional strain, or environmental stress, the principle of maintenace—feeding to maintain the dog's weight at a constant level—continues to apply. The maintenance diet fed prior to such situations will not always meet the dog's altered needs in the new situation. The thing most likely to become deficient in a maintenance diet is energy. Remember, however, in an energy-deficient diet all nutrients are diverted and used for energy first. When a food becomes deficient in energy it frequently becomes deficient, secondarily, in protein and other nutrients as well. Only by feeding a diet designed to meet the dog's specific requirements can you be assured of keeping your dog healthy when its situation changes from simple maintenance to one more demanding.

Environmental Stress

The most frequent change in a dog's life is its environment. The changes occur from minute to minute and hour to hour. Most of these changes are so subtle that, individually, they don't place an immediate demand on a dog. The cumulative effect of all these changes, however, may create a daily demand on the dog that is far greater than simple maintenance. There are a few changes in a dog's environment that do create an immediate and appreciable demand for additional energy and nutrients. In either case, cumulative or immediate, a dietary change must be made to adjust to these environmental changes.

Whether it is a hard keeper or an easy keeper, every dog experiences an increased need for energy during the winter months. For the apartment Poodle, the increase may be so small it is insignificant. For the Beagle kept outdoors, in an unheated house, its energy needs may increase as much as 90 percent during the colder months. Figure 6 illustrates this seasonal pattern of increased energy need. To compensate for this changing energy need a seasonal adjustment of energy levels should always be made in a dog's diet.

A reduced environmental temperature is not the only climatic stress a dog encounters. The optimum environmental temperature of

30

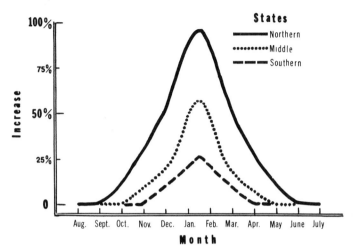

States
Northern
Middle
Southern

Figure 6. As the weather becomes colder, more energy is needed by a dog to keep warm. This graph shows the percentage of the summer diet that is needed during the winter months in different parts of the country.

a working dog is between 40°F and 80°F. The working dog's energy requirements increase as the daily temperatures go above these optimum limits. As the daily temperature increases, the blood flowing to the lungs increases to aid in the control of the body's temperature. A proportionate decrease in the blood flowing to the digestive tract results. This produces a loss of appetite and the dog refuses all, or a portion, of its daily diet. As a consequence working dogs in the tropics may actually consume less, rather than more, fuel as they need to. During high temperature periods (90°F to 120°F), military guard dogs may experience a weight loss of 12 to 20 pounds as a result of this reduced food consumption. To prevent this the U.S. Air Force now feeds their guard dogs a food specifically designed to meet these dogs' unique changed needs. Only a highly concentrated food can adequately meet such needs. The Air Force's special food provides the guard dogs with their elevated caloric need in a minumum quantity of food, yet still meets all of their other nutritional requirements.

31

As a result of studies on the guard dogs in southeast Asia it was found that relative humidity also plays a role in increased energy needs when temperatures rise above 80°F. As the relative humidity increases, the dog's need for a concentrated diet increases accordingly. A diet sufficient to provide a working dog all of its energy needs when the daily temperature and humidity remain below 70 will need three times more calories in the same amount of food when the temperature and humidity reach 90.

Work

While not the most frequently encountered change, work is nevertheless among the most important changes creating additional requirements on the dog. The amount of increased demand is greatest, the length of need the longest sustained, and the dietary adjustment the most often overlooked during work than it is during any other changes encountered by the dog.

Work has been defined as any activity for which energy is expended. Under such a broad definition every dog becomes a working dog. Just staying alive requires an expenditure of energy. The heart beats, the lungs breathe, the kidney and liver work, and the 100-million tiny fires burn. The maintenance of body weight, while engaged in the minimal activities necessary to obtain food, find shelter and eliminate wastes, requires an expenditure of energy.

Hunting birds for six hours also requires an expenditure of energy. An expenditure far in excess of that required to stay alive or maintain body weight, however. After a few hours in the field a Pointer's lungs breathe twice as fast and its heart beats twice as fast. Every muscle in the Pointer's body has contracted and relaxed hundreds and hundreds of times. Its brain has discharged impulses at high rates of speed to maintain such sustained activity. The cellular fires burn brighter and brighter. As they do, the liver and kidneys work harder and harder to eliminate the wastes from their flames.

For the purposes of this book we will define work as any activity that requires energy in excess of simple maintenance. The amount of excess energy required depends on the amount of physical activity involved in the work. Dogs in excellent health and top physical condition can, for brief periods, increase their energy production to support physical exertion by as much as 50 times that of simple maintenance. The duration of such increased energy expenditure is not limited by fuel, but by the dog's inability to take in oxygen at a rate fast enough to support such energy use.

Greyhounds during a race may consistently expend energy at levels 50 times that of maintenance. The duration of this expenditure is for such a brief period of time, however, that the dogs usually will not require an increase of more than 30 to 40 per cent in their daily calorie intake. Pointers working in front of a hunter, on the other hand, rarely reach a rate of expenditure any greater than five or 10 times their maintenance requirements, but they sustain this expenditure for greatly extended periods of time. A hardworking Pointer, hunting for six to eight hours a day, may well require three times the number of calories it would for simple maintenance. If a working dog is to maintain this performance it will have to be fed a diet that provides these extra calories.

An energy expenditure of eight times the basal metabolic rate is about the upper limit of sustained performance for most dogs. An expenditure above this level can only be expected from a dog that is in excellent physical shape and training. When these upper limits are reached, a dog will be using about four times the number of calories it needs just to maintain its body weight. Anytime an otherwise healthy dog is consuming an equivalent of four to four and one-half times its maintenance energy needs, yet it still is losing weight, that dog is being overworked, overstressed or overtaxed emotionally.

Far too often the increased needs brought about by an increase in the dog's activity are overlooked by the dog feeder. One of the most exasperating experiences I've ever had was trying to convince a college football coach, who insisted that his two-legged athletes eat all their meals from a training table during football season, that his four-legged athletes needed a special feeding program during quail season.

Water is among the most necessary nutrients to be increased if the working dog is to meet its increased needs. The cell must have water in order to burn fuel. While it sounds paradoxical, without water present the millions of tiny fires in a dog's body would quickly go out. And, as the fires burn hotter and hotter during work, more and more water is needed. Of all the nutrients required by a dog, water is the one most essential for extended endurance during work. Dogs given a constant supply of water during work will have their endurance increased by as much as 75 percent over dogs without water.

33

This is a point well to be considered by hunters and racing dog enthusiasts. A dog's endurance, when the dog is provided adequate water, can be a fantastic thing. There is, on record, a non-stop sled run of 140 miles which lasted nearly 40 hours! The dog is capable of such feats of endurance only because there is an adequate supply of water available to assist its cells in reconverting its body stores to energy.

Even a dog has its limits of endurance, however, and like all mammals, dogs must have rest periods between periods of work in order to recover.

The consumption of carbohydrates just before working will not increase a dog's endurance. The efficiency with which the dog works will be increased, however. Dogs that have fasted for five days and then eat a high-carbohydrate meal just prior to work are able to perform with equal proficiency as those not fasted—they just can't keep up the pace nearly as long. The feeding of high levels of carbohydrates also hastens the period of recovery from work exhaustion.

Emotional Stress

Closely related to environmental stress, and often accompanying it, is emotional stress. Working guard dogs are trained to be under constant tensions. Such emotional stress places demands for energy production above that used for physical exertion. The combination of physical exertion and emotional stress can place extraordinary demands on a dog's energy needs. A guard dog in top physical condition can lose as much as 10 percent of its body weight in an eight-hour night on duty. Such drastic changes in weight, if uncorrected, will affect directly the dog's efficiency and state of health.

Guide dogs for the blind undergo a tension and stress situation similar to that of guard dogs but to a lesser degree. The guide dog's increased needs must be met in much the same manner as those of the guard dogs, but with the amount and kind of food being adjusted to meet the increased needs of each dog on an individual basis.

Another stress and tension pattern that is of considerable interest to many dog feeders is that experienced by dogs being campaigned on the show circuit. These stresses include travel, changing surroundings, altered sleeping quarters, loss of rest and missed meals. The tensions are created by such things as interruptions of daily

34

routine, strange dogs and people, tired or irritable owners and handlers and judges with cold hands!

Although not nearly as severe, the stresses and tensions experienced by dogs on the show circuit affect them the same way stresses and tensions do guard and guide dogs—by causing a loss of weight and condition. For a dog that has been carefully brought to show condition and bloom, a loss of weight or condition can be disastrous. To keep its prize-winning form, a show dog must be fed a diet designed to provide it with the energy necessary to meet the changing situations it encounters in its campaign from ring to ring.

The things that can cause environmental and emotional stress in a dog are almost as numerous as there are dogs themselves. Some of them are so minor in magnitude that no adjustments in the quantity of maintenance diet are needed to compensate for the change. Other situations causing tension and stress may reach the magnitude of that in military guard dogs. Dogs that experience the upper extremes in such situations must be fed a diet specifically designed to meet their greatly increased needs. Most environmental and emotional stresses are somewhere in between, and the dog feeder must judge the magnitude and adjust the diet accordingly. He can evaluate how well his judgment is by regularly weighing the dog to see that the dog is maintaining its weight at a constant level.

Reproduction

Malnourishment of the bitch, both prior to and during pregancy and during lactation, causes the unnecessary death of thousands of pups every year. To the dog feeder who is also a dog breeder, understanding this single fact and knowing what to do about it can make the difference between operating in the red or the black.

A wide range of fetal abnormalities are produced if pregnant bitches are subjected to dietary deficiencies during pregnancy. Some of these periods are so critical that a deficiency of certain nutrients for no longer than six days duration can result in abnormalities. Equally critical is the fact that some malformations have definite "cut-off" dates after which, no matter what is fed or done, the abnormality no longer can be corrected. All of this points out the importance of feeding a brood bitch a well-balanced, adequate diet before she is bred, during her pregnancy, and while she is nursing her pups.

35

To meet accelerated demands of pregnancy the bitch draws upon tissue stores deposited within her body before she conceived. Bitches fed improperly balanced diets, with marginal levels of nutrients and energy, will not have enough stored amino acids, minerals, vitamins and energy to support healthy fetal growth. Diets of low digestibility are regarded as being among the primary causes of low conception rates, abnormal fetuses, and functional changes of the mammary glands.

The time for, and the amount of, an increased supply of nutrients and energy during pregnancy will depend upon the condition of the bitch at the time of conception. Bitches which have been properly fed to maintain body stores prior to pregnancy will probably need very little dietary increase during pregnancy. Slight increases, if they are needed, will begin about the fourth week of pregnancy. Bitches that have been fed marginal or inadequate diets will not fare as well. They may begin to show weight loss at about the fourth week of pregnancy. A marked increase in appetite may also appear about this time. In such cases, the deficiencies which developed before con-

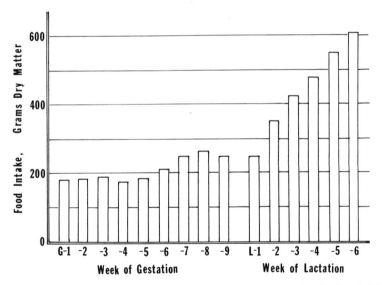

Figure 7. A bar graph illustrating the changes that occur in the feeding habits of a bitch during pregnancy and lactation. While a modest increase in food intake may occur during the last three weeks of gestation, the greatest increase comes during lactation when it may reach 300 percent of the bitch's usual food intake.

36

ception cannot be remedied by feeding an adequate diet during pregnancy. All that will be accomplished by overfeeding a pregnant bitch is to make her too fat at whelping time. Only the current needs of the bitch—that amount to prevent weight loss—should be met until she whelps.

The real need for an increase in dietary energy and nutrients comes with the onset of lactation. By the time the pups are four to five weeks old the bitch will require two and one-half to three times the amount of energy and nutrients every day that she required before she became pregnant, Figure 7. There are some veterinary physiologists who feel that lactation places the greatest stress possible on the bitch. Without doubt, it places the greatest test upon the adequacy of her diet.

By keeping accurate weights of a bitch prior to conception, during pregnancy and during and after lactation, it is a simple matter to determine how her body weight at weaning compares to her body weight at conception. Bitches that are fed properly during pregnancy and lactation should not lose more than about 10 percent of their body weight during reproduction. This is one of the most critical tests that even a dog feeder can use to test the adequacy of a diet.

PART II

WHAT A DOG IS FED

Chapter 4

A Balanced Diet

THE word "diet" is used throughout this book to mean the sum total of what a dog consumes. When modified by the word "daily" it means the total of what a dog consumes in a 24-hour time span, from midnight to midnight.

A dog's daily diet may be a single food, taken from a can or bag, and fed with nothing else added. It may also be fresh ingredients like meat, eggs and milk mixed with cereals and lard or oil to which are added several vitamin, mineral or other supplements. Most American dogs' daily diet consists of one or more commercial foods with a handful of table scraps thrown in. The diet may or may not have a vitamin and mineral supplement added. It may also have hamburger or horsemeat added to improve the palatability. Such diet combinations may or may not be nourishing to a dog. Merely mixing together a number of ingredients which supply, more or less, the nutrients a dog needs does not guarantee that the dog is getting an adequate and balanced diet.

Balance in a dog's diet refers to the same thing that balance on a druggist's scales refers to. When the needle remains in the center, the amount on each arm of the scales is correct. If one side has too little, or too much, the arms fall out of "balance" and the needle moves to one side or the other.

The only difference between the druggist's scales and a dog's diet is the number of balance arms and their length. On a druggist's scales there are only two arms of equal length. One is a fixed-weight

41

arm on which is placed the brass weight, the other is a variable-weight arm upon which is heaped the material being weighed. A dog's diet has one fixed arm, representing the dog's daily needs, but a variable arm for each nutrient needed in the diet. Some of these nutrient arms are not only connected at the center to the big daily-need arm, but are also connected to each other. Because of these inter-connections, a change in the amount of one nutrient heaped onto the diet not only affects the overall diet, but also may have a direct effect on one or more of the other nutrients already in the diet.

Typical of this nutrient inter-relationship in a dog's diet is the calcium-phosphorus-vitamin D complex. Calcium and phosphorus are the primary minerals used by the dog for building bones. They are absorbed and used best by a dog when they are fed in a ratio of about 12 parts of calcium to every 10 parts of phosphorus, and in sufficient quantity to constitute about one percent of the diet as calcium and 0.9 percent as phosphorus.

When calcium, phosphorus and vitamin D are present in the proper ratio and amounts, practically all of these two minerals will be absorbed from the diet. Once in the blood, they will also be used better by the body because they will be supplied to the cell in the proper balance, Figure 8.

When calcium and phosphorus are not supplied in the proper

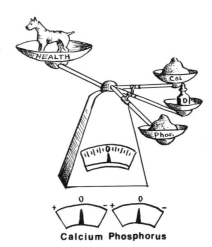

Figure 8. When calcium, phosphorus and vitamin D are present in a dog's diet in adequate and proper balance, a dog remains healthy.

42

ratio, the mineral present in the greatest amount will reduce the amount of the other that can be used by the body. Thus, if phosphorus is present in a ratio of six to one to calcium there is an excess of 80 percent phosphorus. This 80 percent will tie up a proportionate amount of calcium, rendering it unavailable to the body. This will leave only about 20 percent of the calcium in that diet available to be used by the dog. If the calcium in that diet is barely adequate or marginal, it takes only a minor error in the calcium-phosphorus ratio to produce a serious calcium deficiency. Even in diets where calcium is adequate a severe imbalance can produce a deficiency Figure 9.

When calcium and phosphorus are properly balanced, but inade-

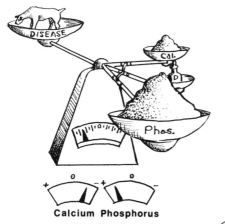

Figure 9. If too much phosphorus is added to a balanced diet, it upsets the diet's balance. Calcium becomes deficient and a disease called hypoparathyroidism results.

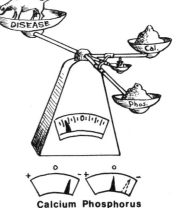

Figure 10. If too little vitamin D is present in an otherwise balanced diet, too little calcium is absorbed. This eventually results in too little phosphorus being used as well. The final result is what appears to be a calcium-phosphorus deficiency and the disease called rickets.

43

quate amounts of vitamin D are eaten, a calcium-phosphorus-like deficiency develops. This is because vitamin D is necessary for the absorption of calcium and without vitamin D the proper amount of calcium is not absorbed, even though it may be present in the diet in adequate amounts, Figure 10.

If calcium and phosphorus are present in adequate amounts but vitamin D is eaten to an excess, the minerals are absorbed from the digestive tract without difficulty. They are also re-absorbed from the bones because there is too much vitamin D in the blood. The bones become riddled with holes while the soft tissues of the body become filled with calcium phosphate deposits. When the kidneys begin to fill up with mineral they stop working and the dog dies, Figure 11.

If calcium is also elevated, large excesses of vitamin D in a dog's diet may not cause the symptoms just described. While the exact reason for this protection remains unknown, it well could be that the vitamin D is used up as it increases the absorption of so much calcium, and, with the calcium being absorbed it does not lie around in the gut to tie up the phosphorus. Once in the blood, the phosphorus becomes the limiting amount, and the excess calcium is rejected by the cells. In any event, large quantities of calcium are excreted in the urine of such dogs, Figure 12.

Large amounts of calcium create other problems, however, Excess calcium tends to exaggerate the need for other minerals, particularly

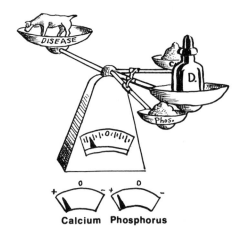

Figure 11. Excessive amounts of vitamin D in an otherwise balanced diet will produce a dissolving of the bones and a re-arrangement of the calcium and phosphorus as deposits in the soft tissues. This disease is caused hypervitaminosis D.

44

the trace minerals. One of these is zinc. Continued high levels of calcium in a dog's diet, like that often seen from the unwise use of vitamin-mineral supplements, can precipitate a zinc deficiency even when adequate levels of zinc are in the diet.

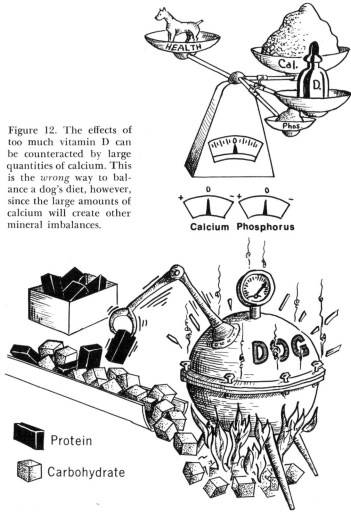

Figure 12. The effects of too much vitamin D can be counteracted by large quantities of calcium. This is the *wrong* way to balance a dog's diet, however, since the large amounts of calcium will create other mineral imbalances.

Figure 13. When adequate amounts of energy are supplied by nutrients other than protein, enough calories will be produced to keep the fires of the body burning brightly, and the dog's metabolic engine "steamed-up" and going strong! At the same time the protein in the diet will be "spared" to be used by the dog's metabolic engine for building blocks instead of energy.

45

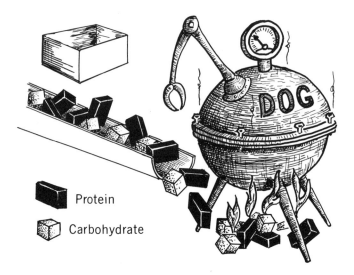

Protein

Carbohydrate

Figure 14. When insufficient amounts of energy are available from nutrients other than protein, protein will be used for energy, also. Protein is the least efficient form of energy for a dog. In instances where protein is not spared, it is burned in an attempt to keep the fires hot enough to at least maintain life.

Minerals have no curb on nutrient inter-relationships. One of the most important relationships in any diet is the one between protein and energy. When the energy in a diet is deficient, protein in the diet will be converted into energy and as a result, protein, too, may become deficient in that diet. When calories from protein exceed 25 percent of the total energy in adequate diets, protein is being wasted. (Notice that this is 25 percent of the calories in the diet, and not 25 percent of the total diet!) Up to 25 percent of the calories from protein will be used to supply nitrogen and building blocks. Any in excess of 25 percent will only be burned for energy, and protein is the least efficient source of energy the dog can eat, Figures 13 and 14.

Such inter-relationships in a dog's diet are endless. . . . thiamine must be increased every time carbohydrates are increased because thiamine is necessary for carbohydrate metabolism . . . as the total output of calories increases, riboflavin requirements increase . . . water intake is directly related to the amount of dry matter eaten

46

. . . the pyridoxine requirement is dependent on the amount of thiamine and riboflavin used in the diet . . . and so on and on.

The immediate reaction of many dog feeders, when they suspect a dietary imbalance, is to drag out the vitamin-mineral supplements. Hopefully, those reading these pages now understand that the nutrient balance of a diet is so critical and complex, and the determination of exactly what nutrients are out of balance is so difficult, that the inept addition of a multi-vitamin-mineral supplement will do more harm than good 99 times out of 100! When an imbalance is suspected, it is far better to discard that diet completely and start all over again with a diet known to be balanced, or at least formulated to be so.

The most abused principle of proper dog feeding is that of nutrient balance. Merely supplying all of the nutrients a dog needs is no assurance that they will form a nutritionally balanced diet. Those nutrients must be present in proper balance to each other if the diet is going to provide a dog with the optimum potential for growth, health and performance.

While we have stressed the importance of a balanced diet, a *totally* balanced diet probably does not exist except in theory. Because a dog eats to meet its caloric need, most dogs do a pretty good job of balancing caloric intake against caloric need. To exactly balance a food therefore, all one need do, theoretically, is to supply each nutrient in proper proportion to the number of calories in the diet. When the diet is consumed to satisfy the dog's caloric need it will automatically satisfy the dog's need for the nutrients at the same time. This, in fact, is the very theory used by those makers of commercial dog foods who are concerned enough to balance their products.

While the method just described works perfectly in theory, in practice it probably never provides a dog with a diet in which every nutrient is precisely balanced. For one thing, every dog may not eat the precise number of calories it needs on the very day it needs them. For those nutrients that are needed on a more critical, day-to-day basis, a deficiency may develop. Another obstacle to exactly balancing a diet by using calories as a reference is the fact that while a change in the environment may create a sizable change in a dog's need for calories, it may leave the need for most nutrients almost unchanged.

The greatest difficulty in balancing a diet for a dog, however,

47

whatever the method used, is our own lack of knowledge about the exact nutrient inter-relationships within a dog's diet.

Fortunately, what the dog feeder lacks in understanding, the Dog Maker made up for by giving the dog a highly flexible digestive and metabolic system. A system which can excrete some excesses while storing others for a rainy day. Healthy dogs can, therefore, compensate in many cases for the not-so-balanced diets they may be fed. This is done with little strain on their health in most cases. In cases where the dog is already in poor health or the balance of the food is so poor that even a healthy dog cannot compensate, the 100-million tiny fires begin to grow dim and cellular activity slows down. If a balanced diet does not soon replace the unbalanced one, the fires will go out, cellular activity stops, and the dog dies.

How, then, can a dog feeder assure himself of feeding the proper ingredients in a combination that will provide his dog with adequate nourishment?

To be satisfactory for any dog, a food must have at least these four characteristics:

1. *Sufficient energy* to carry on the dog's daily activities.
2. *Adequate nutrients* to support the phase of the life cycle for which the food is being fed.
3. *Usable nutrients* to insure adequacy and balance is maintained.
4. *Acceptable* enough to the dog to be eaten in sufficient amounts to provide the energy and nutrients needed.

Energy

Carbohydrates, fats and proteins all supply energy to a dog. The percentage of each nutrient in a food determines the amount of energy in that food. The amount of energy contained in a dog food is called the food's *caloric density*. The more calories that are available from the food the higher that food's caloric density. The higher the caloric density, the less food a dog will have to eat to meet its energy requirements.

Energy is the first thing that should be considered when deciding what to feed a dog. If the caloric density of a food is so low that the dog cannot eat a sufficient amount to meet its caloric need, then all of the nutrients that the dog eats will be converted to energy. If there are insufficient amounts of nutrients in the food to furnish all of the calories the dog needs, then the dog will not gain weight and

48

will remain hungry all of the time. It will eat almost anything, including dead animals, feces, carrion or garbage to fill the hollow feeling within its belly.

A food of an even more insidious nature is the one that contains just enough nutrients to be converted to supply all of a dog's energy needs, but in so doing is left without enough nutrients to supply the dog its nutrient needs. Dogs eating such foods are likely to maintain weight and show no hunger while starving to death all the same. Then, as a full-blown deficiency of one of the nutrients develops, the dog will abruptly reduce its food intake or stop eating altogether. By the time the trouble is recognized it is often too late to rectify, even by feeding a balanced diet. This will especially be true if the dog is a growing puppy.

ADEQUATE NUTRIENTS

Any dog must have certain nutrients if it is to maintain perfect health and performance. Once a diet contains sufficient calories to meet the dog's energy needs the second most important thing is that it contain all of the nutrients needed by a dog and in amounts adequate for whatever phase of life cycle the dog is in. These nutrients, remember, are water, proteins, fats, carbohydrates, minerals and vitamins.

Water

When offered an unlimited supply of water, most dogs drink considerably more than their minimum daily requirements. A number of factors affect the quantity of water drunk daily by a dog. First, for the proper digestion and absorption of nutrients, a dog will need to drink about a quart of water for every pound of dry matter it eats. This amount will vary depending on whether the food is canned, semi-moist or dry. Most canned foods already contain water at about one quart per pound of dry matter. Dry foods, on the other hand, only have about 10 percent water in them, or about 4 ounces in every pound of dry matter. This amount of water is so small that dogs eating only dry foods must drink at least a quart of water every time they eat a pound of food. If the dog is unable to obtain this much water it will reduce the amount of food it eats to balance the dry matter intake to whatever amount of water it is able to drink.

Similarly, a reduction in food intake may result in a reduction of

49

water intake. This reduction may go unnoticed in dogs eating only canned foods. A reduction in intake of $\frac{1}{4}$th pound of canned food will result in a reduction in intake of only one ounce of dry matter and only $2\frac{1}{2}$ ounces of water. The amount of water the dog drinks will probably remain unchanged. A reduction in intake of $\frac{1}{4}$th pound of dry food, on the other hand, will result in a reduced intake of almost 11 ounces of water. The change this amount of water will make in daily drinking habits will be readily apparent.

Once food has been eaten, a dog will use the water absorbed with it for burning the calories the food contains. For the first 500 calories burned each day a dog uses about 14 ounces of water. For the second 500 calories, it uses about 12.5 more ounces of water. After the initial 1000 calories are burned the dog will need about two ounces for every additional 100 calories it burns.

Such things as environmental temperature, relative humidity, muscular exercise, the amount of salt in the diet, disease, fever, etc., all affect the quantity of water a dog drinks.

The easiest way of supplying a dog with all of the water it requires is not by trying to calculate all of these needs. Simply keep plenty of clean, fresh water before the dog all of the time. There is little danger in a healthy dog drinking too much water. Any excess is rapidly and efficiently eliminated.

Proteins

There are three common causes of protein deficiency in a dog's diet.

1. *Insufficient total protein* in the diet. This cause is frequently seen in kennels of hunting dogs where owners attempt to economize. Such items as cornbread, biscuits, oatmeal, boiled potatoes and cheap, dry dog foods composed mostly of cereal, may make up as much as 90 percent of these dogs' diet.

2. *Imbalanced, poor-quality dietary protein.* Imbalanced rations containing inexpensive proteins of low biological value are frequently found among the 10-cent-a-can dog foods. The protein in such foods are usually gelatin, collagen, or those found in tankage or cereal wastes. A typical product is an example made from rejected pinto beans from a canning plant for humans' food.

3. *Bulky, low-energy diets* which cause the marginal amounts of protein present to be converted to energy. Foods, either canned or dry, containing too little fat or too much cereal wastes, tendons, tra-

50

cheas and similar indigestible materials are usually the cause of this type of protein deficiency.

The nutritive value of a protein depends on its distribution of amino acids, and on its digestibility. For the dog, both of these factors seem to be more satisfactory in proteins from animals than in proteins from plants. The limiting factor in the cereal proteins is usually an amino acid, *lysine*. This same amino acid is normally abundant in animal proteins. By blending animal proteins and plant proteins together, in the proper ratio, it is possible to provide a protein blend that has a higher biological value than either of the two proteins used to make up the blend. Most commercial dog foods do combine cereal with animal proteins, but it is often done in a haphazard manner. The optimum blend possible is usually not reached in these cases and the biological value potential of the blend is never realized.

Table I lists the MDR, for maintenance, of the essential amino acids of the dog. The least amount of a "perfect" protein which would supply all of the amino acids, in the amounts listed in Table I, is 0.57 grams per pound of body weight per day. Such a protein actually exists in nature. It is that of whole egg. The arrangement of amino acids in whole egg protein is so close to that of a perfect protein for a dog that whole egg protein is 100 percent utilized by the dog.

TABLE I

amino acid	MDR (mg/lb body wt/day)
arginine	22
histidine	10
leucine	48
isoleucine	32
lysine	31
phenylalanine	23
methionine	9
threonine	20
tryptophan	6
valine	30

The minimum daily requirements of the essential amino acids, listed in milligrams needed per pound of dog for a 24-hour period.

Fats

Fats should be incorporated into a dog's diet in sufficient amounts to make up between 25 and 30 percent of the calories in the food.

51

This will amount to about 12 to 16 percent of the dry weight of the diet. In addition to the fundamental requirement for energy, fat in the diet should also supply sufficient amounts of linoleic acid so that it constitutes about two percent of the calories. Linoleic acid is the most important essential fatty acid in dogs.

If lard, horse fat or vegetable oil are used to furnish at least 15 percent of the calories in a dog's diet, their content of linoleic acid is high enough to insure adequate amounts of essential fatty acids in the diet. Mutton fat or beef tallow will supply energy, but not the essential fatty acids a dog needs because both contain such low levels, themselves.

If too much fat is added to a dog's diet, or is added to the food of a dog that does not require additional energy, the results can be disastrous. The additional calories will cause the dog to reduce the quantity of food that it eats and this may, in turn, create multiple deficiencies. For example: If a can of food containing 500 calories per can, and balanced to that caloric density, is fed to a dog needing exactly 500 calories, the dog will thrive. If, however, you should pour a tablespoonful of corn oil over that food, the addition of 125 calories will cause the dog to reduce its intake of food by 125 calories, or about 25 percent. At the same time the dog will also be reducing its intake of all nutrients by 25 percent and a multiple deficiency will develop.

If that same dog is taken squirrel hunting and increases its daily energy need by 25 percent, the addition of a tablespoonful of corn oil each day will *prevent* the development of any deficiencies that might occur because of a lack of calories in the diet.

When fat is constantly incorporated into a diet in moderate excess, obesity develops. When large excesses of fat are incorporated, it will cause a *weight loss*. Deficiencies develop when too much fat is added because too little food is eaten and many of the nutrients will not be consumed in adequate amounts. In the foods designed for maximum stress the greatly increased fat content is balanced by increasing the concentration of the other nutrients in the same proportion.

Carbohydrates

A large variety of carbohydrates can be used efficiently by the dog. Foremost among these are sugars and starches. Sugars are easily digested "as-is" by a dog, but the starches are better utilized if they are

52

fed cooked. The heat breaks the starches down into dextrins, which can then be easily converted into sugars in the dog's intestines. Starches from oats, corn or potatoes are particularly poorly digested unless cooked, but all cereal or flour-made products should be boiled, baked or toasted before being fed to a dog.

A number of authorities have condemned milk sugar (lactose) and table sugar (sucrose) as causes of digestive upsets and scours in dogs. It is more likely that the presence of a particular type of bacteria causes the digestive upset—regardless of the type of sugar fed. The sugar merely serves as a food source to these bacteria as they multiply and produce toxins from the protein in the diet. Buttermilk, which contains respectable quantities of lactose, is actually used to treat digestive upsets, as soon as the putrefactive bacteria have been controlled by suitable antibiotics. Buttermilk is also fed daily, to dogs prone to digestive upsets, as a preventive measure because it promotes the growth of acid-forming bacteria. These bacteria, in turn, inhibit the growth of the putrefactive bacteria.

The level of carbohydrate should be no higher than 50 percent of the dry weight of the diet. Restricting it to this amount assures room in the diet for enough protein, vitamins and minerals. Then, by adding sufficient fat to provide adequate energy, the proper protein-energy balance can be made to prevent the protein in the diet from being wasted as energy.

Vitamins

The part that vitamins play in nourishing a dog was not discovered until about 50 years ago. As a consequence, vitamins have received unduly large amounts of publicity in relation to their nutritional importance. Almost any commercial dog food that will nourish a dog will contain adequate vitamins just from its natural ingredients. Nevertheless, few commercial dog foods do not have vitamins added to them. Most vitamins are now made synthetically, and all are relatively inexpensive. Today, a vitamin deficiency in a dog fed a balanced commercial food is almost unheard of.

Because of the widespread use of concentrated vitamin supplements and potent single-vitamin therapeutic preparations that are available to any dog owner, vitamin *poisoning* is becoming a far more serious threat to most American dogs than vitamin deficiencies. Over-consumption of a vitamin, in amounts sufficient to cause a toxic reaction, is called *hyper-vitaminosis.*

53

Vitamins are commonly divided into two categories, depending on whether they will dissolve in oil or water. The division is strictly for convenience, having little to do with their activity in the body. The *fat soluble* vitamins are those that dissolve in oily bases and require fat in the diet for their absorption. These are vitamins A, D, E and K. *Water soluble* vitamins are those that dissolve in water, and are the B-complex vitamins and vitamin C.

Table II lists these vitamins, giving their major natural sources for the dog and the dog's requirements for them.

TABLE II

Vitamin	*MDR (per lb body wt)*		*natural sources*
	maintenance	*growth*	
A	45 IU	90 IU	fish liver oils, egg yolk, liver, corn.
D	5 IU	10 IU	sunlight, irradiated yeast, fish liver oils, egg yolk.
E	1 mg*	2 mg	egg yolk, corn, milk fat, cereal grains.
K	no dietary need		yeast, liver, soy beans, fish.
C	no dietary need		orange juice, fresh fruits and vegetables.
B_1 (thiamine)	8 mcg	16 mcg	yeast, liver, whole grains.
B_2 (riboflavin)	.02mg**	.04 mg	milk, yeast, whole grains.
Niacin	.10 mg	.18 mg	whole grains, yeast, meat scraps, fish meal, eggs.
B_6 (pyridoxine)	.01 mg	.02 mg	whole grains, milk, meat, fish, yeast, liver.
Pantothenic acid	.2 mg	.4 mg	yeast, dairy products, liver, rice.
Folic acid	2 mcg	4 mcg	yeast, liver.
Biotin	no dietary need		most natural ingredients.
B_{12} (cobalamin)	.3 mcg	.5 mcg	liver, fish meal, meat scraps, dairy products.

A list of the minimum daily requirements for the vitamins needed by a dog, and the more important natural sources of each.
* MDR for vitamin E will vary according to the quantity of fat in the diet.
** Riboflavin MDR varies depending on how much energy is burned during the 24-hour period.

Minerals

Minerals, like vitamins, have received a large amount of investiga-

54

tion and the dog's requirements for most minerals have been fairly well established.

Table III lists the minerals needed by a dog and gives the more common natural sources and the dog's MDR for each.

TABLE III

mineral	MDR (per lb body wt) maintenance	growth	natural sources
Calcium	120 mg	240 mg	milk, bone meal, dicalcium phosphate, canned salmon.
Phosphorus	100 mg	200 mg	milk, eggs, chicken, canned salmon, bone meal, dicalcium phosphate.
Sodium			salt, most natural ingredients.
Chloride			salt, most natural ingredients.
Potassium	100 mg	200 mg	most natural ingredients, potassium chloride.
Magnesium	5 mg	10 mg	natural ingredients, magnesium carbonate, magnesium oxide.
Iron	0.6 mg	0.6 mg	liver, blood, soy beans, yeast, iron carbonate.
Copper	0.07 mg	0.07 mg	natural ingredients, copper sulphate, copper carbonate.
Cobalt	0.025 mg	0.025 mg	liver, organ meats, eggs, dairy products.
Zinc	0.050 mg	0.100 mg	natural ingredients, zinc oxide.
Iodine	0.015 mg	0.030 mg	iodized salt, sodium iodide, potassium iodide.
Manganese	0.050 mg	0.100 mg	natural ingredients, manganese oxide, manganese carbonate.

A list of the minimum daily requirements for the minerals needed by a dog, and some of the more important natural sources of each.

In the practical application of dog feeding the minerals which seem to be the most critical for the dog are calcium and phosphorus. One reason for this is because most of the major ingredients of dog foods (e.g. meat, meat by-products, soybeans, casein and eggs) contain very low levels of calcium, minimal levels of phosphorus and a reversed ratio. Another reason is because much of the phosphorus in a cereal grain is unavailable to a dog. It is tied up in an indigestible complex with phytic acid. Calcium and phosphorus supplements are cheap as dirt (and, indeed, some are made from ground chalk, marble and other earth-mineral deposits) and are often added to a

55

dog's diet in such huge quantities by the dog feeder that calcium and phosphorus become toxic. In addition, their excesses create multiple deficiencies in other minerals.

Although calcium and phosphorus are the most critical, all of the minerals in a dog's diet should be considered as a single entity by the practical dog feeder. If one mineral is obviously inadequate or imbalanced, they all should be considered inadequate or imbalanced. Rather than trying to add one or two minerals to balance a diet, the dog feeder should discard the whole mineral complex of the diet. In some instances it may be better to discard the entire diet, and start all over again. This time, however, special care should be given to provide a diet in which all minerals are in adequate amounts and in the proper ratio to one another.

UTILIZABLE NUTRIENTS

How well a dog utilizes a nutrient depends on two things, the nutrient's digestibility and its biological value, Figure 15.

All nutrients are not utilized to the same degree by every animal species. A top-grade alfalfa hay contains almost all of the major nutrients a dog needs except enough fat. That could be supplied easily by tossing a few tablespoonsful of salad oil over the leaves. Yet how many people feed their dog alfalfa hay? The reason they don't is because the dog cannot *digest* alfalfa hay. While alfalfa hay may contain most of the essential nutrients for a dog, those nutrients just aren't in a form that is available to the dog. Gelatin, on the other hand, is almost completely digestible by a dog, but its biological value is 0 because it is completely lacking in two essential amino acids. While it may be in a readily available form, the dog cannot use gelatin to grow, repair or replace because it lacks these amino acids.

Digestion is the process by which nutrients are converted from the eaten state into a state that can be absorbed from the dog's digestive tract and be transported by the blood to the body's millions of cells. Here the nutrients will serve as fuel and raw materials. No matter how skillfully a dog's diet is designed, or to what extent one goes to keep it balanced, if the ingredients used to make the food are indigestible by a dog, the dog will still starve.

Digestibility is the degree to which an eaten nutrient is absorbed. It is measured as the percentage of the nutrient eaten that is not passed out in the feces. Nutritionists determine how digestible a

56

food or nutrient is by actually measuring the amount eaten, then measuring the amount passed in the stool, and comparing the two.

A dog feeder can get a rough idea of the digestibility of a food by comparing the volume and consistency of a stool to the volume of food that was eaten to produce that stool. Dogs eating a special dietary food, made from highly concentrated ingredients that approach 100 percent digestibility, may not produce a stool but every third day. It will be well-formed and firm. Such a stool is not composed of the eaten food, but primarily from the residue of intestinal secretions, cells from the intestinal wall and the bodies of myriads of bacteria. At the other extreme are dogs fed an inexpensive dry food made from cheap, indigestible grain and animal by-products. These dogs will produce several stools per day, the total volume of which may be greater than the volume of food that was eaten to produce it! This expansion is caused by the large amount of material that passes through unchanged along with any water it absorbs, as well as the intestinal secretions and cellular debris already mentioned.

Digestibility is as important to a dog feeder as it is to his dog. He pays for the amount of food that comes in the bag, not the amount his dog digests and absorbs. Every ounce of food that winds up in the stool costs the dog feeder the same amount as the food that winds up as muscle or energy. If the nutrients in a food are only 50 percent digestible the actual price paid for the nutrients a dog is able to use is twice the shelf price. And, don't be fooled by price. Some cans of 10¢ dog food are filled with chicken feathers, wheat hulls and straw—all virtually indigestible by a dog. Even if the dog feeder only paid five cents per can for these indigestible nutrients he would be pouring his five cents down the drain. In fact, dog feeders who insist on feeding cheap, indigestible dog foods do exactly that every time they wash a run or flush a stool down the drain!

In the dog, nutrients from animal sources are generally considered to be more digestible than those from plant sources. This is particularly true with proteins. While a completely adequate diet can be made for the dog using nothing but plant proteins, most practical diets for a dog should contain a larger percentage of its proteins from animal sources than from plant sources.

While the most digestible proteins come from animal sources, about the only sources of carbohydrates are the plants. Although tiny amounts of an animal carbohydrate called glycogen are found in muscle and liver, it plays an insignificant role in the dietary intake of carbohydrates in a dog's diet. Plant carbohydrates occur in several different forms, each having a different degree of digestibility by the dog. These forms include sugars, starches, cellulose, lignins and gums.

Most sugars are easily digested and are practically 100-percent utilized by a dog for energy. Starches make up the largest part of a plant and basically are long chains of sugars tied together. In order for starches to be used they must first be broken down into dextrins (shorter chains of sugars), and then into sugars. The first step, breaking starches into dextrins, is the most difficult for a dog. A few starches are readily usable by a dog, but only because the dog has the correct enzyme needed to break that starch down into dextrins. All starches can be made useful to a dog if they are cooked first. Heating, in the presence of a little water, *dextrinizes*, or breaks down almost any starch. Dogs can then convert the dextrins into sugars with relative ease.

Cellulose is not digestible by a dog. The dog has no enzymes to break down cellulose into its more digestible components. Cellulose makes up the second largest part of the carbohydrates in a plant. Any starches or sugars that are trapped in cellulose envelopes also become unavailable to a dog. Animals that eat plants for most of their diet are able to utilize cellulose because they have certain bacteria in their digestive tracts that pre-digest the cellulose into forms that can be used by the animal. Dogs do not have these bacteria.

Gums and lignins are totally indigestible carbohydrates, but make up only a small fraction of the total carbohydrates in a plant.

When measuring the amount of carbohydrates in a dog food, the starches and sugars comprise the digestible part and are sometimes called the *nitrogen free extract* (NFE). Cellulose, lignins and gums make up the indigestible portion and are called the *crude fiber*.

Fats, as a group, are highly digestible by a dog. As the fat molecule becomes larger and larger it becomes harder and harder for a dog to digest, but fortunately, most animal and plant fats have small molecules.

Minerals from plants are more difficult for a dog to digest than those from animal sources. Phytic acid in plants ties up some minerals, particularly phosphorus, into insoluble *phytin complexes*. When water, at room temprature or warmer, is added to foods made from plants, it activates enzymes already present in the plants. These enzymes break down the phytin complexes, freeing the minerals for the dog to use. This is one of the reasons why soaking a dry dog food before feeding it improves its digestibility.

Another reason some plant minerals are less utilized by a dog is because they are contained within indigestible cellulose envelopes. Hot water also helps release these minerals.

Even minerals from animals are not always satisfactory. Finely ground bone may readily furnish much of the minerals a dog needs. That same bone, ground coarse, or crushed into large chunks, will be much less digestible. This is because there is much less surface area on the coarser material for minerals to be dissolved.

The most consistently usable source of a mineral for a dog is probably the refined inorganic mineral itself, or some compound containing it. One of the most suitable sources of calcium and phosphorus, for example, is feed-grade dicalcium phosphate in a fine grind.

Vitamins, too, vary in usability within a diet. Vitamins A, D and E are only soluble in fats. Unless sufficient fat is present in a diet, these vitamins will pass through the intestinal tract unabsorbed, no matter how much of them the dog eats. The water-soluble vitamins usually present no problem. One B-vitamin, biotin, is rendered indigestible by raw egg white.

Biological Value (BV) is a term more often used by nutritionists than dog feeders. It is one of the terms most often misunderstood by dog feeders. It shouldn't be. Simply stated, the BV of a nutrient is the degree of that nutrient's ability to furnish a dog whatever it is the nutrient is supposed to furnish. Therefore, the BV of a fat is the degree of that fat's ability to furnish calories and essential fatty acids to a dog. The BV of a protein, on the other hand, is not its ability to supply energy, but the degree of its ability to furnish amino acids.

The greater the BV of a nutrient, the less of that nutrient is required to meet the dog's MDR for that nutrient. Protein serves as an excellent example, Figure 4. Whole egg protein is the protein that has the greatest ability to supply a dog with amino acids. It has a BV for the dog of 100. Only 0.57 gram of whole egg protein is needed, for each pound a dog weighs, to meet its MDR for amino acids. Horsemeat protein, with its BV of 87, is required at the rate of about 0.75 gram per pound. Soy protein has a BV of only 68, so it is required at about 0.9 gram. Proteins having a BV below 60 cannot supply enough amino acids to meet a dog's MDR, no matter how

59

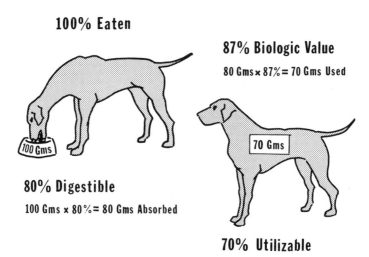

100% Eaten

87% Biologic Value

80 Gms x 87% = 70 Gms Used

80% Digestible

100 Gms x 80% = 80 Gms Absorbed

70% Utilizable

Figure 15. If 100 grams of a nutrient are eaten, and the nutrient is 80 percent digestible, then 80 grams of the nutrient will be absorbed by the dog. If this same nutrient has a biological value of 87 percent, then 70 grams of the nutrient that was absorbed will be used by the dog. Since 70 grams of the original 100 grams is retained and used, the nutrient is 70 percent utilizable.

much of them are eaten. Figure 4 gives the quantity of protein of a particular biological value that is needed to meet the MDR for amino acids in a dog.

When protein is used for energy as well as supplying amino acids, its BV is lowered considerably, since supplying energy is not one of its jobs. That is one of the main reasons why it is important to have sufficient calories from fats and carbohydrates in a dog's food. Remember, if energy is needed, all food will be used for energy first, and every ounce of a nutrient that is used for energy—rather than for what it was intended—reduces its biological value.

ACCEPTABLE FOOD

Many dog owners seem to be obsessed with the idea that the most important thing about a dog food is that their dog gulp it down as if it were the dog's first meal in a week. It *is* important for a dog to eat its food. No food, regardless of its nutritional adequacy, is of any value unless eaten by the animal for which it was intended. On the other hand, an inadequate food will fail to support a dog's life regardless of how fast or how much of it the dog eats. When a food is adequate it does not have to be delicious. As long as the food is

60

acceptable enough to a dog so that the dog will eat enough to obtain its daily nutritional needs, the food meets acceptability requirements.

Factors affecting acceptability may be either positive or negative. A negative factor is one which, because of its presence, renders the food unacceptable to a dog. It is a dominant factor, usually, and no matter how many positive factors are present, the presence of that single negative factor ordinarily renders the food totally unacceptable.

A positive factor may be either an absence of negative factors, or the presence of something that tends to make the food more acceptable to the dog. While the presence of a single objectionable factor usually converts an otherwise acceptable food into an unacceptable one, the addition of a single positive factor frequently will not produce any great magnitude of change in the dog's attitude toward the food.

Factors affecting palatability are always positive in nature, since palatability is merely accentuated acceptability. Palatability usually occurs as the result of the total effect of a number of positive factors in the same food. In the rare instances where a single positive factor does have a marked effect on palatability, it usually is converting an already acceptable food into a palatable one.

An excellent example of a single positive factor markedly changing a food from acceptable to palatable is salt in human foods. Salt also serves as an excellent example of the fallacy of *anthropomorphism*, that is, using man's tastes when choosing for a dog. In some trials we recently conducted we discovered that given the same food, with and without salt, dogs preferred the saltless food almost two to one.

When foods are being formulated, most people remember to consider the acceptability of the final product. Many of them forget, however, that it is far more important to try to please the dog's palate than to please their own.

When the dog feeder tries to make changes in the acceptability of a food, flavors and odors are the things he usually thinks of. In most instances, flavors and odors are much more important as negative factors than as positive ones. The most often overlooked factor affecting the palatability of a dog's food is the food's texture. The texture of a food is affected by its moisture levels, its fat content and types and amounts of carbohydrates, and by the overall effect of the

61

interaction of all the ingredients that are mixed together in the food.

To illustrate to yourself just how important texture really is, consider what would happen if I were to give you a cracker that was damp and soft. It would not even be acceptable, much less palatable. In contrast, if I were to give you a piece of cake that was dry and crisp you would find equal fault with it. From your own personal experience with cakes and crackers you can see how important texture can be. But, don't get caught in the trap of assuming that the dog likes his crackers crisp or his cakes soft. Remember the saltless food.

The above example also points out the importance that experience has on the determination of whether a food is acceptable or not. Many foods that are unacceptable to a dog, initially, will become acceptable as it gains more experience with them. Do not give up on a balanced food the first time your dog turns his nose up at it . . . try it again and again until he has had a chance to learn to like it.

Chapter 5

Non-Commercial Foods

THE dog feeder has at his disposal two major groups of foods for feeding dogs, commercial foods and non-commercial foods. Commercial foods will be discussed in the next chapter.

Non-commercial foods, as considered here, are not necessarily foods which are *not* associated in some manner with a commercial enterprise. Nor or they foods that do not cost money. The term "non-commercial", as used here, refers to those foods which are not a part of the commercial pet food industry or are not sold exclusively as a food for a dog.

The first food fed to a dog was a non-commercial food, the uneaten remains of some caveman's meal. Some of the earliest records provide both descriptions and pictures of dogs being thrown food from the table. Verse 27 of Chapter XV of the Gospel of St. Matthew reads, "The dogs eat of the scraps that fall from the table." It is likely that most of these scraps thrown to modern dog's early ancestors were an array of unbalanced morsels, unfit or unwanted by human masters. Some of the more obvious skeletal and growth defects from improper nutrition are faithfully depicted in some of the earliest drawings and figures of dogs.

For over 3000 years dogs eked out an existence from the food left them by the masters who had domesticated them. Gradually, as dog-raising became a more respected activity, elaborate formulations of natural ingredients were compounded for feeding dogs. These formulations were meticulously designed to duplicate exactly the dog's

63

wild diet. The carefully guarded formulations were handed down from generation to generation. A few that were inherently balanced have survived. But, for the most part, the preparation of a dog's diet from complex formulas and elaborate ingredients have disappeared in favor of the more convenient, less expensive and far better balanced commercial foods.

The explanation given for using non-commercial foods by those who still use them is usually economy or better nutrition. While it may be possible for both economy and better nutrition to result from a diet of non-commercial foods, an examination of most such feeding programs quickly reveals that neither economy nor better nutrition prevail. Indeed, in many instances, the dog feeder is unknowingly providing his dog with a poorer quality nourishment at a price higher than he would have to pay for commercial foods.

Table Scraps

Until about 20 years ago most dogs could still eke out a living on table scraps. With the advent of modern merchandising methods, both the quality and the quantity of the usable scraps has declined. Meats are sold already trimmed and boned, carefully wrapped in cellophane and cardboard, and ready for cooking without additional alterations. Frozen foods have eliminated trimmings from vegetables, and dairy and poultry products come from cartons and coolers, not cows and chickens. Everything is prepackaged in convenient quantities so that purchases can be adjusted to family appetites with almost no leftovers.

The scraps from a meal made from these pre-trimmed, pre-battered, pre-buttered, pre-cooked and pre-packaged foods consists of only bits and pieces which are either inedible or unwanted by human beings, Figure 16. Such bits and pieces make neither a balanced nor an adequate diet for a dog. The true value of today's table scraps are succinctly brought home when the would-be scrap feeder asks himself, "What would I do with these scraps if I didn't own a dog?" If his answer would be to save them in the refrigerator for his own next meal then a dog can probably eat the scraps, too. If he would throw the scraps into the garbage can, then he is literally feeding his dog garbage when he feeds table scraps.

There is an even greater danger in table scraps. In spite of their poor nutritional quality, table scraps frequently are quite palatable to a dog. All too often such table scraps are used with the idea of

64

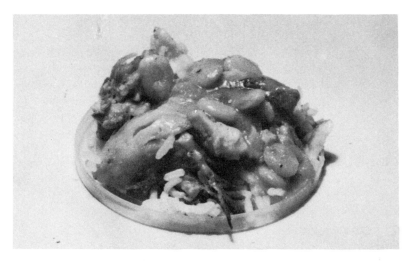

Figure 16. Table scraps. The inedible or unwanted items left by human beings.

increasing the palatability of a less palatable, but better balanced, commercial food. Unless the scraps are finely chopped and blended with the commercial foods, most dogs will simply pick out the table scraps and leave the balanced food behind. Most table scraps are fats and carbohydrates, yielding lots of calories and little else. As a consequence, the dog obtains a sizeable portion of its daily caloric need from the useless scraps and loses his appetite entirely for the commercial food. By refusing to put table scraps on the food, a dog feeder may feel he is forcing his dog to eat a food it does not want. But, in the long run, most dog feeders will agree that it is better to starve a dog with concern than to kill it with kindness.

Natural Ingredients

Originally, dog feeders who fed natural ingredients were attempting to replace the natural diet of the dog. Today such a task would be impossible to perform—if, indeed, it ever was. Natural ingredients used today are no longer the foods eaten by an animal "naturally" in the wild, but have become modifications of those original foodstuffs to more conveneient or longer-lasting forms. The human diet consists of a large selection of such modified natural foods, most of which have been tried for feeding a dog. Besides these human foods, there are still a few natural ingredients available to the dog

65

feeder that are not normally considered to be human foods. Examples of such foods are horsemeat, hog livers and bone meal.

Energy Sources

All natural foods containing nutrients are energy sources, since most nutrients can become energy. Some natural foods supply more energy than others and are customarily used as energy sources. These are the foods containing the largest quantities of fats and carbohydrates. Fats are the primary energy source in any diet for a dog. Most meats come with the fat already attached, especially in the chopped and ground varieties. Fats also can be found in nature in the pure form as vegetable oils or as tallow and lard. Carbohydrates, while not as concentrated an energy source as fats, are lower in cost. Carbohydrates are useful to dilute the protein in high-meat diets or lower the caloric density of diets containing too much fat.

Vegetable oils: Probably the most universally useful source of energy for a dog is corn oil. Corn oil supplies 9 calories in every gram, 250 calories in every ounce, 124 calories in every tablespoonful, and 62 calories in every teaspoonful. When used as the only fat in a food it also furnishes about ten times the amount of essential fatty acids needed by a dog. Corn oil is inexpensive, easily obtainable and has a reasonably good keeping quality. Other vegetable oils that can be used satisfactorily as an energy source for a dog are oleomargarine, olive oil, peanut oil, safflower oil and soybean oil.

Animal fats: While most animal fats contain just as many calories as vegetable oils, only two contain essential fatty acids in amounts sufficient to supply a dog's needs. These are the fat of the pig, commonly called lard, and horsefat. The tallow of beef and mutton should never be used as the sole source of energy for a dog because of their low content of essential fatty acids. Animal fats contain about 126 calories in every tablespoonful.

Cereal grains: One of the major sources of carbohydrates, both for dogs and man, is the cereal grains. The useful carbohydrate in these grains is predominantly starch. Starch can also be purchased in pure form, and contains about 29 calories per tablespoonful, or about 464 calories per cup. Other sources of carbohydrate energy from cereal grains can be obtained from dry and cooked breakfast cereals, boiled rice, hominy grits, corn meal, and in the milled form, as flour.

66

Cereal grain products should never constitute more than about 50 percent of the dry matter of a dog's diet.

Potatoes: Except for the fact that potatoes have more water in them, the amount of carbohydrates in potatoes is almost the same as in the cereal grains. Potatoes can be used interchangeably with those cereals that are fed in the boiled state. Like cereals, potatoes should never constitute more than 50 percent of the dry matter of the diet.

Bread: As a source of carbohydrates in a diet, white or whole-wheat bread ranks among the better "natural" foods available to a dog feeder. It usually is fortified with vitamins and minerals, is palatable to most dogs and is always available and inexpensive. Economy can be even greater when the bread is bought a day old. Some feeders of natural ingredients insist that bread should be toasted before being fed to a dog. While such a practice makes the slices easier to crumble and mix with the rest of the diet, the starches in bread have already been subjected to cooking and about all toasting does is to enhance the tastiness of the bread.

Specialty flour products: A carbohydrate source frequently overlooked by a dog feeder is the specialty product made from flour—noodles, macaroni and spaghetti. These have an energy content comparable to other cereal grain products. And, like rice and hot cereals, they have the advantage of being able to be added dry to a food, then being cooked after the water has been added. This gives the capability of mixing a large amount of dry food at one time, then adding water and cooking small amounts as it is needed.

Protein Sources

Meat is, without question, the most common natural ingredient fed to a dog. It is also the most common source of protein. It is not the only source, however, nor is it the best. Eggs, milk, and plant proteins also make up a large reservoir of protein sources available to dog feeders.

Meat: There are a few dog feeders who foolishly insist that meat is the only thing a dog should ever be fed. Meat, alone, is entirely inadequate for a dog. The foremost deficiency in a diet of meat is its lack of calcium. If the meat is trimmed of fat there is also likely to occur a deficiency in energy. There are numerous other deficiencies, but none as dramatic as these two.

Meat, nevertheless, is the single most important source of protein fed to dogs. Thousands of tons of horsemeat and beef are used each

67

year in producing commercial dog foods. Hundreds of tons more are fed as a supplement to commercial foods or in home-made rations. When fed as an addition to a balanced commercial food, meat can be added up to 10 percent of the weight of the mixture. When added in any greater amounts it will dilute the commercial food to the extent that the diet will no longer be balanced or adequate. When used as the sole source of protein in a home-made ration, meat should constitute at least 25 percent of the total weight of the diet. No home-made ration should ever contain more than 75 percent of its weight as meat, however.

All meats except pork can be fed to a dog either cooked or raw, but will usually furnish more nourishment in the raw state. Vitamins are destroyed by the heat of cooking. Fat also is driven out of meat during cooking, and unless it is poured back into the ration, it will become lost as an energy source. The only real justification for feeding a dog cooked meat in a homemade ration is because it is pork, or because the dog does not like raw meat. Dogs having a *genuine* dislike for raw meat are few and far between.

The nature of the animal from which the meat comes does not seem to be too important where protein is concerned. Nutritionally, most proteins from different animals seem to be about equal. For years it was contended by some dog feeders that pork could not be fed to dogs. Feeding experiments do not bear this out. In fact, pork liver is probably among the most nutritious livers commonly available to the dog feeder. The only restriction which pork has when being fed to dogs is that it be cooked.

Eggs: Eggs for feeding dogs can be bought by the dozen in the grocery store, by the hundreds from hatcheries or by the thousands from egg ranches. Regardless of how many or where they are obtained, an egg should never be fed to a dog raw. Raw egg whites react with the vitamin, biotin, and prevent a dog from using it. In fact, feeding raw egg whites is the exact way scientists produce experimental biotin deficiency in a laboratory.

Cooked, whole eggs provide the best possible protein available to a dog. If egg was the only protein being used in a food it would only have to be added in amounts of about two ounces (about one egg) for every pound of food. While this amounts to only about two percent protein in the diet, it is still sufficient because egg protein is of such high quality. When using eggs to increase the value of protein in a commercial food for an adult dog, therefore, never add more than one egg to each pound of food, or it will be wasted.

Milk: Much controversy has raged over feeding milk to dogs. Milk has been accused of causing diarrhea and other digestive upsets. While it may produce these problems in large amounts, if milk is kept to about two ounces of fluid milk or two tablespoonsful of dry milk per pound of food, few problems will be encountered. The value of the milk, when fed in proper amounts, exceeds the risk of upset. Milk supplies calcium and phosphorus in the proper ratio and amounts, a host of vitamins, and also a protein which approaches the value of whole egg.

Cottage cheese: Cottage cheese is little more than the major protein fraction of milk, casein. It does not have the same value as the protein of whole milk because the lactoalbumin, normally present in whole milk, has been washed away in the whey. The value of the protein in cottage cheese compares favorably with that of horsemeat. Cottage cheese offers the dog feeder an inexpensive, readily available source of quality protein for his dog.

Cheese: Another dairy product made from casein is cheese. Cheese, unlike cottage cheese, also contains a considerable amount of fat. The fat makes cheese a valuable source of energy as well as of protein. Because they are made as human foods, and are sold in competition with other human foods, cheeses are among the more expensive protein sources for feeding dogs. For dog feeders who wish to spend the extra money, cheese is a worthwhile consideration.

Fish: Fish is not commonly used in dietary formulations for dogs, but there is no logical reason to eliminate it from consideration as a protein source for a dog. Indeed, fish protein is one of the better proteins, for the money, that a dog feeder can use. Fish, too, should always be cooked before being fed. In this case the heat destroys a chemical found in many fish that will destroy vitamin B_1 (thiamine) if left unchanged.

Vitamin Sources

Vegetables: While a few vegetables may serve as natural vitamin sources, most vegetables have little value to a dog. Dogs can only digest about 30 to 50 percent of most of the vegetables eaten by man. Many of these vegetables are practically all water. What roughage they may contain can just as easily be obtained from cereal grains. Vegetables contain too little fat to be of any value as energy sources. Any plant protein they contain is likely to be of low biological value to a dog. The only important vegetable sources of vitamins for a dog are listed in Table II of the preceding chapter.

Fruits: Fruits are of even less value to the dog than vegetables are. The main vitamin for which fruits serve as a natural source is vitamin C, a vitamin that is not required in a healthy dog's diet. The healthy dog produces enough vitamin C from glucose to meet its MDR.

Other vitamin sources: Several other natural sources of vitamins are available to a dog feeder. Some of these, like eggs, cheese, bread and fish, have already been touched upon under other headings.

Of all methods, by far the most accurate and efficient way to provide a dog's MDR for *each* vitamin when compounding a diet from natural ingredients is by using a vitamin mix and calculating the exact amount to add that will provide an adequate supply of vitamins.

Mineral Sources

The minerals, like the vitamins, are best balanced in every diet by using a mineral mix in amounts calculated to supply an MDR for each mineral, and balanced to the caloric density of the diet. In natural diets most of the trace minerals are found in adequate amounts in the natural ingredients. It is important that the major minerals —calcium, phosphorus, potassium, magnesium and sodium—be balanced during diet formulation to insure that they are present in the diet in adequate amounts and in the proper ratio.

Bone meal: Bone meal contains calcium, phosphorus and magnesium in almost the exact ratio required by a dog. As long as it is fed in a finely ground form, most of the mineral it contains will be usable by the dog. Bone meal should be added at about $\frac{1}{2}$ ounce for every pound of raw meat put into a dog's diet. It should never be added in excess of $\frac{1}{2}$ ounce per pound of the total diet.

Because it is inexpensive and easily available, bone meal is too often fed as the cure-all for any dietary mineral problem. This invariably leads to a greater imbalance in the mineral portion of the diet, not to its correction.

Other mineral sources: Milk and cheese are probably the only

70

important sources of calcium and phosphorus among the foods not fed especially as sources of these minerals. Magnesium is found in nuts and beans, potassium in almost any natural ingredient. Most trace minerals in a natural diet are derived from the natural ingredients.

Nature's Mystery Food—Liver

Newborn puppies, dying from the "failing puppy syndrome", have a tablespoonful of chopped liver added to their mother's diet. Overnight, the pups snap out of it and start gaining again. Orphan puppies, stunted because their formula is inadequate, have a little liver puree added to that formula and those same puppies suddenly begin to grow and gain weight. A young, adult male, starting his second year at stud is listless, uninterested and underweight. A teaspoonful of raw liver daily returns the stud to his original luster and aggressiveness. A dog struck by an automobile fails to respond, even though surgery has successfully corrected its injuries. About a week after the operation a tablespoonful of liver is prescribed three times weekly. By the end of the third week all of the dog's lost weight has been regained and healing of the external wounds appears complete.

All of the dogs described above had one thing in common—liver was added to their diet. Perhaps liver should be called a "miracle" food rather than a mystery food. But, whatever you call it, the recoveries described were the results of liver, and whatever it is that enables liver to produce such "miracles" remains a "mystery".

For years veterinary nutritionists have referred to the "unidentified liver fractions" and their seemingly miraculous effects. Whatever it is in liver, known or unknown, few canine nutritionists deny that liver does something special when it comes to a dog's diet. If there *is* one single food that every dog should have in its diet, that food would have to be liver.

As a matter of reference, and for those who would enjoy probing a little deeper into the mysteries of dog feeding, Table IV lists a comprehensive analytical breakdown of the nutrients found in beef and pork liver. While there may be some fractions in liver as yet unidentified, one thing about liver is no mystery. It contains more nutrients in one package than any other natural food available to man or beast.

71

TABLE IV
The Nutrient Content of Beef and Pork Livers

Nutrient	Beef	Pork	Comments
water %	69.7	72.3	similar to commercial foods
protein %	19.7	19.7	having a BV better than meat
fat %	3.2	4.8	
carbohydrate %	6.0	1.7	
crude fiber %	0	0	
total ash %	1.4	1.5	
calcium (mg) *	7	10	
phosphorus (mg) *	358	362	
iron (mg) *	6.6	18.0	
sodium (mg) *	110	77	
potassium (mg) *	380	350	
copper (mcg)*	2450		about 5x more than most sources
cobalt			
vitamin A (IU) *	43,900	14,200	
vitamin D (IU) *	34	44	same as milk, more than plants, less than fish-liver oils
vitamin E			
vitamin K		115-230	
vitamin B_1 (mg) *	0.26	0.40	
vitamin B_2 (mg) *	3.33	2.98	
niacin (mg) *	13.7	16.7	
folic acid (mcg)*	294	221	10x more than most foods
pantothenic acid (mcg)*	5660-8180	5880-7300	5x more than most natural sources
biotin (mcg)	100		10x more than most natural sources
vitamin B_6 (mcg)*	600-710	290-590	about equal to most natural sources
choline (mg) *	480-700	470-620	5x more than most natural sources
vitamin C (mg) *	31	23	

* in 100 grams of liver.

72

Chapter 6

Commercial Dog Foods

THE earliest commercial dog foods were in the form of a baked biscuit. They appeared immediately after the Civil War, about 1866, in England. How much the food technology learned during the war was involved in their appearance is not known, but the hard, dry dog biscuit closely resembled the Civil War soldier's "hardtack". This early biscuit was made primarily from cereal products and baked in a thin sheet on a bread tin. Scoring the dough allowed the baked sheets to be broken into biscuits of more convenient size. Baking the starches made them more usable than they were in raw natural mixes and also provided them in a more uniform mixture.

It was soon found that if the biscuits were "kibbled", or uniformly crumbled into small pieces, they would absorb water or other liquids much faster, and this would make them more palatable. The kibbled biscuit was far more convenient than the perishable home-made rations of natural ingredients. Although still unbalanced, the kibbled food's ability to better nourish a dog was immediately noticed. When fresh meat was added to the kibbled food its nutritional qualities far exceeded any other known formulations of the day.

In the United States another form of dry food was evolving, the dog meal. Primarily a by-product of the human breakfast food industry, meals were composed of dried cereal flakes, unprocessed cereal grains and a new twist—dried meat scraps. American manufacturers were attempting to incorporate meat into their products, in a dry form, to make their foods more "complete" for a dog. By adding the meat themselves, American dog food makers were able to control the amount of protein that went into the product, thereby protecting their food's balance. By adding the meat in dry form they were able to maintain the moisture of the product below the perishable level of ten percent.

While convenience has become the major factor in the popularity that commercial foods enjoy today, the original efforts were directed at providing a better means of food preservation. Besides drying, another food preservation technique was being investigated by food technologists of the early 1800's. Based on earlier work done in 1787 by Nicolas Appert, a French candymaker, the canning process was developed. In 1820 the first canning plant in the U.S. was established in Boston. By the 1850's the canning of meat, as food for humans, had become a common commercial procedure.

It was not until 1922 that a group of American businessmen involved in exporting horsemeat for human consumption conceived the idea of converting some of the unexportable cuts into dog food. The cuts that went abroad constituted only a small part of the horse's carcass and large surpluses of horsemeat were available for such an enterprise.

The original group attempted to develop a scientifically nutritive food for dogs. The response to their efforts was neither immediate nor overwhelming. Not until one of the men with a basket of canned dog food on his arm, went about Chicago soliciting sales from veterinarians, did canned dog food begin to be accepted. Once it did catch on, sales mushroomed. By 1932, only ten years after its conception, nearly 200 brands of canned dog food were being sold.

Today, nearly 1500 makers sell some 10,000 labels of pet foods in dry, canned, soft-moist and frozen varieties. It is not at all uncommon nowadays to find 30 or 40 different dog foods in a single grocery store display. Pet food volume today exceeds the ready-to-eat cereal and instant breakfast sales combined . . . a clear case of the offspring outgrowing the parent.

Less than 15 percent of the dog-owning public still feed their dogs non-commercial foods exclusively. Every recent survey of dog feeding practices has indicated this fact. Furthermore, of the 85 percent of the dog owners who use commercial foods, 30 percent feed nothing but commercial foods. This means that more than half of

74

the dog owners in the U.S. feed some combination of commercial foods and non-commercial foods.

Dog foods sold commercially are usually divided into four types on the basis of the method by which they are preserved. This classification also corresponds to the amount of moisture the food contains. The four types are:

Dry foods   5% to 10% moisture
Soft-moist foods   20% to 25% moisture
Canned foods   65% to 78% moisture
Frozen foods   60% to 70% moisture

Each type of commercial food can be further divided. This division can be made on the basis of the nature of the ingredients or the processing method. These are:

dry	soft-moist	frozen	canned
meal	ground	ration	ration
biscuits	chunk	all-meat	all-animal-
kibbled	ribbon		tissue
expanded			chunks
			stew

Each type has its own peculiar characteristics and its own advantages and disadvantages. Each has its own proponents and opponents. While the author has his own preferences, each type and style of food is discussed here from what is hoped to be an unbiased viewpoint.

Dry Dog Foods

Dry meals: Early dry meals were little more than hog rations. Indeed, many may have been just that. By combining carbohydrates from cereals such as ground corn, cracked wheat and rolled oats, together with some dried tankage and a vitamin-mineral mixture, an early dry meal was made.

Today's dry meals, Figure 17, are greatly improved. The carbohydrate sources are heat-treated to dextrinize the starches and improve their digestibility. Toasted corn meal, wheat flakes and oat meal are used instead of raw cereal grains. The tankage has been replaced by meat and bone meal having a standardized protein and fat content. These two major ingredients, cooked cereal and meat meal, are blended together in amounts pre-calculated to supply more nutritious protein and a better protein-to-calorie ratio. Sufficient amounts

75

Figure 17. Dry meal dog food.

of fat are added to increase the caloric density. With modern equipment's capabilities, vitamins and minerals can be more accurately measured and more uniformly blended throughout the meat and cereal mixture.

Dry meals are sometimes pelleted to make them easier to handle and feed. These are usually milled into pellets of $\frac{1}{8}$th inch to $\frac{1}{4}$th inch in diameter that break at about $\frac{1}{4}$th inch to about $\frac{1}{2}$ inch lengths. The pellets may also be milled much larger, crumbled, and then screened to obtain a uniform particle size. Pellets can be fat-coated, which increases their caloric density and enhances their palatability.

A typical formula for a dry meal is listed in Table V.

76

TABLE V

The formula for a dry meal dog food.

ingredient	percent
Corn or wheat flakes	50.0
Soybean meal	16.5
Meat meal	12.0
Liver meal	5.0
Nonfat dry milk	5.0
Bakery products	3.0
Dry yeast	3.0
Tomato pomace	2.5
Dicalcium phosphate	1.5
Salt	0.5
Vitamin mix	0.5
Trace mineral mix	0.5
	100.0

Biscuits and Kibbles: When cereal grains and dried meat scraps are ground together into a flour, they can be blended with water or other suitable liquids to form a dough. This dough can be baked into a biscuit. Baked dog foods are produced in much the same manner as baked foods for humans. The necessary amounts of grain flours, meat meals, dairy products, vitamins and minerals are blended together in a paddle mixer to form the dough. The dough is rolled into a continuous sheet and fed on conveyor belts into band ovens. Such ovens allow a continuous flow of dough into, and baked product out. The baked sheet is usually cut into large rectangular pieces which are placed into crumblers or "kibblers" and broken or kibbled into more or less uniform-sized fragments, Figure 18. Before being packaged, better quality kibbled products are passed over screens, called "scalpers", which eliminate the smaller particles and fines from the product being packaged.

An alternate method for baked products is to push the dough through an extruder with a rotary molder or stamp that presses out characteristically shaped biscuits from the dough, Figure 19. These frequently are made from different colored doughs, each designating a different flavor or variety. The shaped biscuits are fed into the band ovens, baked, then collected at the other end and packaged. Sometimes shaped biscuits are dropped from the stamp onto tin sheets. The sheets are then placed into conventional industrial bakery ovens and baked. When baked in this fashion, the biscuits

77

Figure 18. Kibbled biscuit dog food.

Figure 19. Shaped biscuit dog food.

78

are taken to a tempering or drying room to develop a final hardening before they are packaged.

A typical formula for a baked dog food is found in Table VI.

TABLE VI

The formula for a baked food.

ingredient	percent
Wheat flour	33.0
Whole milk	22.0
Soybean meal	10.5
Meat meal	8.0
Lard	8.0
Wheat germ meal	5.0
Liver and glandular meal	5.0
Dried vegetable pomace	3.0
Dicalcium phosphate	2.5
Baking powder	1.0
Salt, iodized	1.0
Vitamin mixes	0.5
Trace mineral mixes	0.5
	100.0

Expanded Dry Foods: By mixing raw grains, meat meal, vegetables and dairy products with steam, inside a blending pressure cooker, these ingredients can be cooked, while at the same time being whipped into a homogeneous mass. Using this technique allows the addition of ingredients not used in other types of dry foods.

Following the heat-mixing process the homogeneous mass is pushed through a die and expanded with steam and air into small, porous nuggets, Figure 20. As it comes from the die, the expanded nugget still contains a large amount of moisture and is soft and sponge-like. To prevent the nuggets from sticking together, they are dropped through heated air streams or passed through a low heat on a slow-moving belt. This hardens the nugget, giving it a crunchy, palatable character. An alternate method used by some manufacturers is to produce a large expanded nugget that is then kibbled to produce smaller sized fragments of expanded food, Figure 21. Most "kibbled" foods on the market today are of this type rather than the kibbled biscuit.

The dried, hardened nugget or kibbled fragment is usually passed

79

Figure 20. Small nuggets of expanded dry dog food.

Figure 21. Expanded dry dog food that has been kibbled.

80

through a spray chamber and coated with a liquid fat, carbohydrate or milk product. This coating process enables the manufacturer to add needed calories to the food that cannot be added before it is expanded. When water is added to a nugget so coated, this coating greatly enhances the odor and palatability of the food.

Products which are designed to be expanded must be formulated to contain at least 40 percent carbohydrates or the expansion process won't work. Some manufacturers also add plasticized binders such as lignin extracts, cellulose gums or verxite to improve the nugget's physical quality.

Because of their fat coating, most expanded foods are packaged in multiwalled bags having at least one ply serving as a grease barrier. Some of the substances used as grease barriers are glassine, vegetable parchment, or plastic coated paper. In extreme cases, even plastic sheets may be used.

A typical formula for an expanded dry food is found in Table VII.

TABLE VII

The formula for an expanded dry dog food.

ingredient	percent
Ground corn	30.0
Soy grits	15.0
Meat and bone meal	14.0
Wheat grits	10.0
Lard	7.0
Ground oats	6.0
Ground grain sorghum	6.0
Wheat middlings	5.0
Wheat germ meal	3.0
Brewer's dried yeast	1.0
Salt (iodized)	1.0
Dried whey	1.0
Vitamin mixes	0.5
Trace mineral mixes	0.5
	100.0

Soft-moist Foods: By adding preservatives and humectants to the meat ingredients cooked in a pressure blender the amount of water that can remain in the finished product, without encouraging spoiling, can be higher than that of dry products. Foods so processed are called *soft-moist* foods.

81

Figure 22. Soft-moist dog food extruded to resemble hamburger.

Six basic ingredients are necessary for the proper formulation of soft-moist foods—soybean meal, sugar, fresh meat or meat by-products, animal fat, preservatives and humectants. The six are mixed together, with appropriate vitamin and mineral mixes, in a paddle mixer. The fresh meat by-products, which amount to about 30% of the total, are added last because they turn the mixture into a doughy, sticky consistency. At that stage the mixture is fed into a blending-cooker and cooked. This heating, while blending, dextrinizes the raw starches, reduces the mixture to a homogeneous mass, and pasteurizes the product. Thorough blending also assures a constant discharge temperature.

Inside the cooker the mixture reaches a temperature of about 200° F. and contains almost 30 percent moisture. As it is extruded from the cooker, forced air quickly dries the mixture to about 25 percent moisture, while at the same time cooling the product to 80° F. This combination produces a satisfactory consistency for packaging and handling operations. The hot mixture may be extruded in various shapes and sizes, Figures 22, 23 and 24.

Figure 23. Soft-moist dog food extruded to resemble cut pieces of sausage.

Figure 24. Soft-moist dog food extruded in alternate white and red ribbons to resemble chunks of meat.

83

Figure 25. Hamburger style soft-moist dog food packaged in pillow-pouched package (left) and patty (right).

Packaging of soft-moist foods may consist of wrapping individual patties in cellophane sheets, sealing portion-controlled servings in pillow-pouched bags or covering a dozen or so chunks of product with sealed films of cellophone and placing them into plastic-lined cardboard boxes, Figure 25.

Unrefrigerated dog food usually spoils at moisture levels above 10 percent. The secret to keeping a dog food at levels as high as 25 percent moisture is the addition of humectants and preservatives. Humectants are ingredients that take up water and jealously keep it from being used by bacteria or other micro-organisms. Propylene glycol and sorbitol, two commonly used humectants, can also be used by the dog's body to supply energy. Preservatives are chemicals added to create an environment that is unsatisfactory for the growth of any micro-organisms that are present. They, too, tend to reduce the usefulness of the water content to micro-organisms. Sugars and syrups are used in soft-moist foods as preservatives, but also serve as flavor enhancers. Sugars and syrups are also excellent sources of energy. Sucrose is the sugar most often incorporated into soft-moist foods. This sugar occasionally causes a loose stool to develop in a dog.

84

Table VIII lists a typical formula of a soft-moist food.

TABLE VIII

The formula for a soft-moist dog food.

ingredient	percent
Soy flour	31.0
Meat by-products	28.0
Sucrose	21.0
Wheat bran	3.0
Dicalcium phosphate	3.0
Horsemeat or beef	3.0
Dried nonfat milk	3.0
Tallow	2.0
Water	2.0
Propylene glycol	1.5
Salt (iodized)	1.0
Sorbates	0.5
Vitamin mixes	0.5
Trace mineral mixes	0.4
Artificial coloring	0.1
	100.0

Canned Foods

Another way of preserving fresh, wet ingredients is to seal them into containers that prevent any re-contamination and then destroy any micro-organisms of spoilage already in the food. This is the method used when dog foods are sealed in tin-plated steel cans and the sealed cans are subjected to a heat-sterilization process.

Ration-type canned foods: In ration-type canned foods, Figure 26, the fresh meat and meat by-products are put into grinders that chop them into small uniform-size pieces. This ground mixture is then fed, along with the ingredients that need no grinding, into blenders. At the same time animal and vegetable fats and water sufficient to process are added to the mixture. The water is added to the mixture until it gives it a satisfactory fluidity. The food mixture must be liquid so it will pour, to allow for proper can filling.

In order to obtain a proper vacuum in each can as it is sealed, the liquid must be poured at a temperature of at least 160° F. To produce this temperature the blenders are either enclosed within a steam jacket or the steam is infused directly into the mixture. In the

Figure 26. Ration-type canned dog food.

Figure 27. The "head space". A remnant of the air space upon which a vacuum was drawn when the can was sealed.

blenders the ingredients are mixed, while being heated, and then pumped to the can fillers.

Modern can fillers are able to fill and seal cans at 500 to 800 per minute. Each can is filled leaving a small slack space. This space is left so that a little air is present inside the can upon which a vacuum can be drawn. The remnants of that air space are often seen in ration-type canned foods when the lid is removed. It appears as a small, dark, rounded depression in the center or along the edge of the food mass, Figure 27. This spot is frequently mistaken by dog feeders as a spoiled area in the can. Its presence is perfectly normal, and it has no effect on the nutritional quality of the can's contents. The darkened surface is caused by oxidation of the food and is completely harmless to the dog.

A typical formula for a ration-type canned dog food is given in Table IX.

TABLE IX

The formula for a ration-type dog food.

ingredient	percent
Whole ground chicken	15.0
Soy grits	12.0
Ground corn	7.0
Spleen	6.5
Lard	4.5
Beef	3.0
Beef blood	3.0
Lungs	1.5
Dicalcium phosphate	0.8
Vitamin mixes	0.6
Trace mineral mixes	0.1
Water	46.0
	100.0

All-animal-tissue foods: Once these foods were called "all meat" or "100% meat" dog foods. Since 1969 no dog food can legally be labeled as "all" or "100%" anything unless it does, in fact, contain all or 100 percent of whatever it says it does. For a food to qualify as "all" or "100%" meat it must be made *wholly* from the lean skeletal or heart muscle of the food animal. The foods commonly called "all meat" of "100% meat" contain not only meat, but organ tissues, adipose tissues, lungs, udders, gullets and similar animal by-prod-

87

Figure 28. An all-animal-tissue dog food.

ucts, Figure 28. Since "all meat", therefore, is an incorrect name for these foods, we have chosen to use a term less misleading. In this book we will refer to those foods made from meat and meat by-products as "all-animal-tissue" foods.

In all-animal-tissue foods, slabs and chunks of raw ingredients are chopped into more or less uniform-sized pieces by knives, and dropped onto conveyor belts. In some instances the pieces are cooked by special methods before canning. The can-filling machines for all-animal-tissue foods are equipped with a rotating knife. When the can is full, the knife slices the contents off even with the top, but allowing a small space for fill slack.

No formulas are necessary for all-animal-tissue foods since they contain only one major ingredient, the meat and by-products of animals. Some may have a flavoring agent added, and all must have a little charcoal put in to denature the food to keep it from being sold for human consumption.

Chunk-style Foods: Because some dog feeders objected to the presence of recognizable pieces of trachea, blood vessels, lungs, etc. in cans of food they had to feed their dog, Figure 29, another step was added to the process of making all-animal-tissue foods by some manufacturers. The chopped mixture is fed into a steam-charged blending cooker and macerated into a smooth, homogeneous mass. This mass is extruded as a "chunk" of the mixture. These chunks are either dropped into a boiling water bath or blast-heated to firm the outside surface of the chunk and hold it together.

Each can is filled with these chunks, Figure 30. The chunks are covered with a gravy or juice and the can is sealed.

Besides producing a much more attractive food product, the chunking process has another distinct advantage over the all-animal-tissue foods. During the blending, measured amounts of minerals and vitamins can be added to produce a balanced formulation. One of the greatest disadvantages of an all-animal-tissue diet is that it produces diseases related to its deficiencies in minerals and vitamins. The ability to add needed vitamins and minerals retains the advantages of the high-meat foods, but allows the manufacturers to produce a balanced, adequate food that will nourish a dog even when fed as an exclusive diet.

A typical formula for a chunk-style dog food is given in Table X.

TABLE X

The formula for a chunk-style dog food.

ingredient	percent
Meat by-products	35.0
Meat	20.0
Liver	15.0
Steamed bone meal	7.0
Lard	6.0
Soy bean meal	5.0
Corn flour	4.5
Beef blood	3.9
Malto-dextrins	2.0
Mineral mixes	1.5
Vitamin mixes	0.1
	100.0

Stews: These foods are made strictly to appeal to the dog feeder who knows what a stew is. For a dog, whose digestive system is not equipped to handle whole, unskinned peas or slices of carrots,

89

Figure 29. An easily recognizable section of artery in an all-animal-tissue canned food.

Figure 30. A chunk-style canned dog food.

90

Figure 31. A pet stew dog food. Note the peas and carrots.

Figure 31, the stew may not be as appealing. The stew is processed much like the all-animal-tissue foods. Along with the meat and meat by-products, peas, potatoes and carrots are also dropped onto the conveyors and mixed together. The mixture is then metered into a can, and the can is sealed.

Retorting or Cooking: Regardless of whether the food they contain is ration-type, animal tissue, chunk style or stew, once the cans are filled and sealed they must be sterilized to prevent spoilage. This is done by heating their contents to at least 250° F., for several minutes while the atmospheric pressure is raised to 15 or more pounds per square inch. This heating destroys some of the nutritive value of the food, especially certain vitamins. The less time and temperature to which the contents of the can must be subjected and still destroy the micro-organisms, the greater the nutrient quality retained.

Most canned foods are sterilized using a device known as a *retort.* This is nothing more than a great big oversized pressure cooker. The cans are stacked on shelves in racks which are then lowered into the retort. Once filled with cans, the retort is closed and tightly sealed. The temperature within the retort is brought up to 250° F.,

91

using steam under pressure. The length of heating time depends on the size of the retort and the number of cans. When the cans have been heated long enough to bring the center of every can to 250° F. for at least three minutes, the heat is turned off. The pressure in the retort is kept constant by compressed air while cold water is rapidly admitted into the bottom of the retort. The purpose of the cold water is to reduce the cooling time as much as possible. When the cans have cooled to about 100 to 110° F. they are removed from the retort, labeled, boxed and sent to the warehouse.

A more uniform method of sterilization has been developed, using a *continuous cooker*. The two most common methods of continuous cooking used in the dog food industry employ machines known as the reel-type cooker and the hydrostatic cooker.

The hydrostatic cooker serves as an excellent example of continuous cooking. Sealed cans from the can filler are continuously introduced into one side of the cooker while sterilized cans are being removed from the other side. The cans are moved along by a chain-driven belt, first through a pre-heating stage, then through a pressurized cooking stage in which the time and temperature are carefully regulated, and finally through a cooling stage, Figure 32. The temperature at which the cooker is kept determines how long a can must move through the cooking stage. By adjusting the speed at which the belt moves the can along, an operator can determine the exact length of time during which each can is exposed to the critical cooking stage. The use of the continuous cooker allows a dog food manufacturer a method of processing each can at the same temperature and time as every other can, regardless of the day or size of production.

The cooking process of the canning procedure accomplishes two important functions. First, the heat favorably alters the nature of some of the ingredients. The cereal grains are dextrinized and hydrolyzed. Plant proteins and carbohydrates are freed from their unusable forms by the action of heat and by enzymes that are present in the plants. The physical structure of some of the carbohydrates and proteins is altered so that they absorb water, swell and form a plastic, semi-solid mass in the ration type foods or a thick gravy in chunk and stew type foods. In foods that are not subjected to heat before filling (cold-packed foods) the sterilization procedure is the only form of cooking they get.

Secondly, the heat, under pressure, kills most of the micro-organ-

92

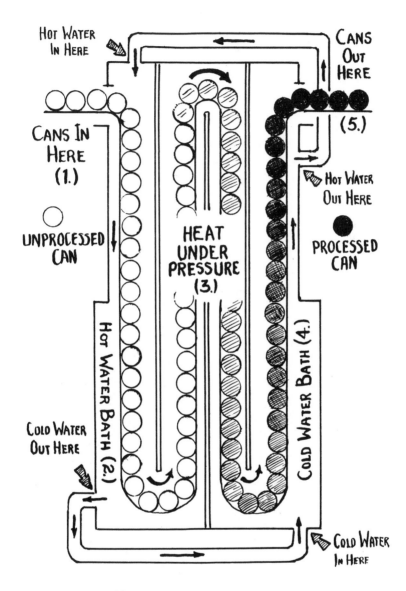

Figure 32. Schematic diagram of can flow of cans of dog food being sterilized in a continuous cooker.

isms within the can. The sterilization process is particularly designed to destroy the germ that causes botulism, *Clostridium botulinum*. This germ thrives in cans sealed away from all air, and forms protective spores when subjected to heat lower than 250° F. Most micro-organisms that contaminate cans of food are much less resistant than the botulism organism. If the sterilization kills the *Clostridium*, it's a pretty good bet that it has killed everything else in the can, too.

Cans that have not undergone proper sterilization become apparent very quickly. As the bacteria grow, they produce gases. These gases build up inside the can, unable to escape because of the seal. Such cans are easily recognizable, and are called "swellers" or "puffers" by people who work with canned food products, Figure 33. When the gases reach enough pressure within the can they burst through at places of least resistance—usually the lids or side seams. Under proper conditions, these cans may create a real hazard, building up pressures as high as 120 psi before they burst.

Frozen foods: A final method of preserving dog foods is by freez-

Figure 33. The can on the left is a "sweller" in its earlier stages. Note the dome-shaped appearance of the lid.

ing. When the temperature of a food is dropped below 32° F. the growth of bacteria is greatly retarded. The food can be kept, unspoiled, as long as the food remains at the lowered temperatures.

To prepare a frozen dog food the fresh meat and meat by-products are fed into a hogger which grinds them into a uniform-size particle. The ground meat and by-products are transferred to a mixing vat where they are mixed with a pre-mix of vitamins and minerals and the dry cereal ingredients, if there are any. Once these constituents are mixed, blood, lard and water, in pre-calculated quantities are metered into the mixing vat and the whole mixture is heated to 180° F. while being stirred.

The purpose of this heating is to kill any *Salmonella* organisms, the bacteria that cause typhoid-like upsets in animals. Besides killing the bacteria, the heat serves to dextrinize the starches and partially cook the fresh ingredients.

The heated mixture is then fed into a press which forms the mushy mixture prior to packaging. It then is metered in measured amounts into boxes, or stuffed into casings. The boxes are closed and sealed, the casings twisted shut. Both are packed into large shipping cartons and frozen in walk-in freezers at a temperature of $-20°$ F. or below. It must be maintained in the frozen state until it is fed or it will spoil shortly after being thawed.

Advantages and Disadvantages

There are advantages and disadvantages with all four types of commercial foods. The fact that a food has a disadvantage does not mean it is unsatisfactory, since in any individual case the food's advantages may outweigh its disadvantages. Can openers may be no disadvantage whatsoever with cans used in a family kitchen, but a forgotten opener on a hunt into the Canadian backwoods might prove a distinct disadvantage if only canned food had been taken along.

Canned

Advantages	*Disadvantages*
1. Requires no refrigeration (long shelf life).	1. Expensive form of preservation.
2. Durable container (no infestation).	2. Is three-fourths water.
3. Usually highly palatable.	3. Heavy, inflexible container.
4. Ingredients more digestible than most dry foods.	4. Left-overs spoil if unrefrigerated.
	5. Requires a special device to open cans.

95

Soft-moist

Advantages
1. Requires no refrigeration (moderate shelf life).
2. Usually highly palatable.
3. Ingredients equally digestible as canned foods.
4. Contains only about 1/4th water.
5. Packed in convenient, portion-controlled container.

Disadvantages
1. Deteriorates after package is opened.
2. Causes digestive upsets in some dogs.
3. Spoils if it gets wet.
4. Expensive form of preservation.
5. Requires water be supplied for drinking to maintain adequate intake.

Dry Foods

Advantages
1. Requires no refrigeration (moderate shelf life).
2. Does not spoil after package is opened.
3. More nutrients and energy per pound of food.
4. More economical than foods with higher moisture content.

Disadvantages
1. May contain insufficient fat (too little energy).
2. Processing heat may destroy vitamins.
3. Digestibility of nutrients may be low.
4. Must supply adequate drinking water.
5. Fat may become rancid with storage.
6. Insects and other vermin may contaminate.
7. Will spoil if it gets wet.

Frozen Foods

Advantages
1. Potentially, the highest digestibility of nutrients.
2. Usually highest in palatability.
3. Provides nutrients in closest to fresh form as possible.

Disadvantages
1. Requires special equipment to store.
2. Spoils after package is thawed.
3. Is more than one-half water.
4. Requires thawing before feeding.
5. Nutrient quality may suffer from "freezer burn" if package tears.

Specialized Foods

Most of the commercial dog foods made and sold in the United States are designed and formulated for maintenance. An increasing number of foods are being made expressly for a particular phase of the dog's life cycle other than maintenance. These foods constitute a sub-group of commercial foods, the *specialized foods*.

Dietary Animal Foods: The first specialized food developed was

96

designed to be used in the management of a specific disease suffered by dogs. The pioneer in this field was Mark L. Morris, DVM. In the late 1930's a disease known as "hemorrhagic gastroenteritis" was responsible for more than 50 percent of the deaths of American dogs. Through the assistance of a Rutgers graduate student, Dr. Morris discovered that the disease was being caused by diseased kidneys. Unable to perform their function properly, the diseased kidneys could not eliminate the excessive waste products created during the metabolism of poor quality dietary protein. These waste products built up in the dog's blood, producing disease and death.

Dr. Morris reasoned that the build-up of toxic waste products could be reduced if a proper diet was fed to the afflicted dogs. To be successful, such a diet would have to contain a minimum amount of the highest quality protein possible and ample energy to spare that protein from being used as energy. Using a combination of eggs, cottage cheese, farina, and a balanced vitamin and mineral mix, Dr. Morris put together a food that would meet these specifications. The food could be fed in his hospital or it could be canned and sent home with the dog owner.

The response to eating the food was dramatic in the sick dogs! Initial response by veterinarians was less overwhelming. As the word of the success of Dr. Morris' new food spread, however, enthusiasm within the veterinary community spread, too. Finally the demand for Dr. Morris' new food became greater than he could supply. He was forced to give up his practice and devote his full time to commercial production of the specialized food.

Dr. Morris limited the sale of his new food to veterinarians. They alone were qualified to diagnose and treat the disease for which the new food had been developed. Subsequent additions to this line of foods have likewise been restricted to veterinary sales for the same reason.

This class of pet foods, designed for the management of disease, has been designated as "Dietary Animal Foods" by the United States Department of Agriculture to distinguish them from ordinary dog foods designed to be used for maintenance only. Such a distinction enables these specialized foods to contain less salt, or less protein, or less something else that ordinary maintenance foods must contain. This capability is an absolute must if a dietary food is going to be able to do the job it's supposed to do for the sick dog.

The only useful dietary animal foods are still sold only to veteri-

97

narians. These foods should be fed only at the veterinarians' directions. Such a precaution insures that an adequate diagnosis has preceded their use and proper evaluation will accompany their results. Some of the dietary animal foods available to veterinarians for treating their patients are:

1) *Restricted-protein diet*: An updated version of Dr. Morris' original food for kidney disease. It contains a high-quality protein blend having a biological value of nearly 90 in some brands. The quantity of protein is kept at a level only slightly above that needed to supply a dog its MDR for amino acids.

2) *High-protein, high-energy diet*: Because growing dogs have a requirement for nutrients and energy almost double that needed to maintain an adult dog, this food was designed to provide the growing dog with an ideal diet to support its growth.

3) *Bland, low-residue diet*: Every ingredient in this diet is put there because of its high digestibility and biological value. It is a diet designed to be fed to dogs having a gastro-intestinal upset. With such upsets, the intestinal tract does not function as well as it normally does. Its ability to digest and absorb nutrients is considerably reduced. Any residue from a poorly digestible food further irritates the already upset intestinal lining.

4) *Low-calorie, high-residue diet*: Dogs, like man, suffer from obesity. And, just as with man, the only solution to the problem is eating a lowered intake of calories. By increasing the residue in these foods with a low-energy bulk, the dog is kept from feeling hungry all of the time.

5) *Hypo-allergenic diet*: The two main ingredients from which this food is made are mutton and rice. Neither is commonly eaten by American dogs. By using them as a base, a food can be made to which American dogs are less likely to have been sensitized. Hypo-allergenic diets are used primarily as a diagnostic aid, since even mutton and rice can cause allergies if eaten often enough.

6) *Low-salt diet*: Animals with congestive heart failure retain large quantities of sodium in their body. Sodium causes a retention of excessive fluids in the dog's abdomen, lungs and limbs. By restricting the intake of sodium, much of this water retention can be prevented.

Laboratory and colony foods: Another type of food designed to meet a specialized need is that developed especially for laboratory and colony dogs. These foods are fairly recent additions to the commercial dog foods. For years people raising colonies of dogs limped by with whichever food maker got the lowest bid. These foods were usually supplemented with whatever happened to be the director's favorite food supplement.

With the passage of humane treatment laws for lab animals, the cost of research dogs has increased greatly. Most colonies are demanding that foods be adequate to protect their increased investment. Specialized lab animal foods have been the result.

In addition, researchers have discovered that the food fed an experimental animal has a lot to do with the outcome of the investigation. A food that is non-uniform, and is constantly changing in chemical content, can produce a significant error in the results. As a consequence, more and more laboratories are demanding that foods be constant and uniform. The only way to accomplish this is to produce the food by a rigidly fixed formula, allowing no substitution in either ingredients or their quality.

Obviously, such foods are going to cost somewhat more than ordinary maintenance foods. In the long run, however, when specialized lab foods are properly fed, they actually offer most laboratories and dog colonies a slight savings.

More important to most dog owners is the fact that several of these specialized foods are also ideal for use by breeders, kennel owners and dog feeders in general. The specialized lab foods that are of particular interest to most dog feeders include the following:

1) *Colony maintenance rations*: This food was designed to be fed to non-reproducing colony dogs and research dogs between projects. The only difference between it and most premium brands of commercial dry foods is its better nutrient digestibility and uniformity of ingredients.

2) *Lactation rations*: This food, too, looks much like a commercial dry food, Figure 34. It is quite different, however, because it was designed specifically for the reproducing bitch during that period while she is nursing pups. Food for a lactating bitch must contain the additional energy and nutrients she needs in a more concentrated form than maintenance foods. This is the only way to insure that the dam continues to receive all she needs without requiring her to eat tremendous quantities of food.

3) *Growth rations*: This food is designed for dog colonies that raise their own dogs. It is also highly suitable for breeders and other dog raisers who wish to provide their pups with the best diet availa-

99

Figure 34. A specialized food for lactating bitches. It is a nugget-type, expanded dry food. The maintenance and growth foods look almost identical.

ble. It combines both the puppy's increased need for energy and nutrients and its inexperienced digestive tract as the considerations for formulating the diet.

Stress diets: The increase in the use of military dogs during the last 20 years has prompted the development of a food especially designed to meet the greatly exaggerated needs of these guard dogs. The food designed for use by military dogs in southeast Asia, Figure 35, is now available to civilian dog owners*. Such a food will prove of great use to owners of hunting dogs, racing dogs, and especially to owners of civilian guard dogs.

These maximum stress foods are designed almost exclusively for dogs having a greatly increased need for energy, but relatively slight increase in the need for other nutrients. They are foods of extremely high caloric density, having their nutrients greatly concentrated to enable them to be consumed in adequate amounts in the small quantities of food eaten.

* Maximum Stress Diet, Riviana Foods, Inc., Topeka, Kansas.

100

Figure 35. The maximum stress diet. This food is made by a special process allowing it to be highly concentrated and contain large amounts of energy.

Figure 36. One of the four simulated bitch's milks now sold commercially.

101

Simulated Bitch's milk: Some of the most difficult dogs to successfully feed are newborn puppies. At one time it was made even more difficult by the lack of a suitable food for the puppy.

The obvious food for puppies is bitch's milk. Unfortunately, the bitch, unlike the cow, is hardly an ideal subject for milking. The quantity of milk produced is small; the collection is difficult. Even if one does have a lactating bitch available, it is much easier to get the bitch to adopt the pups and let them do the milking themselves. The problem, of course, is that most of the time a lactating bitch isn't available.

In the late 1930's, Dr. G. C. Supplee, then Director of the Borden Research Laboratories, and his associate, J. H. LeWare, conducted a 14-month-long investigation into the nutritional requirements of puppies. The outcome of their efforts was a formulation simulating the nutritional characteristics of bitch's milk. Their original formulation was marketed in powder form by Gaines Food Co. under the name of "Formula 107-A", and as a liquid called "Ken-L-Lac" by Chappel Bros. Today at least four simulated bitch's milk formulas are available, Figure 36.

Simulated bitch's milks have been responsible for saving the lives of thousands of hand-fed and orphaned pups. It is an excellent example of how modern scientific technology and commercial dog foods have made the dog feeder's responsibility of meeting every dog's dietary needs easier and easier.

102

Chapter 7

Evaluating a Dog Food— Physical Examination

THE first question every dog feeder must answer is, "What food should I feed my dog?"

There are only about a dozen brands of dog food distributed nationally, but thousands of regional and local brands. Many of the latter are known only to the dog feeders living in the counties around which the dog food is made. Such foods may never be sold more than a few hundred miles from their point of origin. Some of these foods are highly nourishing to a dog; others are completely worthless.

Because there is such a variety (i.e.: types, brands, ingredients, prices, etc.) of dog foods available to any dog feeder, there is only one sensible way to answer the question about what food to feed. That way is to evaluate those foods available and choose the best one, based on the results of your evaluation.

Such a suggestion may sound like a profound statement of the obvious, but, not one dog feeder in a hundred has chosen the food he is feeding by a formal evaluation. Plenty of dog feeders refuse to buy a particular brand because of their experience with its poor performance. Rarely does a dog feeder buy a food because he attributes any of his success at dog-raising to that food. Too many dog feeders buy their food by impulse, or upon the suggestion of others, even

103

when those suggestions may come from the advertising agency of the dog food company.

The proper selection of a dog food is the most important thing a dog feeder does. Why then, when the procedure seems such a necessary step to proper feeding, do so many dog feeders refuse to subject the food they feed to a critical evaluation before they feed it to their dog? Probably because they don't know how. Companies making dog foods, who do know how, have traditionally provided only "feeding instructions," never instructions for a procedure that might enable a customer to discover a product that was superior to their own.

The widely held belief that any food, simply because it is the product of the American pet food industry is automatically adequate and nourishing to a dog, is pure myth. A feeling of security because the food has been purchased from your trusted local grocery is based on even less reality. There is only one way to select a food that you can be confident will provide your dog with adequate nourishment. That way is to subject all of the foods available to you to a critical evaluation program. The time taken to correctly make a food evaluation is time well spent, and the procedure should never be slighted.

Evaluating a dog food is a simple, straight-forward procedure of comparing certain characteristics of one food with those of other foods available. The procedure offered here is not foolproof. Nevertheless, it has enough built-in flexibility that innovative dog feeders can adapt it to best fit their own situation and further reduce their margin of error.

When making an evaluation, the four characteristics of a satisfactory dog food, discussed in Chapter 4, should be used as the minimum standards that any food must meet. Once again, these are:

1) A food should contain sufficient energy for daily activity.
2) A food should contain adequate nutrients, in proper relationship to each other.
3) A food should contain ingredients that are usable by a dog.
4) A food should be acceptable in a sufficient quantity to fully supply items 1 and 2.

The Evaluation Procedure

Start by making a list at the grocery store, feed store, or wherever you obtain your food. The list should include all of the brands,

104

from the least expensive to the most, of the type or types of food you intend to evaluate. The list should include at least the brand name, the size of packaging available, and the cost of each size of package.

A proper evaluation is made in five steps. The steps should always be taken in the same sequence. These steps are:

1) Screening based on retail cost.
2) Screening by label examination.
3) Evaluation by physical inspection.
4) Final evaluation by feeding trials.
5) Selection based on true feeding costs.

STEP 1. Screening by Retail Cost: For many dog feeders, cost has often been the only step in their food evaluation program. Until you have had some experience in evaluating dog foods, you may also feel there is little else but the price to compare between one dog food and another. Price is used only for preliminary screening. You cannot make an intelligent decision about true feeding costs until you have learned more about how the food ranks with regard to the four minimum standards and the food's actual performance.

If economy is your only consideration when buying a dog food, then make your evaluation by comparing the three or four cheapest brands on your list. If expensive, prestigious foods are your objective, then make your evaluation from among the highest priced three or four brands. If the proper nourishment of your dog is your prime consideration, include all the foods on your list in your evaluation.

There is one exception to the foregoing. If you are evaluating canned foods you should begin by *eliminating from your list any brands that retail for 12¢ per can or less.* Table XI lists a typical cost breakdown for a can of food sold in a grocery store. A quick look at the costs involved in canning a 12-cent-a-can food explains why canned foods in this price range are better left out of your feeding program.

The fixed costs of canning remain the same whether the can retails for 12¢ or for 30¢ per can. The 6.7¢ fixed costs listed in Table XI is what it costs a dog food maker to put a sealed, processed and labeled can of water, in a 48-can carton on his factory dock. The main things determining what the can retails for are advertising and promotional costs, manufacturer's profit, retailer's markup and ingredient cost.

105

TABLE XI

The Typical Cost Breakdown of a Canned Dog Food

item	cost	item	cost
Can and lid	$.035	Advertising	$0.002-.040
Label	.002	Commissions	.003-.012
Carton	.004	Transportation	.010-.010
Labor	.003	Mfgr's profit	.012-.035
Overhead	.013	Retailer's markup	.018-.052
Administrative	.010	INGREDIENTS	.008-.084
	$0.067 fixed costs		$0.053-.233 flexible costs

$0.067 fixed	$0.067 fixed
0.053 flexible	0.233 flexible
$0.120 store price	$0.300 store price

The figure in Table XI of most interest to the dog feeder is the ingredient cost. How much of a 50¢-per-pound ingredient do you think can be put into a can of dog food for 0.8¢? How many nourishing foods do you know of that cost less than one cent per pound? Even when expense is your main concern, you must remember that unless a cheap food actually nourishes your dog, it would be even less expensive, but equally effective, simply not to feed your dog at all!

The variations between quality and costs among dry and semimoist foods are not as dramatic as those between canned foods. All price ranges should be considered when evaluating the dry and soft-moist foods.

STEP 2. Sreeening by Label Examination: On the label of every container of dog food there are six things that might assist you in evaluating the food in that container (Figure 37). These are:

1) The *brand and product name* of the food.
2) The *name and address* of the organization responsible for making or distributing the food.
3) The *net weight* of food in that container.
4) The *manufacturer's guarantees* for the food in that container.
5) The *ingredients* used in manufacturing the food.
6) If the food is *nutritionally complete* for a dog, a statement on the label to that effect.

Brand and Product Name. A manufacturer may market several

106

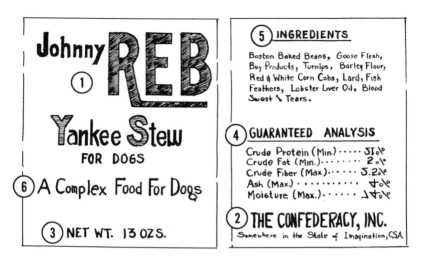

Figure 37. A hypothetical dog food label, illustrating the six items that might help you evaluate the food. They are: 1) brand and product name, 2) name and address of manufacturer or distributor, 3) net weight, 4) the manufacturer's guarantees, 5) the ingredients, and 6) a statement of nutritional completeness, if appropriate.

products under the same brand. He may also make several brands. The product and brand name enables you to identify the food again when your evaluation discloses it to be of poor or high quality.

Name and Address. Every label of a dog food must contain the name and address of the manufacturer or major distributor of that food. This sometimes is confusing, since the distributors are not always the manufacturers of a food. There are some dog food makers who do nothing but make dog food for someone else. This is referred to as "private label" manufacturing. Many large grocery store chains have their pet foods custom-packed by someone else. In such instances the quality of the product rests with the maker, and no longer reflects the amount of pride a food chain may have in its own label.

If the street address of the maker or distributor is not listed in the telephone directory of the city shown on the label, the address must be placed on the label, too. Use the address on the label to request analytical and feeding test data about the food. It also should be used for directing any complaints you may have regarding the food.

107

Net Weight. A statement of the weight of food that is to be found within the container must appear in a conspicuous place on every label. This figure can be used to calculate the cost per pound or per ounce of food, rather than cost per container. Remember that just because two foods are offered for sale in the same size container does not mean that both containers will contain the same amount of food. Net weights of different foods in identical size cans may vary anywhere from 14 ounces to 16 ounces. You get almost 15 percent more for your money when there is 16 ounces in a can than when there is 14 ounces.

Most cases in which similar sized containers contain different weights of product are not deliberate efforts to mislead. Usually the can, box or bag is a standard size into which each manufacturer simply puts as much of his product as the container will conveniently hold. Dry foods that are fully expanded, and processed into large nuggets, will occupy more space per pound than smaller or less expanded nuggets. Foods containing more water will weigh less per can than those containing more meat and grains.

Consumers who wait until they get home to discover that they just bought eight pounds of food in the same size sack they bought 10 pounds of another brand last week, have only themselves to blame. The net weight of every container of dog food is plainly printed on the label.

Guarantees. The decision of what analytical information is required on a dog food label is set by each state's feed control officials. In general, every state requires at least the following items to be declared in the "guaranteed analysis" on a dog food label:

The minimum percentage of crude protein,
the minimum percentage of ether extract
the maximum percentage of crude fiber, and usually,
the maximum percentage of water, and
the maximum percentage of ash.

Additional guarantees can be made, but if so, must be included in the guaranteed analysis panel. Common among such guarantees are minimum percentages of calcium and phosphorus, maximum percentages of salt and minimum percentages of one or more vitamins, Figure 38.

While the guaranteed analysis does not tell the precise amount of a particular nutrient in a food, it does give a rough guide to the food's composition. Even with their built-in tolerances, it is unlikely

108

GUARANTEED ANALYSIS

Crude Protein, not less than............23%
Crude Fat, not less than................7%
Crude Fiber, not more than.............5%
Ash, not more than...................10%
Calcium (Ca), not less than.............1%
Phosphorus (P), not less than..........1%
Salt (NaCl), not more than..............1%
Dry Matter, not less than.............90%
Moisture, not more than..............10%

Figure 38. A dry dog food label showing extra guarantees of minimum calcium and phosphorus and maximum salt.

that many manufacturers will vary too far from their own guarantees. Those nutrients required to be listed at minimum quantities are usually ingredients that are more expensive, and are added in the least amounts possible. Those required to be listed at their maximum allowables are usually the less expensive or filler-type ingredients and are added in the largest amounts possible.

In most instances the guaranteed analysis is satisfactory as a guide from which a rough calculation of caloric density can be made. Foods containing fat in quantities less than seven percent per pound of dry matter will have a caloric density so low that, unless the dog eats excessive quantities, the food will be unable to satisfy the first minimum standard, adequate energy. *Eliminate from your list any canned food that does not have at least three percent fat or any dry food that does not have at least seven percent fat.*

Manufacturers customarily set their guarantees with rather wide tolerances. This is done because many dog foods are made from open formulas that allow substitution of ingredients. Such substitutions enable the manufacturer to take advantage of fluctuating ingredient costs. By setting the tolerances between the guaranteed analysis and the actual analysis relatively wide, reasonable substitutions can be made without danger of exceeding the guaranteed limits.

The one listing that will almost always be the same level as the maximum shown on the label is the one for water. The only ingredient in a dog food that is less expensive than water is air. By using the moisture figure in the guaranteed analysis you can obtain a fairly accurate estimate of how much food you are getting for your money. Paying 75¢ out of every dog-food dollar for water is uneconomical. Consequently, *eliminate from your list any canned food that contains more than 75 percent water.*

The absence of a guarantee for a nutrient does not rule out its presence, but without a minimum guarantee you have no way of knowing the nutrient is present in adequate amounts. Therefore, *eliminate from your list any food that does not have a guaranteed minimum for, or has a guarantee of less than, 0.30 percent Calcium.*

Ingredients Panel: The terms used to describe the ingredients used in commercial dog foods can be confusing, especially to those unfamiliar with them. These terms are defined in the *Official Publication* published by the Association of American Feed Control Officials (AAFCO). This group was originally formed to regulate the manufacture of cow, horse and swine feeds. Their regulation of dog foods has evolved over the years, and they have adopted many of the feed terms for use in dog foods. An abbreviated list of these ingredients and their description is found in the appendix.

Every ingredient used in making a dog food is supposed to be put on the label of that food. To avoid misrepresentation, each ingredient should be listed in descending order, by weight, so that the ingredient listed first is present in the food in the largest amount, and the ingredient listed last will be present in the least amount.

The regulation regarding the listing of ingredients is largely unenforceable. In many instances the physical identity of an ingredient is lost entirely during processing. This is particularly true in the expanded dry foods, the soft-moist foods and the extruded chunk-style canned foods.

The real value in an ingredients list is not what it contains, but in what it does not contain. Most manufacturers are reluctant to include among their list of ingredients items they do not include in their food. Therefore, *eliminate from your list any canned food or soft-moist food that does not include an animal protein source*

110

among the first two ingredients, or a dry food that does not include an animal protein source among its first three ingredients. You should also *eliminate from your list any food that does not have at least one cereal grain among its ingredients.*

Statement of Nutritional Completeness. The Federal Trade Commission (FTC) has decreed that no manufacturer can claim on his label, or state in his advertising, that a food is nutritionally "complete" or "balanced" for a dog unless that food:

"(1) Contains ingredients in quantities sufficient to satisfy the estimated nutrient requirements established by a recognized authority on animal nutrition, such as the Committee on Animal Nutrition of the National Research Council of the National Academy of Sciences; *or*

(2) Contains a combination of ingredients which, when fed to a normal animal as the only source of nourishment, will provide satisfactorily for fertility of the male and female, gestation and lactation, normal growth from weaning to maturity without supplementary feeding and will maintain the normal weight of an adult animal whether working or at rest, and has had its capabilities in this regard demonstrated by adequate testing."

These same regulations, basically, were adopted by the Association of American Feed Control Officials (AAFCO) on August 6, 1971. AAFCO supervises the state by state regulation of pet foods. In addition to the FTC requirements, AAFCO added two more stipulations.

First, products that are designed to be used only for a limited purpose (eg., maintenance of adult dogs or feeding of growing puppies) must have a statement of that limited purpose placed conspicuously on the label. Even limited purpose products cannot be called "complete, perfect, scientific, or balanced" unless the food ". . . contains ingredients in quantities sufficient to satisfy the estimated nutrient requirements established by a recognized authority on animal nutrition for such limited qualified purpose or . . . have had its capabilities in this regard demonstrated by adequate testing."

Second, if a food product contains ingredients in amounts that deviate from those nutrient requirements estimated by a recognized authority, or in the event that no estimation has been made for a particular life stage by a recognized authority, the foods must have their capability of supporting those stages of the animal's life cycle demonstrated by testing.

To implement these regulations, AAFCO has, with the American

111

Veterinary Medical Association and the Pet Food Institute, formulated a testing procedure which must be used to satisfy the "adequate testing" requirements.

Consequently, after January 1, 1973, *all dog foods which do not have a label statement claiming that food is either "complete," "perfect," "scientific" or "balanced" for the dog should not be considered for further evaluation.*

STEP 3. Physical Inspection: The foods remaining on your list that have not been eliminated by preliminary screening should now be subjected to a physical inspection. The inspection should be performed when enough time is available to allow all the foods of one type to be examined at the same time. This is the only way a valid comparison can be made between each food.

The physical inspection of a dog food encompasses an examination of both container and contents. The procedure differs slightly according to the type of food being examined.

Canned Foods. Some equipment is helpful when inspecting canned foods. The tools needed for a routine examination are:

1) A can opener.
2) A paper plate.
3) A table knife.
4) Paper towels and napkins.
5) A plastic garbage bag.

To begin, tear off the label and examine the can. It should be bright and shiny, and free from any rust spots, dirt or grease. Some cans may be ribbed, others may be straight sided, Figure 39. The ribbed cans are made from a thinner gauge metal and ribbed to give the can added strength.

On one end of most cans of dog food will be an identifying code number stamped into the lid, Figure 40. This code usually designates the product and the day and month the food was produced. If several plants make the same product, the specific plant may also be identified. Any time a complaint is sent to a manufacturer about his product it should always include the code number from the can or cans of food you are referring to in your complaint.

Other observations may also be made from a can. A good example is the can lid illustrated in Figure 41. It came from a can that retailed at three-for-27¢! This is a case in which the manufacturer obviously attempted to economize by using a lid which was designed, and even lithographed, for another purpose. The can was

112

Figure 39. Dog food cans showing straight-sided and ribbed types.

Figure 40. Identifying code number in the lid of a can.

113

Figure 41. Lid from a can originally destined for use with a liquid human product, but ultimately used for a dog food.

slightly smaller than most dog food cans, too. Such a maneuver by a maker does not, in itself, condemn his product. But it does indicate, usually, his general attitude about making and selling dog foods. Such evidence, coupled with other findings, may well serve as a reason to eliminate such a product from your list. In this particular case, the food was eliminated at the outset of the evaluation because of its low retail price.

After you have examined the unopened can, open one end and remove the lid. Observe any odors that come from the can just as it is opened. It should smell fresh and wholesome, although not necessarily appetizing. Remember, your tastes and those of your dog differ. The contents of the can should never smell putrid, rancid or sour.

Check to see how much separation has occurred in the contents during *curing*. A canned product "cures" between the time it is sealed and cooked, and when you open it. Fat is the thing that ordinarily separates first. When it does, it rises to the top and congeals as a pasty, whitish or yellowish, greasy-feeling substance on the can's lid. If you open the can on the end that was up during curing you will be able to see this layer of congealed fat, Figure 42.

114

Figure 42. Layer of fat, congealed on the lid of a dog food can. The right-hand edge of the lid has been cleaned for contrast.

In ration-type foods there may appear the small, round or oval-shaped, dark-colored depression or hole called the "head space," Figure 27. The head space is an artifact of a small air pocket purposely left in the can when it was filled. This air pocket provides the space needed to draw a vacuum during sealing, which extends the product's shelf life. The head space is often mistaken by the dog feeder as due to spoilage, mold growth or contamination, but it does not affect adversely the quality or wholesomeness of the food in any way.

Once you have made a visual and nasal inspection of the opened end of the can, empty the contents onto the paper plate.

If the product is ration-type it will probably be in the form of a solid, pudding-like mass. The proper way to remove this mass for a physical examination is to cut the remaining intact lid all the way around, then use it as a base to push the food mass out of the can. The food should slide with relative ease from the can as pressure is applied inward on the lid.

The outside of the freshly expressed surface of the food mass should be smooth and relatively uniform in appearance. Whole

115

grains and small chunks of meat appearing on the surface are desirable. The type of grain frequently can be identified and the presence of meat can be confirmed. While the absence of such particulate matter does not rule out their presence, the gross recognition of meat and grain certainly confirms their presence.

Once the outside surface of the food mass has been examined, lay it on its side. Cut through the middle of the mass, lengthwise, observing the texture of the product as you cut. The slice should extend only about two-thirds of the way through the mass, the remaining one-third being broken open rather than cut. This allows for both a cut surface and a broken surface for you to inspect. Foods containing large particles will have an uneven tug on the knife and their broken surface will be uneven, Figure 43. More homogeneous masses will have a much smoother broken surface, Figure 44. The presence of a uniform texture in the mass usually means that some of the meat or cereal by-products have been ground finely to conceal their identity. A uniform texture does not necessarily mean that an

Figure 43. The uneven, broken surface of a piece of dog food containing whole grains, large chunks of meat and ingredients in a coarse form. Contrast with Figure 44.

116

Figure 44. The smooth, broken surface of a piece of dog food containing all of its ingredients, including grains, meat and meat by-products, ground so finely that most of it is unrecognizable. Contrast this with Figure 43.

ingredient is present or absent. It simply serves as an excellent means to conceal that fact.

The sliced and broken inner surface should not appear greatly different from the uncut outer surface. Any change in color between the surface next to the can and the inside of the mass may indicate that the food has reacted with the inside of the can in some way. In the cheaper grades of foods, in which the cans may not be enameled, the bare metal may cause chemical reactions with the food. This produces a darkened surface, which may or may not have an effect on the nutritional quality of the food. A darkened surface may also indicate that the food was cooked too long or at too high a temperature, and the outside got cooked more than the inside. Such excessive cooking may destroy vitamins and reduce the protein quality of the food.

Pick up and roll a small piece of freshly cut food between the thumb and forefinger. The bit of food should roll into a ball, but

117

should not be so sticky that large amounts of food cling to your fingers. It should not be so wet that it is mushy, nor so dry that it crumbles apart as it is rolled into a ball.

Take a small amount of ration-type food on a knife blade and spread it across the surface of the paper plate, as you would butter on bread. The presence of any number of ingredients, some desirable, some not, can be revealed this way. You may be surprised at how much you can find within a couple of thinly spread knifefuls of food, especially after you've had a little practice at the art. Some of the more readily recognizable items found in a thin spread of ration-type food are illustrated in Figures 45 through 49.

The presence of grass awns, grain hulls, hair or feathers and of foreign materials such as sand, wire or wood chips, can often be discovered. The presence of a single strand of horsehair or a lone grain of sand is usually of no importance. Large numbers of such materials in a can of food indicates that somewhere in the manufacturing process these materials are gaining access to the food in such quanti-

Figure 45. A highly desirable ingredient in a canned dog food is *whole* grain. These are grains of barley.

118

Figure 46. Another desirable ingredient in dog food is muscle tissue. This is the real "meat" of any dog food, and can be positively identified by the bundles of individual muscle fibers. Here a single fiber has been isolated and exposed.

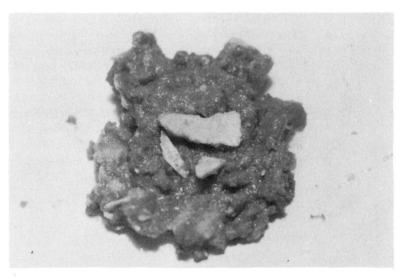

Figure 47. Fragments of bone in a canned food may range in size from almost powder to several milimeters in length. Those shown here all came from the same can, but were actually taken from different knifefuls of food.

119

ties that they might prove harmful. It can also indicate that the manufacturing process or its quality controls are so sloppy that other, even more dangerous, items are gaining access to the food.

When undesirable plant and animal matter is found, examine additional samples from the can. If they, too, contain such material, examine a couple more cans of the same product. *Eliminate from your list any food that contains substantial amounts of undesirable plant and animal matter in three or more consecutive cans examined.* When foreign materials are discovered, examine additional samples from the same can. *Eliminate from your list any food that has three or more pieces of foreign material in the same can.*

Don't be alarmed or reject a food because of the presence of small chips of bone, Figure 47. Bone is frequently used to decharacterize meat by-products to prevent them from being sold for human consumption. Bone also is an excellent source of protein, fat and minerals.

If the food is a meat and meat by-product, chunk style, or stew, pour the contents directly into the plate without removing the intact lid.

Figure 48. Undesirable ingredients also show up in cans of dog food, like this chicken claw. Numerous others were found in the same can, which probably indicates that ground chicken feet were one of the ingredients.

120

Figure 49. Any foreign matter found in a can of dog food is undesirable. It does not become a matter of concern, however, until it reaches such levels as to present a hazard to the dog eating it. It may also indicate a laxity in the quality control of the manufacturer. This hair (arrow) has been magnified with a lens to be better seen.

With meat and meat by-product foods, ascertain how much of the food is meat and how much is by-product. The simplest and most direct way of doing this is by actual count. Go through and divide the can's contents, one piece at a time, into a meat and a non-meat pile. Everything that can be identified as genuine muscle meat goes into one pile. Into the other pile goes all the pieces of cartilage, gristle, gullets, udders, intestines, etc., Figure 50.

Figure 50. A can food made from meat and meat by-products that has been separated into a pile of meat (right) and a pile of by-products (left).

121

If the label read "meat and meat by-products" the muscle meat pile should be larger or contain more pieces than the non-meat pile. If the label read "meat by-products and meat" the non-meat pile will be larger. The FTC *GUIDES* state that a manufacturer cannot label a food using an ingredient's name unless that ingredient makes up the largest proportion of that food. Any violation of the FTC regulations should be reported directly to the FTC.

With the chunk-style meat products, the chunks should be uniform in size, shape and color. Most will have smooth, thick gravy or sauce poured over them, filling the can. When a chunk is cut through, do not expect to see hunks of meat, or even a meaty texture. The chunk is not chopped meat alone, but a mixture of ingredients in which all physical integrity of each individual ingredient has been lost entirely. The evaluation of the chunk-style foods is among the most difficult for this very reason. Considerable reliance must be placed on the integrity and past performance of the maker of such products.

Dry Foods: Once the label of a dry food has been examined, turn your attention to the container itself. The best place to make a con-

Figure 51. When fat in a dry food soaks through its container it is called "grease-out". Grease-out spots cause the fat to turn rancid more rapidly and serves as an open invitation to vermin infestation. This brown paper sack was filled half-full of dry meal to illustrate how grease-out appears in porous materials.

122

tainer examination is at the retailer's, when you are making out your list of foods to evaluate.

Dry foods come in boxes, sacks and commercial-size bags, depending on the quantity of food being sold. Most dry food containers are laminated with several layers. One of these layers is usually a grease retaining layer, designed to keep the fat from penetrating the rest of the container. Grease retaining layers are made from parchment, waxed paper or plastic sheets. Inspect all of the containers of dry food at the store where you buy your food to see if there are any areas of "grease-out" where the fat from the food has soaked through the container to the outside, Figure 51.

Grease-out allows fat in the food to come into contact with the air and rancidity occurs more rapidly. In addition to causing accelerated rancidity, grease-out spots also serve as an ideal invitation to insects and vermin. *Do not put on your list any food in which more than 25 percent of its containers are found with areas of grease-out.*

Every container of dry food, whether it has grease-out or not, should always be inspected for the tell-tale holes left by insects, rats and mice. If only one brand shows evidence of vermin infestation it might be better not to include that brand on your list. If numerous containers from most brands show evidence of some vermin infestation, it may be best to change the place where you get your food.

Each container should also be examined to determine how well it was able to withstand the rigors of transportation. One of the quickest ways to cut corners in dry food making is to reduce the cost of the container by using lighter weight paper stock. Such practices don't show up until the packaged product is handled en route to the market. Of course, a single damaged container means nothing. But, the appearance of numerous damaged containers in the same brand is likely to indicate that the manufacturer is not giving the shipment of his product the concern it deserves. When more than 25 percent of the containers of the same brand are damaged you should make a note of that fact on your list. If several shipments arrive with 25 percent or more of the containers damaged you should probably eliminate that food from further consideration.

As with canned foods, the physical inspection of dry foods on your list should all be made at the same time for the most accurate comparison.

The first thing to do when opening a container of dry food is to smell its contents. Some of the smells which are easily identified are

123

the appealing aroma of a fresh, uncontaminated food; the sour smell of rancid fat; the pungent odor of rat urine or mouse urine; the acrid smell of insect infestation and the musty odor of mold. In cases where the food has become damp, the repugnant odor of putrefaction may also be present. The presence of any of these odors but the first is reason enough to discard *that containerful* of food. It is enough to *eliminate that brand from your list, if the first three out of five containers examined have the same fault.*

With every brand that smells satisfactory, pour the first few inches of food in the container into a plate, bowl, bucket or other suitable receptacle. Next, pour all but the last couple of inches of food in the container into your feed bin, barrel or any other receptacle large enough to hold it. Finally, pour the remaining few inches of the food out into another plate or bowl. Compare the first few inches, side by side, with those from the bottom of the container. Contrast the size of the food particles from the top of the container with the size of those at the bottom. They should be almost identical. Examine the portion poured from the bottom of the container to determine the amount of *fines* present. Fines are the tiny particles of food that are broken off during processing, handling, bagging and transport, Figure 52. In the better grades of dry dog food, most fines

Figure 52. The tiny particles of food that break away from an expanded or kibbled dog food during manufacture or transport are called "fines". These are the fines from a kibbled biscuit product.

124

are removed during manufacture by sifting devices called "scalpers". The only fines found during your examination should be those resulting from bagging operations and during transport, and these should be minimal. *Eliminate from your list any food in which more than 50 percent of the bottom few inches in a container are fines.*

If the product is a dry meal, spread a handful into a thin layer on a dull white, pale green, light blue or gray surface to enable you to examine it more carefully. Try to identify as many ingredients as you can from the thinly spread layer. Cracked corn, oatmeal, wheat flakes, bone meal, meat and bone scrap, and numerous others can usually be identified, even by the unskilled eye, Figures 53 and 54.

Once you have gained some skill at this sort of detective work it may be possible for you to actually do a crude analytical study by separating each of the various ingredients into little piles. You may even be able to get a rough idea of the percentage of each ingredient the meal contains from the size of the piles. A magnifying glass will be of great help when performing these more detailed inspections of a dry meal.

The ability of a dry food to absorb water is one of the more accurate quantitative means of evaluating these foods' physical qualities. A satisfactory dry food should be capable of absorbing at least twice its own volume of water within 30 minutes. To perform a water absorption test on a dry food the following equipment is needed:

1) A mixing bowl
2) A measuring cup
3) A collander or strainer
4) A drain pan
5) A source of water
6) A plastic garbage bag

Place one cup of the dry food to be tested into the mixing bowl. Pour two cups of tap water over the food. Without stirring or mixing, allow the mixture to stand for 30 minutes. At the end of the 30-minute period pour the food and the water into the collander or strainer, over the drain pan. In a satisfactory dry food, no water should drain from the mixture. *Eliminate from your list any food from which more than $\frac{1}{4}$th cup of water drains during two minutes.*

Examine baked and kibbled foods for the presence of burned spots on the biscuits. The presence of a single burned biscuit is not sufficient evidence, alone, to indicate that a food lacks nutritional adequacy. But, the presence of large numbers of burned biscuits

125

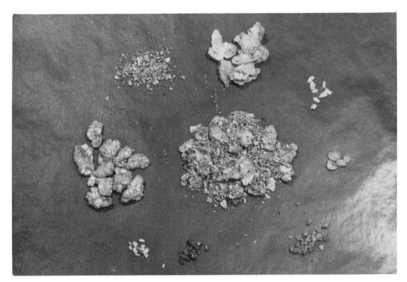

Figure 53. Dry meal, spread on dark surface and separated into its recognizable constituents. These eight piles may double in some foods, but this meal is typical of most dry meals sold today.

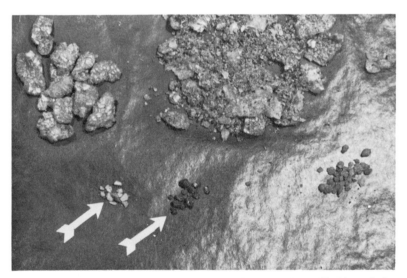

Figure 54. Close-up of some of the constituents shown in Figure 53. Of particular interest are the two small piles marked by the arrows. These are meat and bone scraps and indicate that an animal protein is a constituent of the meal.

126

may indicate that the food has been cooked at too high a temperature, in which case nutrients are apt to be destroyed. *Eliminate from your list any baked or kibbled food in which more than 25 percent of the biscuits have burned spots on them.*

If dry products are damp, soft or stale, it may mean that they have been improperly processed, gotten damp in transit, gotten damp during storage, or that they are old. Dry products that become damp, quickly deteriorate from the action of mold, and eventually bacteria. Sometimes the only indication that mold is beginning to attack a dry food is the musty odor smelled when a bag is opened. At other times it may be seen as a white, hairy beard or a bluish-green or black velvety coating over the food. Any food found to be moldy should be destroyed immediately and never fed to dogs.

Soft-moist Foods: Most soft-moist foods are sold in grocery stores. Since the marketing container is a reflection on the grocer as well as the manufacturer, any outside containers that arrive at a store damaged usually never reach the shelves. Consequently the examination of a soft-moist container is limited to the cellophane, controlled-portion inner wrapper.

The cellophane should be soft and pliable, and it should not be off color. Pillow-pouched bags should contain a small amount of air that does not escape under moderate pressure. Wrapped sheets should be tightly sealed at the back of the patty.

A careful inspection should also be made through the unopened wrapper for any dull or furry, gray or black spots; or for any shiny or moist, whitish or yellowish spots. The first is mold growth, the second bacteria. Soft-moist foods have been advertised as canned foods without the can. A more appropriate description might be canned foods without the canning process. Genuine canned foods are subjected to a heat great enough to destroy both mold and bacteria. Soft-moist foods are not subjected to such heat and many species of both mold and bacteria remain viable in soft-moist foods. A little water is all either needs to get started, and away they go, held in check only by the inhibitors within the soft-moist food.

Once the visual inspection of the wrappers and wrapped surface of the food has been made, tear open the cellophane. Observe all odors at the time of opening the wrapper. Pick up a piece of the food and squeeze it. Regardless of the type, it should be soft, spongy and tender. It should have a slight lubricated feel, but should not feel moist on the surface.

None of the results of your inspection can be used to eliminate any brand of soft-moist foods. About the only thing a physical examination of a soft-moist food is useful for is to eliminate individual packages of food. The only way a satisfactory evaluation of soft-moist foods can be made is by feeding tests.

All of the foods that have not been eliminated by the screening tests should now be subjected to the series of feeding tests described in the next chapter.

Chapter 8

Evaluating a Dog Food— Bioanalysis

WHILE price, label and physical inspections are excellent methods of screening out undesirable foods, they do not provide any answers about the actual nutritional value a food has for a dog. *There is only one way to accurately determine a food's nutritive value—feed it to a dog and see what happens.* The proof of the pudding may be in the eating, but the proof of a dog food is in the results of the eating.

Digestibility Trial

The first feeding test that should be performed on each food is a rough determination of its digestibility. The test is performed by feeding the food being evaluated to a dog for five days. During the last three days of feeding, the nature and volume of the dog's stools are carefully observed.

Such an undertaking may, at first, seem to be a pretty objectionable chore. You will soon discover that you have forgotten all about the esthetics and *almost* don't notice the odor. Instead, you will become absorbed in how much you can learn about the food you are feeding just by examining what has happened to it while it was inside the dog. You will learn to ignore your prejudices and view the dog's stool for what it really is . . . the food you fed yesterday after it has done its job of nourishing your dog.

129

The digestibility trial is performed as follows:

STEP 1) Determine from Table XII the correct amount of food to feed each day. Feed that exact amount of the food to be evaluated to your test dog for six days. Weigh and record how much food the dog eats each day. On the third day begin a careful observation of each bowel movement the test dog has. Note the stool's color, odor and any unusual features. *Eliminate from your list any food that produces loose stools for two or more consecutive bowel movements. Any foods that produce stools that contain so much undigested material they resemble more closely the food from which they came than they do a dog's stool should also be eliminated.*

Otherwise, the formed stools should be collected in plastic bags for weighing. Clear sandwich bags make this job less objectionable, even for the experienced food tester. Each bag should be labeled and refrigerated for 12 to 24 hours before it is weighed.

Divide the weight of the total stools produced for one day by the weight of the food eaten the day before. The percentage of the food fed that appears as stool is a relative figure of the food's digestibility. The percentage should be compared to the figures listed in Table XIII and the food accepted for further testing or eliminated according to the table.

TABLE XII

The quantity of each type of dog food that should be fed
to a dog of given weight during a digestibility trial.

If dog weighs:	feed this much dry food	SM food	can food	If dog weighs:	feed this much dry food	SM food	canned food
2 lbs	1.5 oz	1.5 oz	3.5 oz	25 lbs	9 oz	10 oz	1 lb, 8 oz
3 lbs	1.5 oz	2.0 oz	4.5 oz	30 lbs	10 oz	11 oz	1 lb, 11 oz
5 lbs	2.5 oz	3.0 oz	7.0 oz	35 lbs	11 oz	12 oz	1 lb, 14 oz
7 lbs	3.5 oz	4.0 oz	9.5 oz	40 lbs	12 oz	13.5 oz	2 lb, 0 oz
10 lbs	4.5 oz	5.0 oz	12.0 oz	50 lbs	14.5 ozs	1 lb, 0 oz	2 lb, 7 oz
15 lbs	6.0 oz	7.0 oz	1 lb, 0 oz	60 lbs	1 lb, 0 oz	1 lb, 2 oz	2 lb, 13 oz
20 lbs	7.5 oz	8.0 oz	1 lb, 4 oz	70 lbs	1 lb, 2 oz	1 lb, 5 oz	3 lb, 0 oz

TABLE XIII

The relative digestibility of a dog food, based on the relationship of the stool produced to the quantity of food eaten to produce it.

wt. of stool ÷ wt. of can food eaten	wt. of stool ÷ wt. of dry food eaten	evaluation
.10	.20	
.15	.60	
.20	1.00	Accept
.25	1.40	
.30	1.80	
.35	2.20	Eliminate
.40	2.60	

If the collection and weighing of stools is more than you feel you can handle, there is another, but less accurate way of estimating digestibility. Instead of actually collecting and weighing the stools, try to estimate their total volume for a 24-hour period. Likewise measure the food fed by volume as well as weight, for comparison to the stool volume. Follow the directions already given for eliminating foods on the basis of the stool's physical characteristics. In addition, compare your observations to the following descriptions to arrive at an approximate digestibility of the food.

Extremely poor digestibility: Volume of stool produced greater than volume of food eaten to produce it. Stool appears almost identical to the food as it appeared when it was fed. Many elements in the stool still in the same form they were in when the food was fed. Odor of the stool may bear more resemblance to the food from which it came than to that typically associated with a dog's stool. The number of stools may be double or triple the number normally produced by the test dog. *Eliminate these foods.*

Poor digestibility: Volume of stool produced equal to or slightly less than quantity of food required to produce it. Stool still bears considerable resemblance to the original food, but would rarely be mistaken as anything else but a dog's stool. Still numerous elements appearing in the same form as in the food. The number of stools are slightly to moderately increased. *Eliminate these foods.*

Average digestibility: Volume of stool produced 50 to 75 percent of the quantity of food required to produce it. Stool bears little resemblance to the original food. It would never be mistaken for anything but a dog's stool. If the appearance were not enough, the typical odor would immediately confirm its nature. An occasional grain might still be recognized, but for the most part the structure of the stool is indeterminate. The number of stools produced are normal. These foods should be subjected to further tests.

Good digestibility: Volume of stool produced 25 percent or less of the quantity of food required to produce it. Stool bears no resemblance to the original food that produced it. Odor and appearance of stool are those usually associated with a healthy, well-fed dog. The number of stools produced are normal. These foods should be subjected to further feeding tests.

Complete digestibility: Volume of stool less than ten percent of the quantity of food required to produce it. Stool bears no resemblance whatsoever to the food required to produce it. The stool's appearance might be described as "cigar-like". Odor may be almost absent. In most instances there will be only one stool every two or three days. These foods are usually found only in the class of dietary animal foods and most of them have already been subjected to large batteries of feeding tests to determine their adequacy.

Digestible Energy Trial

The second feeding test to which every dog food should be subjected is one that makes certain the food has ample energy to maintain the dog's body weight. To perform this test, first weigh the test dog. Next, follow precisely the feeding instructions on the food's label to determine the quantity of food to feed your test dog. Feed exactly this amount every day for at least three weeks. Weigh the dog weekly on the same day and at the same time of day.

If the test dog eats all of the food fed each day and . . .

1) loses weight for three consecutive weeks, *eliminate the food from your list because it does not contain adequate digestible energy.*

2) maintains its weight constant within five percent for three consecutive weeks, the food is adequate.

3) gains weight for three consecutive weeks, the food is higher in digestible energy than originally calculated and can be fed in a lesser quantity.

4) gains or loses one week, then reverses the next week by an amount greater than five percent, feed two additional weeks (a total of five in all) to see if a trend can be established. If the unequal pattern continues, *eliminate the food from your list on the basis of*

132

non-uniformity, and have the dog's physical condition checked by a veterinarian just to be sure the variability is not being caused by disease.

If the dog does not eat all of the food every day and . . .

1) loses weight for three consecutive weeks, *eliminate the food as unacceptable to the dog.*

2) maintains or gains weight for three consecutive weeks, reduce the quantity being fed to just that amount being eaten and feed two more weeks to confirm the dog's ability to maintain its body weight on that quantity of food.

3) gains or loses one week then reverses the next week by an amount greater than five percent, follow item four, above.

Acceptability Trial

Although palatability and acceptability are not true measures of nutritional adequacy, at some time or another you may wish to find out which food your dog likes best. The easiest way to find out is to feed the foods in question, two at a time, and let your dog tell you which one he prefers.

Offer the same quantity of each food that you would if it were the only food being fed to the animal. In other words, the dog will be receiving twice as much food every day as it needs. Feed the two foods for five days, carefully recording the amount of each food the dog eats. At the end of the five days add up the total amount of each food eaten. Determine to what percentage the total of each food made up the dog's total diet over the five days. Do this by adding the two foods' totals together and dividing that sum into each of the two individual totals. For example:

	Food A		*Food B*
1st day:	12 ounces	1st day:	10 ounces
2nd day:	6 ounces	2nd day:	10 ounces
3rd day:	4 ounces	3rd day:	12 ounces
4th day:	0 ounces	4th day:	16 ounces
5th day:	0 ounces	5th day:	14 ounces
Food A total	22 ounces	Food B total	62 ounces
	Grand total	84 ounces	

$$\frac{22}{84} \quad 26\% \text{ total diet} \qquad \frac{62}{84} \quad 74\% \text{ total diet}$$

133

If one food makes up at least 60 percent of the dog's five-day diet, that food is definitely more acceptable to the dog than the other. If neither food makes up more than 60 percent, they probably can either be fed successfully. In our example, food B made up 74 percent of the five-day diet. In this instance, food B was considerably more acceptable to the test dog than food A.

If you have more than two foods to compare, use the food from the first pair tested that was eaten in the greatest quantity to compare against the third food. Then use the "winner" of that pair to compare against the next food, and so on, until you have determined which food your dog likes best.

Growth Studies

A test of a food's nutritional adequacy that is far more accurate than those already mentioned is the food's ability to support growth in puppies.

Dog feeders who don't feed puppies, or have no breeding bitches, don't actually need to test their food's ability to support growth. But, any food that will support growth will also support any adult dog's maintenance needs and many of its working requirements. Moreover, a growth study is actually the shortest way to determine if a dog food has a true capability to support maintenance of an adult dog.

To obtain a growth study, one must first obtain a growing dog. An entire litter of puppies is even better. The best age to use pups to test a food's growth capabilities is at weaning, but puppies up to nine weeks of age can be used successfully.

To start, weigh each puppy. Feed all of the puppies the same food, without adding any form of supplementation. Enough food should be offered so that every pup eats as much as it wishes and there will always be a little left over. Remember, the idea of this test is not to determine how much food is needed. It is designed to see whether or not the food, *in any quantity*, will support the puppies' growth.

The pups should be weighed weekly and their growth compared to a standard growth curve. Standard curves for various-sized breeds are found in the appendix. The average of all the pups weights can be plotted on a graph similar to that shown in Figure 55. This graph can then be compared to one of those in the appendix for a dog of similar breed or size as the test pups. *Eliminate from your list*

134

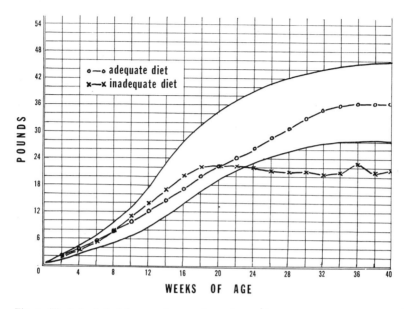

Figure 55. A food that is not adequate for a dog will not support puppy growth. This graph illustrates the weekly weights of two different groups of puppies, one being fed an adequate diet and one an inadequate diet.

any foods that fail to produce a rate of growth equal to or better than that in the standard chart.

Any food that will support puppy growth will also support adult maintenance. Since the needs of puppies for growth are double the needs of adults for maintenance, the fact that a food does not support a puppy does not mean it would not support maintenance. But, by feeding only those foods that are capable of supporting growth, you can always be certain that the food you are feeding will support maintenance in adult dogs.

Successive Generations

The ultimate test to which any food can be put is that of supporting several generations in succession. If you really want to put a food through its paces, feed it exclusively and without supplementation, to three successive generations. This will require a minimum of two years, starting with a six-week-old female puppy and feeding the food to her, her pups, and her pups' pups. If there is any weak-

135

ness in the food whatsoever, feeding it to successive generations will invariably bring that weakness to the surface.

While few dog feeders would ever initiate such a long testing procedure on the food they feed, they still should be able to evaluate a food through successive generations. By feeding the same food long enough, and by keeping accurate records of the food intake, body weights and reproduction success of their dogs, any dog feeder can perform a feeding trial through successive generations.

In each example of these feeding tests, only one dog has been used as a test dog. Mathematically, two dogs are probably better than one and four dogs are better than two. One hundred dogs would be better still! But the most important fact still remains that one dog is better than none! And, until this book was written, *none* was the number being used by most dog feeders to test the food they fed.

While I would never be last to advocate the use of two or four dogs as a test battery, I will always be among the first to advocate that any testing is better than no testing at all. After all, the most meaningful tests you can perform are with the dogs you are actually going to feed, whether it is only one dog or a dozen.

PART III

HOW A DOG IS FED

Chapter 9

Equipment

UNTIL now we have spoken almost entirely about only one of the items needed to properly feed a dog—its food. This chapter will discuss some of the other items needed for using that food in a proper feeding program.

Scales

Scales are the dog feeder's most useful piece of equipment. Throughout a dog's life its body weight is a constant and accurate reflection of its nutritional state. By frequent weighings at regular intervals, a dog feeder can keep a running check on how well he is doing his job of supplying his dog with its nourishment. In fact, with nothing more than a set of scales, a notebook, a few sharp pencils, a balanced food, a suitable container and this book, a complete feeding program can be tailored to every dog you own or feed.

In addition to weighing the dog, a dog feeder also uses scales for weighing food. The simplest, yet most accurate, way for the average dog feeder to measure and control the amount of food he feeds is to weigh that food. In instances where highly accurate measurements of the dog's actual intake are desired, the scales are used to weigh the food offered to the dog, then to weigh the amount of that food the dog did not eat. The difference is an accurate measurement of the amount of food the dog did eat.

The dog feeder who makes up his own diet, or uses a mixture of commercial foods to make a diet, must use a scales to measure the exact quantity of each ingredient that goes into his ration. It is impossible to mix an adequate and balanced diet, with any consistency, without carefully weighing each ingredient added. The dog feeder who neglects or refuses to employ scales while formulating a diet is fooling only himself. He will never fool the dog he is feeding!

For weighing most dogs, an ordinary bathroom scales serves perfectly. Weigh yourself and record the weight. Pick up the dog and weigh yourself again, this time holding the dog, Figure 56. Record this weight. Subtract the first weight from the second. The difference will be the weight of the dog you were holding. If the dog you want to weigh is too large to hold comfortably, a grocery or dock scales may be needed to weigh it. For dogs too small to measure accurately on a bathroom scales, a regular baby scales serves quite well.

The baby scales can also be used to weigh out food portions, Figure 57. An even better scales for this purpose, and a must for weighing newborn puppies is an Ohaus balance, Figure 58. The Ohaus Scale Corp. makes several scales that are useful to dog feed-

Figure 56. An ordinary bathroom scales serves ideally as a means for regularly weighing your dog. The technique is not difficult to perform. (See text.)

140

Figure 57. A baby scales serves two purposes for the dog feeder. In addition to the obvious one of weighing baby dogs, it also is handy to calibrate food containers and weigh out portions of food.

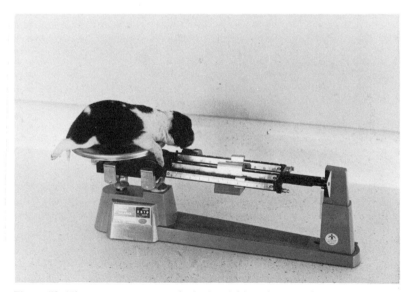

Figure 58. The most accurate method of weighing tiny puppies is with a gram scale. An ounce weighs 31 grams, so you can be 30 times more accurate with this Ohaus balance than you can be with a standard baby scales.

141

ers. Information about them can be obtained from the company's offices. For dog feeders who find themselves having to raise many orphaned or extra pups, one of these scales that is sensitive to small changes in weight is essential to the success of the undertaking.

Food and Water Containers

No food should ever be fed to a dog unless that food is put into some type of a container. The practice of putting food on newspapers, or directly on a cage floor or the ground, serves no purpose except to contaminate the food from the surroundings, contaminate the surroundings from the food, draw flies, increase parasite transmission and soil the dog's coat. The money, time and energy a dog feeder thinks he is saving by such feeding practices are completely wiped out by the loss of one dog, the time spent to clean floors and combat insects, or the effort needed to put a food-soiled coat back into show condition.

Feeding Bowls: No feeding bowl should be used unless it meets the following criteria:

1) It is the correct size for the dog that is using the container.

2) It is designed so that it is easily washed, drained and dried, or can be thrown away after each use.

3) It is made from satisfactory materials.

Feeding containers can be found for sale made from a large number of materials, some good and some bad. An ideal material from which a dog's food container is made should:

1) never be toxic to a dog (This includes the body of the feeding bowl, its coverings, and any paint, decals, printing or other decorations),

2) be capable of withstanding a reasonable amount of abuse from a dog's teeth,

3) be of a substance that is non-corrosive to dog foods, dog urine and the other substances to which a feeding container normally may be subjected,

4) be impervious to soaps, detergents, water, grease and disinfectant solutions,

5) be resistant to breakage, cracking or similar damage under normal wear and tear,

6) be inexpensive.

A material that meets every one of these specifications does not exist. There are four materials, however, that meet enough to be

142

Figure 59. A pair of glass feeding containers, one serving to hold food, the other, water. They are nothing more than ordinary pyrex ovenware, purchased at the nearest super market.

Figure 60. A pottery food container. These are frequently used for feeding rabbits, and can be purchased at any general feed store.

143

considered as suitable for dog food containers. These are glass, pottery, plastic and metal.

Glass containers, Figure 59, are the least suitable of the four. They are unfit for kennels or breeder operations. Their fragile nature makes them unsatisfactory if more than a single container must be handled at one time. The feeding bowl used for one house dog usually is handled individually at each feeding, just as the family's dishes and bowls are. Under such restricted conditions of handling glass containers rarely are subject to breakage. Because of their low cost and attractive nature, glass feeding and watering bowls make satisfactory household food containers.

Pottery containers, Figure 60, enjoy widespread use for rabbits, rats and other rodents, as well as birds. These animals all are fed dry foods. As long as dogs are fed dry foods, pottery containers serve adequately. When containers must be cleaned and handled after each feeding, pottery containers become too heavy and bulky. They, too, can be chipped and broken if handled too roughly. Pottery con-

Figure 61. A typical plastic food container purchased at a pet supply store. This one has two compartments, one for food and one for water.

144

tainers for feeding dogs have largely been replaced by those made from other materials.

Plastic containers, Figure 61, have some of the advantages of both glass and pottery containers. They have some unique advantages as well. But, they also have some serious faults. While plastic bowls can be thrown around and generally withstand considerable abuse, they are quite vulnerable to a dog's teeth. A determined or bored dog can reduce most plastic containers to a sieve, or worse, a pile of shreds. If these shreds are eaten they may cause serious stomach upsets. Some plastics are made from volatile solvents that are irritating to the stomach's tender lining. Some plastics cannot tolerate boiling water, others have a low resistance to certain chemicals, while still others crack when they get cold or fold and bend when they get hot. While every plastic does not have all of these faults, few plastics fail to have at least one.

Metal containers, Figures 62 & 63, are probably the most satisfactory all-round food and water containers available to the dog feeder. Their only major disadvantage is the damage inflicted by a dog's teeth. Even this can be reduced to almost zero when seamless stainless steel is used. Most metal containers come in a convenient array of sizes. They are light-weight, easily stacked, can be handled without fear of breakage, and are probably the least expensive if initial cost is spread over the duration of their effective use.

One of the major advantages of metal containers is their adaptability to proper cleaning procedures. They can be washed in hot soapy water, thrown (literally) into hot, boiling rinse water; extricated with metal tongs and stacked without too much care on top of each other to drain and air dry. All of this can be done without appreciable danger to either the food containers or the dog feeder.

Another obvious advantage of metal containers is that they can be dropped repeatedly without breaking. Eventually such abuse will cause them to bend and then crack and finally become unservicable. But, given the proper care, metal containers will give many years of satisfactory service.

Table XIV summarizes the advantages and disadvantages of the four types of material from which food containers can be made.

Self-feeders: The container used for dispensing food at a uniform rate to dogs on a self-feeding program is a specialized type of food container called, appropriately, a self-feeder.

145

Figure 62. Aluminum feed pans. Notice the variety of sizes and styles available.

Figure 63. Stainless steel feed pans. These are the author's first choice when it comes to food containers.

146

Self-feeders are available in many ranges of materials, sizes and shapes. They can be purchased ready-made or they can be home-made.

The ideal self-feeder is one that is all-weather, will hold enough food for about a week's supply, prevents spillage, protects the food from the elements and is easily cleaned and stored. One of the least expensive and most serviceable self-feeders we have found are those made for feeding swine, Figure 64.

Self-feeders also can be made from several types of materials. The most popular home-made feeders are made from galvanized sheet metal, tin, plywood or some combination of these three. Figure 65 shows how a couple of dog feeders can be made using plywood and metal.

Figure 64. A self-feeder. This one is really a pig feeder, but works ideally for dogs as well. They are available in this or similar types at almost any general feed store.

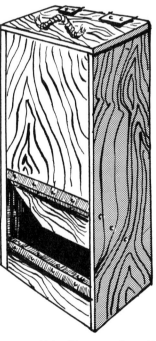

Figure 64A. Home-made self-feeder.

147

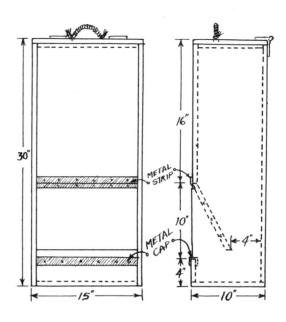

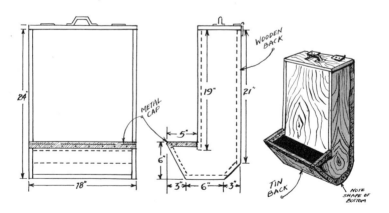

Figure 65. Plans for two home-made self-feeders. The top one can be made with either a wooden or sheet metal bottom and back. Notice that both have metal caps over the exposed surfaces to keep the dogs from chewing on them.

148

TABLE XIV

A summary of the advantages and the disadvantages of the four types of materials from which food and water containers can be made. One and two pluses are degrees of disadvantages, three and four are degrees of advantages. The total number of pluses, therefore, give a relative value among the four substances.

CHARACTERISTICS:						RESISTANCE TO:					
	Expense	Availability	Durability	Ease of handling	Ease of storing	Weight	Boiling H_2O	Soaps, Detergents	Urine	Food	Teeth	Disinfectants
Glass	+++	++++	+	++	+	+++	O	X	X	X	O	X
Pottery	+++	+	++	+	++	+	O	X	X	X	X	X
Plastic	++	+++	+ to +++	++++	+++	++++	O	X	X	X	O	X
Metal	++++	+++	++++	++++	++++	+++	X	X	X	X	X	X

Water bowls: In general, containers suitable for feeding a dog are suitable for watering it. In fact, under most practical situations, containers are used interchangeably.

One type waterer—the automatic—should be mentioned separately. Automatic waterers are devices that have a regulatory gauge which monitors the level of water in the container. Within, or attached to the gauge is an automatic valve that allows water to enter the container when the level drops below a pre-determined amount. Such waterers are particularly suitable in operations where self-feeding is used. Like the self-feeder, automatic waterers do not need to be attended daily and keep daily labor at a minimum. Equally important, the automatic waterer insures the dog feeder

149

Figure 66. An automatic waterer. The large container about the outside houses the heater element which is necessary to keep the water from freezing during the winter.

that ample water will always be available to dogs eating dry food. The only time that automatic waterers give trouble is outdoors during winter months, when they are subject to freezing. By equipping the waterers with a circular heater around their containers, Figure 66, this problem can be eliminated.

Several brands of automatic waterers are available from different makers. Others can be homemade. Either are quite suitable—when they are working.

Mixing Containers: For dog feeders who feed more than a couple of dogs, a large mixing container for mixing their food is essential unless individual foods are fed each dog. These containers should be of durable material and most experienced dog feeders usually consider that none is satisfactory unless made of metal. They should be large enough to contain all of the food being mixed for one feeding,

150

and still have a little extra space, just in case. It is helpful if these containers have their contents marked off in graduated quantities. Since few will have such markings as originally purchased, it usually becomes necessary to pour in water from a container of a known quantity and score or otherwise mark the sides at the various levels.

Container Cleaning: All containers used in the feeding operation should be thoroughly cleaned after each feeding.

All uneaten food should be scraped from the sides and bottoms of food containers and dumped into a plastic garbage can—not down the sink drains! Always observing this rule considerably lessens fouling of the wash water and reduces the amount of detergent needed to clean the containers. Keeping as much food wastes as possible out of the drains reduces the incidence of plugged drains and eliminates most of the sour food odors found in some kennels' diet kitchens.

Food containers scraped free of food, and water containers, should be scrubbed with a brush in hot, soapy water to dislodge any adhering particles of food and to remove all films of grease. The scrubbed containers should then be dropped into a boiling water rinse and left for several minutes before being taken out and dried. Once the food containers are dry, they should be stacked in some out-of-the-way place, ready for the next feeding time.

Utensils

Like any procedure, dog feeding requires certain utensils for a smooth, easy operation. Fortunately, they are few in number, and in most instances even the least experienced dog feeder can get by with only a handful of tools.

Can Openers: They come in all sizes and descriptions—from little, one-time openers in military rations to the heavy-duty electric openers found in restaurants. An elaboration about how to use a can opener to a can-oriented American consumer would be a monument to redundancy. Suffice it to say that the can opener is the most indispensable utensil to the dog feeder who uses any amount of canned dog food. Feeders of canned foods who travel and have forgotten to take along their can opener know only too well the agonizing chore of hacking off the lid of a dog food can with whatever sharp object they can find.

After grinding my way through numerous brands of can openers, I have decided upon one which I feel offers a good investment to any individual opening a large number of cans every day. There

151

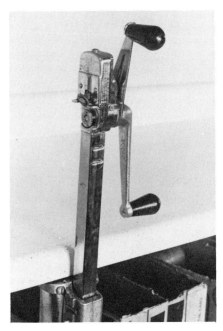

Figure 67. The Dazey can opener described in the text.

Figure 68. These are the two things that make the Dazey opener useful to the dog feeder. On the left is the replaceable feeder wheel, on the right the replaceable cutter wheel.

may be others, but the one I have chosen is the Dazey Heavy Duty can opener, Model 500, Figure 67. This model can be mounted directly onto the diet kitchen table, and once one becomes accustomed to it sticking elbow-high in the middle of things, it becomes almost impossible to get along without. It is hand operated, not electric. One of the most satisfactory features to recommend the Model 500 is the fact that the two moving parts that most frequently wear out on any rotary can opener, the cutting wheel and the feeder wheel, are both replaceable, Figure 68. They can be

152

obtained in quantity from Dazey regional service centers and can be replaced by almost any one after a little practice.

Spoons: The spoons most useful to a dog feeder are of two designs commonly found in most kitchen supply departments at any hardware store. One is a large, long-handled spoon with holes in the bottom, Figure 69, and is used for stirring and mixing the food ingredients. The other is a similar-sized spoon, but without the holes, and is used for dishing out the food into individual containers. Once some experience has been gained with a particular spoon, the dog feeder can scoop out, almost to the ounce, the exact amount of food he wants every time.

Knives: The kitchen knife, Figure 70, has many uses in a diet kitchen. It can be used for cutting large pieces of meat and other ingredients into smaller pieces. It can be used to slice off sections of the food mass from a canned food when accurate fractions of the contents are needed. It can be used to finely chop canned meats, fresh meats or other ingredients to facilitate a more uniform mixing. When bags of dry food are used, the kitchen knife comes in handy

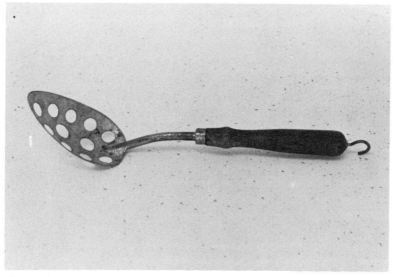

Figure 69. A large cooking spoon with drain holes in the bottom. This one was bought that way, but if you are unable to find one, holes can be drilled in a conventional kitchen spoon to provide the same effect.

153

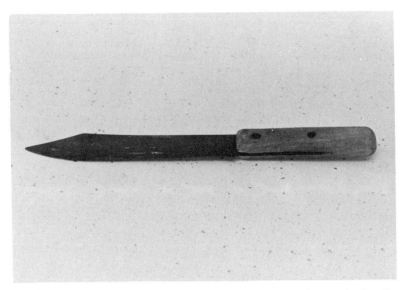

Figure 70. A broad-bladed kitchen knife. This is an inexpensive wooden-handle model, but it has a thousand applications in a diet kitchen.

when you've pulled the wrong string, or the bag top is sealed plastic.

The clam knife, Figure 71, also makes a handy, multipurpose tool in a diet kitchen. It can be used to slice sections of canned foods, and dice them too, if necessary. It will cut into small chunks, large pieces of horsemeat or beef. It also serves as a spatula, mixer, stirrer and sometimes as a lid-pryer. In extreme emergencies it can even be converted into a temporary coffee stirrer. When it is accepted, as such, by guests, it serves as an excellent reflection on how clean you are keeping your diet kitchen and its utensils.

Measuring Utensils: The most important measuring utensil, the scales, has already been discussed in a section devoted exclusively to it.

Another useful measuring utensil is an ordinary set of measuring spoons used by housewives. Metal or plastic, these pre-scaled spoons allow accurate measurement of both liquids and solids from $\frac{1}{4}$th teaspoonful to one tablespoonful or more. Such spoons are particularly useful when adjustments in the food must be made in individual containers.

Also a housewife's kitchen utensil, the measuring cup, can be

154

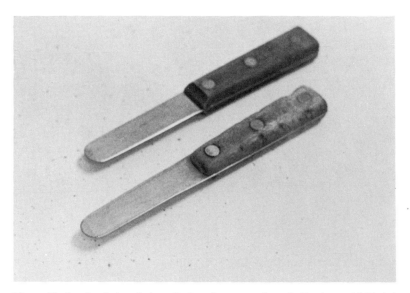

Figure 71. A pair of clam knives. Designed to open clam shells, these stiff-bladed, not-too-sharp utensils are ideal around a dog feeding operation for everything from slicing boiled kidneys to stirring boiled coffee.

useful to the dog feeder as well. These cups should be either metal or plastic, since the possibility of rough handling is increased in a diet kitchen and glass utensils may be broken. By practicing with his scales and a measuring cup, the dog feeder can soon learn to use the measuring cup to "weigh" out portions of either dry food or soaked food.

Because all dry foods should be fed by weight rather than by volume, a handy measuring cup for dry foods can be fashioned from an ordinary dog food can. Open only one end of the can, remove the contents and the label, and wash the can out thoroughly with soap and water. Once it is dry, weigh the can and record its empty weight on its bottom with a felt marker. Next add the dry food you will be feeding into the can while it is sitting on the scales. Stop when you have added one-half pound. The weight on the scales will be eight ounces plus the weight of the can. Mark the outside and inside of the can with a felt marker or quick dry enamel at the exact level of the top of the food. When this mark dries, add an additional half-pound of food to the can and again mark the level on the outside and inside of the can, Figure 57. Now empty the can and fill it once more to the half-pound mark with new food. Weigh it.

155

again and if the weight is equal to within $\frac{1}{2}$ ounce of the can's weight plus eight ounces, the can is marked accurately enough to use. In foods that have a density so light that one full pound will not fit into a dog food can, use a coffee can or its equivalent.

Once marked, the can will serve as an easy and convenient device for the dry food you are feeding. It can be used to "weigh" out as many pounds of food as you need for the day's feeding. If you change dry foods somewhere down the line, it will be necessary to recheck the can to be sure it will still weigh the new food accurately. In fact, it is wise to recheck the can periodically, anyway, since dry food formulations have been known to change without any label changes being made.

Other cans may be calibrated to measure out other items. One that's especially handy is a can that's calibrated to deliver a desired amount of soaked food. It, then, can be used to dish out the correct quantity of food for each dog at each feeding. Such a can will save you a lot of mental gymnastics. This can should be calibrated in the same way as the one just described, except that water, in the correct proportion, is added to the dry food before the can is marked. A can calibrated in this fashion can be used to deliver a known weight of dry food, even after it has been soaked.

Spatulas: Ordinary rubber or plastic cake spatulas, Figure 72, are excellent utensils for a dog feeding operation. They serve to scrape the food out of measuring cans so that accurate portions are given to each dog. They also serve as excellent tools for scraping uneaten food from feeding containers.

Brushes: Copper or brass wire brushes, Figure 73, are the most suitable for washing feeding pans. They last longer. They do not absorb grease or get clogged or dirty as they age. They will corrode if they are not properly rinsed after every use. If such corrosion occurs, the wires break and the brush quickly becomes useless. Like any other utensil used in a dog feeding program, brushes will perform in direct proportion to the care and service they are given by the dog feeder.

Pan Forceps: Because boiling water should be used in cleaning food containers, it is necessary to have some means of removing the rinsed pans without blistering your hands. The least expensive utensil in this category is any one of the several utensil forceps sold by almost any leading scientific equipment company for handling hot laboratory equipment, Figure 74.

156

Figure 72. A pair of rubber cake spatulas. These come in handy for digging out that little bit of food that gets pushed into the corners between the bottom and sides of food containers.

Figure 73. A pair of brass-wire brushes for scrubbing food containers.

157

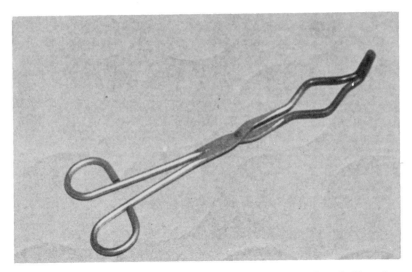

Figure 74. Metal tongs used for pulling hot food containers from boiling rinse water.

Pan Racks: Another method of removing pans from boiling water is the use of racks upon which the pans are stacked for immersion into the hot water. They can be removed from the water safely by handles which stick above the water's surface. The pans are allowed to dry and can even be stored in the racks.

The Diet Kitchen

Every housing facility for dogs, like every housing facility for people, should have a kitchen. It does not need to be an elaborate affair, but must be functional. In order to insure this functionality, every diet kitchen should include at least the following:

Hot and Cold Running Water: This is not likely to be a problem for suburban or urban dog feeders. While many rural outbuildings may have a well nearby, some do not have water piped into the building. Even those buildings that do have water may have no electricity source for operating the thermostat or heater element of a hot water heater. Hot water is essential to the proper handling of dirty food containers. If you are planning a new kennel, or just adding a diet kitchen to an old one, don't forget to incorporate into your plans the facilities for hot and cold running water.

Figure 75. A stainless steel sink, having a drainboard at one end and a partition through the middle. Also notice the open storage area, below.

A Sink: Once you have hot and cold water, you will need something to deal with it. The obvious solution is a sink. The ideal sink for a diet kitchen is made of stainless steel. It should be divided into two equal parts by a partition through the middle, Figure 75. Each side should be large enough to accommodate all of the food containers you will use during any one feeding. The water faucet should be the type that will turn, allowing water to be poured into either compartment. The drain should be oversized to accommodate what food does gain access to it, and the U-neck should not be buried behind an inaccessible wall, posts or equipment racks.

Drainboard: Many sinks come with a drainboard built on. If yours does not, one should be attached. Drainboards can be made from either stainless steel or Formica. If economy is desired, a drainboard only needs to be on one side of the sink. That side should be the one that will be used for rinsing containers. That is the place where draining capabilities are most needed, as the hot, dripping pans come out of the rinse. The same drainboard can serve as a mixing and dishing-out area if the kitchen is small.

Cooking Equipment: In diet kitchens where fresh ingredients like

159

horsemeat, kidneys, livers, etc. are fed, a single or double gas or electric burner should be installed. A five-or ten-gallon pot usually is all that is needed to cook these ingredients. In instances where hot water is unavailable to the kennel or diet kitchen, these burners can also be used to heat water for cleaning food containers.

Garbage Cans: An absolute must in any kitchen is a garbage can. It is of particular importance in dog diet kitchens. It can be either galvanized or plastic, but in any case should be lined with a plastic garbage bag. The size of garbage can needed will depend upon the size of the diet kitchen and the number of dogs that are fed from it.

Miscellaneous Items: A broom and mop should be kept in all diet kitchens. A roll of paper towels should be hung near the drainboard, and some ordinary dishtowels hung nearby are always handy. Finally a storage area should be provided. In it should be kept all of the soaps, detergents and disinfectants used in cleaning the feeding equipment and the kitchen.

Chapter 10

General Considerations When Feeding Any Dog

THE eating behavior of a dog is characteristic of the whole species, not of any individual breed, since all dogs eat the same way. As a result, there are certain general considerations that can be made when feeding *any* dog, whether it has 10 stars or 57 varieties in its pedigree.

The Mechanics of Eating

A dog is not equipped to eat its food the same way a man does. A dog has no hands. Its jaws are suited for biting and cutting rather than chewing. There are few "gag" reflex nerves at the back of a dog's mouth, but many in a man's throat. A dog has fewer taste buds on its tongue, but a much greater sense of smell than a man has. There are many other differences as well.

While the eating behavior of a dog may seem strange or awkward to some dog feeders, to the dog it is the most comfortable and satisfactory way of getting its food from its bowl into its stomach. The normal pattern of swallowing in a dog is often described as "bolting." The dog picks up a piece of food with its front teeth and with a short, quick thrust of its head, tosses the piece of food back onto the top of its tongue. The piece of food is then rolled, unchewed, to the back of the mouth. As the piece reaches the base of the tongue, a

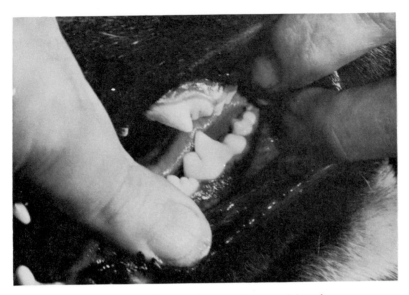

Figure 76. A dog's meat choppers, its carnassial teeth.

reflex causes the back of the tongue to push the food upward and backward into the esophagus. From there it is carried directly into the stomach.

When a piece of food is too large to be swallowed, the dog holds the food with its paws and uses its front teeth to tear off smaller pieces that can be swallowed. If the food is too tough to be torn, the dog will cut it into pieces small enough to be swallowed, using two specialized jaw teeth, Figure 76. These teeth are called carnassial teeth and have large shearing surfaces that act like scissor blades which can cut through such tough substances as muscle, hide, tendon, gristle and even bone. While the powerful jaw muscles of a dog are useful for cutting chunks of food into swallowing size, these muscles are little used for actually chewing those pieces. A dog's teeth are few in number and poorly equipped for mastication.

The Habits of Eating

A dog's eating habits are controlled by three things—its brain, its experiences and its environment. The very first experiment in

162

behavioral psychology was done by a scientist named Pavlov who taught dogs to get ready to eat when they heard a certain sound. Since that initial experiment, scientists have observed over and over how important the things happening around, and to, a dog are when it comes to affecting the dog's eating habits.

Once, when dogs were wild, most of their daily activity was devoted to obtaining a meal. While the need for this activity has practically disappeared, mealtime still constitutes one of the most important events in a dog's life. And, many of a dog's behavioral responses are still linked to its eating routine.

Today's dogs have become creatures of habit. They thrive on monotony and are most comfortable when things remain the same. Few dogs appreciate a sudden change in their sleeping quarters or the surprise of a new food in their bowl. The more that can be done to prevent change in a dog's feeding program, the better it will be for both the dog and its owner. Regularity in feeding promotes good appetite, good digestion and regular eliminations.

Therefore, the first general consideration to be made when feeding any dog should be:

I. A REGULAR FEEDING SCHEDULE SHOULD BE ESTABLISHED AND, ONCE ESTABLISHED, SHOULD NOT BE ALTERED.

Rule 1.) *A dog should be fed at the same time every day.* This is good, sound dietetics for any mammal, whether it be a dog or a dog feeder. Hunger follows a pattern, and by keeping the time of feeding constant you can regulate the time when a dog will be the most hungry. Feeding at the same time each day trains the dog's digestive processes to prepare for food only at that time. Pavlov's famous experiment involved the measurement of digestive juices being produced by dogs that expected to get something to eat because they knew it was time for them to get it. If your dog is fed at the same time every day it is not as likely to eat something fed by someone else because it will be fed at the wrong time.

If you are feeding only one dog, establish a feeding time, and place the food before the dog every day at that time. The selection of the actual time can be arbitrary, and chosen to best fit the dog feeder's schedule. When the feeding occurs is unimportant, so long as it occurs at the same time every day. If more than one dog is being fed, the feeding operation should start at the same time every

163

day, and should progress from dog to dog in the same sequence at each feeding. Watering, likewise, should follow a set pattern.

Puppies have conventionally been fed small portions of their daily diet at frequent intervals during the day. The rationalization behind this is sound, but the frequency of feedings often is too high. Even newborn puppies do quite well when fed only four times daily. Some breeders even reduce this to three times daily, but unless your schedule absolutely prohibits it, a minimum of four feedings should be the limit. The feedings need not be separated exactly six hours apart, but it is desirable to space the feedings as evenly as possible throughout the 24-hour time period. My own schedule usually works out best when I feed around 7:00 A.M., 12:00 noon, 6:00 P.M., and 11:00 P.M. Yours may be different.

The frequency of feedings should not be reduced to three a day until the puppies are weaned. Whether you are feeding newborn puppies four times daily, or weanlings three times, once the pattern of feedings has been set, it should not be changed, but should occur at the same time every day.

Rule 2.) *A dog should be fed by the same person at every feeding.* This rule is not nearly as important where a couple of house pets are being fed by several members of the same family, as it is where large numbers of dogs are being fed by numerous different kennel personnel. It is particularly applicable where dogs are in strange environments such as boarding kennels, veterinary hospitals or show arenas. Dogs that have become accustomed to one feeder may exhibit all sorts of erratic eating behavior if that person is changed. Some dogs will reduce their food intake measurably. A few may stop eating altogether for a short period. Other dogs may eat twice as much as normal! As the dog becomes accustomed to the new feeder, its eating habits will, in most cases, gradually return to normal.

Rule 3.) *Every dog should have its own food and water container.* This precaution is not only sound behavioral psychology, it also is just plain good hygiene. It is especially wise to assign food bowls on an individual basis when your feeding containers are noticeably different from one another. Besides improved feeding technique, certain practical benefits are to be gained from following this rule. In racing stables, for example, where maintenance of body weight is so important, feeding instructions can be written on the bottom or side of each dog's feeding container, right next to its name or number.

164

In fact, when a dog has special feeding requirements, the use of color-coded or labeled food containers can prevent costly errors in your dietary program.

Rule 4.) *A dog should be fed in the same place every time it is fed.* Whether it be the corner of the kitchen, beside the back-door steps, at the rear of a kennel run, or along the left-side wall of a cage, the site where the food container is placed should remain the same every day. In fact, everything that's done with the food container should be identical at each feeding. If you use a push cart or wagon to carry the tub of food to the dogs, always use the same cart and tub. If you prefill food bowls in the diet kitchen and carry them on the cart, don't decide one day to carry the tub of food on the cart and fill each bowl as you reach the dog. It may have become boring to you, but to your dog it has become *the* way of life. A change only serves to disrupt his way of life and to create cause for insecurity. While these things may seem like unimportant trivia to you, they may be of the greatest importance to your dog. It is often just these "little things that separate the successful dog feeders from the unsuccessful ones.

Rule 5.) *No dog should ever have its food changed without a good reason.* Contrary to popular opinion, dogs do not need a change in food from time to time to keep them from growing tired of the same food all the time. Many dogs have lived normal, healthy lives eating the same food throughout their entire lifetimes.

In many instances where a dog feeder thinks a dog has gotten sick and tired of a food, the dog has just gotten sick from the food. Not so sick, perhaps, that it really showed, but sick enough to stop eating. When a dog food is deficient, it is not uncommon for a dog eating that food to lose its appetite. Of course, nutritional deficiencies are not the only thing that will cause a dog to lose its appetite. Feeding a food containing excessive calories, feeding spoiled or contaminated food, and illness are among some of the other things that will cause a dog to stop eating. These and other causes of reduced appetite are discussed in greater detail in the chapter on feeding the sick dog.

Rule 6.) *Uneaten food should not be left for more than 30 minutes.* If you feed only one or two dogs, removing the uneaten food within 30 minutes should offer no problem. In kennel situations where larger numbers are being fed, and it requires more than 30

165

minutes just to make the feeding rounds, you should begin to pick up the food containers just as soon as you have completed feeding the last dog. Pick up the feeding containers in the same order that they were put down. Don't get in such a hurry to get them, however, that you forget to record each dog's food intake.

Rule 7.) *Dogs should have regular elimination times.* Dogs that are kept in relatively close confinement should be taken out for eliminations immediately after feeding. This will establish a regular pattern. Such a pattern promotes regular eliminations, stimulates better digestion and increases food utilization. Perhaps equally important from the kennelman's viewpoint is the fact that a regular elimination time permits the dog's quarters to be cleaned while the dog is absent and allows the least chance for the dog to mess up the newly cleaned cage or run.

The second general consideration to be made when feeding any dog is:

II. ANY TIME IT BECOMES NECESSARY TO MAKE ANY CHANGE IN A DOG'S FEEDING ROUTINE IT SHOULD BE DONE AS GRADUALLY AS POSSIBLE.

If it becomes necessary to change the time at which a dog is fed, the most satisfactory way to do so is by making gradual time changes from the old time to the new. Suppose you change jobs, and start getting home an hour later than when you usually fed your dog. It is far better to start about two weeks before you make the change and feed the dog five minutes later every evening for twelve days, than to abruptly offer your dog its food 60 minutes late the first day you start the new job.

When personnel changes occur in kennels it always helps to make the transition go smoother if the old feeder can accompany the new feeder for several days. This practice is often out of the question, but is a legitimate consideration to be made when the situation surrounding the changing of feeding personnel permits it.

Probably the most often changed item in any dog's feeding routine is the food itself. There are occasions when circumstances dictate that you must make a change in a dog's food. Examples of these are: when you get a new puppy and you don't feed what the previous owner feeds, you change a dog's diet for reasons of health, or there is a discontinuation of a commercial food line. Whatever the reason for making the change, if it is made too abruptly it may cause a digestive upset. The micro-organisms growing in a dog's digestive tract become accustomed to one diet. So does the dog's digestive tract itself. An abrupt change does not allow sufficient time for either to reaccustom themselves to the new diet. Any time a dietary change is anticipated the following procedure will not only prevent gastro-intestinal upsets, but will provide the greatest degree of acceptability of the new food during and after the changeover.

How to Change a Dog's Diet

STEP 1. If a dog is in a new environment, has a new owner, or is being required to undergo some other emotional or physical strain, food changes should be postponed until the stress has been eliminated or the dog has adapted to it. With changes in ownership, the diet fed by the previous owner should be obtained if at all possible and fed until the dog becomes accustomed to its new surroundings.

STEP 2. Once the dog is in a proper emotional state to accept a dietary change it should be accomplished without delay. Start by substituting 25 percent of the old food with new food. Mix the two thoroughly, making every attempt to conceal the new food within the old. This mixture should be fed until the dog eats the mixture with the same relish that it ate its previous food. For some dogs this may be the first time the mixture is fed; for others it may take several days or even weeks. Don't hurry the procedure! After all, the dog may have had 24 months to get accustomed to its old diet. Don't expect it to change all of that in just 24 hours.

Once the dog is eating the 25:75 mixture as well as it did its previous food, proceed to step three.

STEP 3. During the third step, 50 percent of the old food is replaced by new food and slightly less effort is made to coneal it within the old food. Again, when the dog is eating the 50:50 mixture with the same gusto it did its previous food, proceed to step four.

STEP 4. Now 75 percent of the new food is present in the mixture being fed, and little if any effort is made to conceal the new food except to mix it evenly with the orignal food. By now, most dogs will readily accept the increased mixture the first time it is fed. If the dog accepted the 50:50 mixture at the first feeding, step four can be eliminated and you can proceed directly to step five.

STEP 5. This is the final step, the one in which all of the old food is eliminated from the dog's diet. One hundred percent of the new food is fed from then on.

167

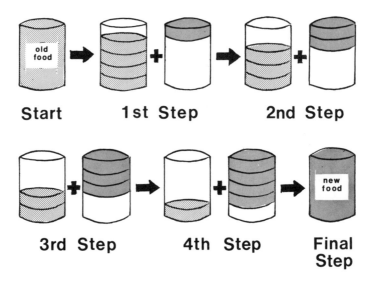

Start   1st Step   2nd Step

3rd Step   4th Step   Final Step

Figure 77. A schematic diagram showing the steps that should be taken when changing a dog from one food to another.

For some dogs this procedure may take only three days and require only steps two, three and five. For others it may take longer and must progress through each step separately. *Do not become discouraged.* With dogs, food likes and dislikes are mostly learned from previous experiences. Changing a food is a process of unlearning and relearning, and such things cannot be hurried.

The third general consideration that should be made by all dog feeders any time they feed a dog has more to do with human behavior than it does with a dog's. That consideration is:

III. NEVER ADD SUPPLEMENTS TO A DIET UNLESS YOU KNOW EXACTLY WHAT IS DEFICIENT IN THE DIET AND EXACTLY HOW MUCH TO ADD TO BALANCE THE DIET.

Failure to observe this consideration will lead to a *greater* imbalance far more times that it ever leads to any improvement. Most of the supplements dog feeders add to a dog's diet are of little value nutritionally, and some are actually harmful. In most cases, supplements are used as a "shotgun" by the dog feeder who does not understand anything about proper dog nutrition. He hopes that, by some hook or crook, he can come up with the right amount of every nutrient if he throws enough junk together. What such a practice

168

actually does is strain the dog's metabolic system as the system works madly trying to kick out all of the excesses being built up from the supplement. Even when his dog's system is successful in eliminating the excesses, the dog feeder still has no way of knowing that his supplementing has provided a minimum of *every* nutrient. His dog's system may be able to eliminate the excesses, but it cannot fabricate the deficits.

The truth of supplementation is that it is an excuse for not really knowing how or what to feed a dog. The fallacy of supplementation is that if, by some miracle, a dog feeder hit upon the right combination as he dumped in a little of this and a little of that, he would never know it. If he didn't know what to do to produce a food and a diet to provide his dog with adequate nutrition in the first place, how can a dog feeder expect to recognize when he has accomplished something he can't even recognize.

If a dog feeder knows how to determine his dog's nutritional needs and how to provide a diet that meets these needs (as you should be able to do, now) he will have no need for supplements, except in isolated cases we will mention shortly.

Vitamin supplements: There are so many ways for a dog's food to contain adequate vitamins that deficiencies of specific vitamins rarely occur today. Every commercial dog food that has a claim on its label that it is "balanced" or "complete" must contain at least the MDR of every vitamin known to be needed by the dog. Within the ration-type canned foods, soft-moist foods and expanded dry products (and these three make up about 80% of all commercial foods sold) almost all can make the claim that they contain the MDR for vitamins.

It is possible for either foods or diets to contain vitamins in an improper balance. The addition of vitamin supplements to even these will be of little help, however, unless the exact deficiency or imbalance is known and precise quantities of the specific vitamin or vitamins are added to balance the ratio. Otherwise the addition of a vitamin supplement will merely substitute one imbalance for another, and the latter may be worse than the first.

A far more dangerous thing can result from the indiscriminate use of vitamin supplements—the overdosage of vitamins. Such an overdosage is called hypervitaminosis, and is particularly easy to produce with vitamins A and D, both of which become toxic in even moderately excessive amounts.

169

The only time that vitamin supplementation is justified is when it is used as an ingredient in a homemade ration known from its formulation to be inadequate in vitamins. Even then, no more than the MDR of any vitamin should be added, since such supplementation is designed only to insure that the dog eating the food will receive at least its MDR for each vitamin.

Mineral supplements: Almost every commercial food contains adequate minerals except some of the all-animal-tissue foods. Although most natural ingredients of dog foods do not contain adequate minerals for a dog, minerals are even less expensive than vitamins and are usually added to commercial food formulas. The addition of mineral supplements to all-animal-tissue foods by dog feeders, in hopes of balancing such foods, is an almost impossible task. The addition of mineral supplements to any other types of commercial foods is a waste of money and unnecessary duplication.

Mineral supplements, like vitamins, are only justified when formulating homemade rations, and the natural ingredients of the formulation do not provide adequate minerals to meet all of the dog's MDR for each mineral.

Fatty acid supplements: It is my opinion that fatty acid supplements constitute one of the biggest wastes of money made by the dog feeder. They are usually bought to improve the dog's haircoat or general condition. The only problem most dogs suffering from dull haircoat or poor condition have, is a lack of total digestible calories—not a deficiency of fatty acids. Many dogs which appear to be responding to a fatty acid supplement are actually responding to the addition of calories to their diet, calories provided by *all* the fats in the supplement. These same dogs very often would have responded equally as well to a tablespoonful of corn oil, Figure 78. In fact, those few that actually responded to an increase in fatty acids would have also responded to the corn oil, since corn oil contains all the essential fatty acids a dog needs.

Fat supplementation: Fat supplementation should not be confused with fatty acid supplementation. Fat supplementation is done for the sole purpose of adding extra energy to the diet. If corn oil is the fat added, more than enough essential fatty acids will be added at the same time.

One of the most universal weaknesses in many dog foods is a marginal or subadequate level of fat. This is due to a combination of several factors, not all of which are the fault of the dog food maker.

170

Figure 78. The best fatty acid supplement, at a price any dog feeder can afford. Corn oil, fed at sufficient levels to provide a dog with the fat and energy it needs, will also provide a dog with more than enough fatty acids.

While fat is more expensive than some ingredients, this is not the only reason dog foods contain too little fat. There are inherent difficulties in the preservation of fats, particularly at high levels, and both dry and soft-moist foods are plagued with rancidity if the fat level is increased above certain limits. Artificial preservatives are available which help prevent rancidity, but they present problems of toxicity when added in large amounts.

Those foods that are marginal or subadequate will probably be eliminated from your feeding program during the digestible energy trial described in Chapter 8. Even foods containing adequate levels of energy may become inadequate for a dog when it is working or stressed. The addition of fat, up to a certain point, can increase the caloric density of such foods to the extent that it will supply enough energy to meet the increased needs of work or stress. When the caloric density of the food has been calculated as described in Chapter 12, and the number of calories required to meet the increased need have been estimated, one teaspoonful of corn oil can be added for every 35 calories the diet falls short of providing the total daily requirement.

171

There are certain hazards when adding fat to a diet. The dog feeder should be familiar with these hazards. First of all, corn oil, lard or bacon drippings are all 100 percent fat and contain about 135 calories in every tablespoonful. If you are feeding a food that is balanced to, let's say 1.35 calories per gram, and you add 135 calories to the diet by the addition of a tablespoonful of corn oil, you will cause a reduction in the amount of food that dog eats. This reduction will be about 100 grams, or the amount necessary to reduce the intake of calories by 135 (1.35 cal./gram x 100 grams = 135 calories). At the same time you will also reduce the nutrients in the diet by the amount contained in the 100 grams. Unless the dog actually needed this 135-calorie increase in energy, the addition of fat may produce a deficiency of those nutrients that are present in only marginal amounts in the diet.

Another hazard of fat supplementation is exactly the opposite of the one just described. Fat produces a noticeable increase in the palatability of many foods to which it is added. An increase in fat level may change a food from one that is being accepted in only marginal amounts to one that is eaten in such quantities as to cause obesity. The increased palatability overrides the dog's usual habit of eating to meet only its caloric needs. The extra fat increases the number of daily calories far in excess of those needed for maintenance.

Whenever a diet is supplemented with fat, a dog feeder must always keep in mind the possible effects of such supplementation. He must regulate his addition of fat so that the final formulation of the diet contains just that quantity of fat necessary to maintain the dog's optimum body weight.

Amino acid and protein supplements: Using amino acid and protein supplements to improve the nutritional quality of a dog's diet has the same thing wrong with it that most other types of supplementation have. It's closing the barn door after the horse is out. The time to make sure your diet contains adequate protein, having a proper amino acid distribution, is when the food is being formulated and tested, not when it is being poured into the feed pan. Once a food has been prepared, pouring a little powder or colored liquid over it rarely turns that food into anything better than it ever was. The chance is a lot greater that it will change a satisfactory food into an unsatisfactory one.

172

Chapter 11

Feeding Methods

THERE are four ways to feed a dog. Each has characteristics that make it a more suitable method for use in some situations than in others. Although he may use only one, a good dog feeder should be acquainted with all four feeding methods. The four methods of presenting a food to a dog are: 1) portion control. 2) *ad libitum*, 3) self-feeding and 4) artificial alimentation.

Portion Control

Any time a definite quantity of food is measured out and fed to a dog, that is *portion control*. Whether it is the housewife counting out five tablespoonfuls from a can, a kennelman serving two dippersful of dry food, or a veterinary assistant carefully weighing out four ounces of a dietary food, they all are using portion control as the feeding method. The portion usually fed in a portion control feeding program is the amount of food calculated to supply enough calories to maintain the dog's optimum weight. Any portion the dog feeder chooses can be used, however.

The greatest advantage of portion control feeding is that it regulates the maximum amount of food a dog eats. Indeed, it is the only method that can be used for this purpose and, as such, is highly satisfactory and widely used as a method for feeding overweight dogs.

Other advantages of portion control feeding are: 1) It permits the feeder to determine precisely how much food any particular dog is eating each day. 2) It allows individualized feeding, enabling the dog feeder to use different types or kinds of food for different dogs, or add anything that needs to be added to an individual dog's food.

173

3) It can be used for making adjustments in a dog's dietary intake because the quantity fed can be increased or decreased each day by a chosen amount. 4) It places the control of the dog's daily food intake into the hands of the dog feeder.

There are also some disadvantages to portion-control feeding. The foremost is the inconvenience and time consumed in weighing out each dog's food with every feeding. A second disadvantage is the complexity of such a program, particularly if many dogs are involved. Without strict and accurate records, it is impossible to conduct a portion-controlled feeding program on more than one or two dogs without forgetting what dog gets what.

Portion control is most often used by feeders of house pets, by feeders evaluating a food, by veterinarians, for feeding easy keepers, for gluttons, and for adjusting a dog's food intake prior to *ad libitum* or self-feeding.

Ad Libitum

The latin phrase, *ad libitum*, means "at pleasure," and is a literal description of exactly how this feeding method works. An ample quantity of food is fed and the amount of it eaten is left to the pleasure of the dog. If the dog eats all that is offered each day, additional food is offered, until slightly more is offered than is eaten. If a dog refuses to eat all that is offered, the quantity offered is reduced until slightly more is offered than is eaten.

Ad libitum feeding allows the dog to set its own food intake and to establish its own body weight. For most dogs this is completely satisfactory because most dogs eat only to maintain their optimum weight. In many instances where a dog's optimum weight is unknown, *ad libitum* feeding is an accurate way of determining that weight. For a few dogs, however, this method is totally unsatisfactory. These are the easy keepers and the gluttons. For these animals, the only successful feeding program is portion control, where the amount fed can be restricted to only that quantity needed to maintain these dogs' optimum weight.

More dogs are probably fed using the *ad libitum* method than any other. In pure-bred kennels, in those kennels where all the dogs are similar in weight, and in colonies of guard and laboratory dogs, the same size feeding is often fed to every dog. The size of these feedings usually has been adjusted by the feeder's experience so that every dog is being fed *ad libitum*. Where dogs of different sizes are being kept, it is not uncommon for feeders to divide the group into three categories, "large," "mediums" and "smalls," and to feed a standard quantity to each category, using an *ad libitum* program.

Two distinct disadvantages accompany any *ad libitum* feeding program. One is if the quantity fed is too small, the dog will lose weight. The other is if the quantity fed is too large, but the dog eats it all anyway, it gets too fat. Because they regularly overfeed their pets, and the food they feed is usually highly palatable to their dogs, feeding too much is the most common error made by feeders of household dogs who use an *ad libitum* system. Most housedog feeders should use a portion control feeding system.

In general, *ad libitum* feeding can be used for most ordinary feeding situations. A few examples are routine kennel feeding, *some* household pets, many breeding situations, colonies of laboratory dogs, and virtually all sporting and guard dog operations. *Ad libitum* feeding can successfully be used in almost any feeding situation where convenience and time are factors, but some record of body weight and food intake on individual dogs is desirable.

Self-feeding

Because of their nature of eating to meet their caloric needs, most dogs can be placed on a feeding program where food remains before them continuously. Such a program is known as self-feeding. An extension of the convenience of *ad libitum* feeding, self-feeding not only enables the dog to decide how much it will eat, but when. About the only thing the dog feeder has to do is choose the food to be fed.

Most dogs with food before them at all times adjust their food intake quite satisfactorily and do not overeat. About one dog in 50 is a glutton, however. The success of a self-feeding program depends on a dog feeder's ability to identify these few dogs that refuse to restrict their own intake. These dogs must be separated and placed on a portion controlled feeding program if their weight is to be maintained at the proper level.

To establish a successful self-feeding program a dog feeder must have the proper equipment, place and attitude necessary for the job.

First, all self-feeding programs require a self-feeder. This piece of hardware is described in Chapter 9 on equipment. Second, it is essential that the dog feeder have a food suitable to be used in a self-feeding program. For all practical purposes, this limits the choice of food to a dry one. Canned foods would spoil and soft-moist products do not deliver properly from the feeder.

175

The best place to put a self feeder is indoors. If this is impossible, it should always be under some type of overhead shelter. While some models of self feeders are made with hinged doors to prevent the entry of sunlight and rain, feeders that are used in the open must always be covered with a roof or they will lead to food spoilage in some form.

Once a feeder and the food to go into it have been chosen, and a place to put the feeder has been found, the change-over to self-feeding can begin. The best time to make this conversion is immediately after the dogs have been fed. As the old individual food containers are picked up, the new self-feeders can be hung and filled with food. While nearly every dog will investigate the new feeder, and most will take a bite or two of food out of curiosity, few dogs will exhibit much interest in the food in the feeder on a full stomach. Any dogs that do are good candidates to watch as potential gluttons. As the dogs' stomachs begin to empty, and the first twinges of hunger appear, each dog will help himself to a few more bites of food from the feeder.

It is important never to let the feeder become empty. Most dog feeders using self-feeding programs refill their feeders about once a week. If you are feeding larger dogs, or several dogs from the same feeder, it may be necessary to refill more often. By watching closely the level of food in the feeder for the first few weeks, you can establish a pattern for refilling. Once a regular refilling pattern has been established, it should be followed closely. By doing so you may be able to "sense" any changes in intake each time you make a routine refill. Remember that a seasonal change is to be expected, and should be allowed for in the refill procedure. This is particularly important with dogs living out of doors.

At about every third refill you should pour all of the food in the feeder out into another container and examine it. If the food is still fresh, does not smell moldy or rancid, and does not have any insects contaminating it, pour it back into the feeder. Refill the feeder to the proper amount, as usual. This precaution prevents you from continuing to feed your dog moldy, spoiled or contaminated food without being aware of it.

In hot or humid climates the examination of the food in a self feeder should be made weekly if the dogs are being fed outdoors. Oldness or staleness in a food not only affects its nutritional qualities, but its palatability as well. In fact, the first place you should look when dogs on a self-feeding program reduce their food intake

176

or lose weight is inside the feeder. Seven times out of ten the cause of the food reduction or weight loss will be found right there.

Self-feeding programs are especially useful to dog feeders with large numbers of dogs to feed, although it is quite successfully used by people who feed only one dog. It reduces a tremendous amount of the labor and time associated with individual feeding programs. As a consequence, self-feeding is probably the most economical method of feeding large numbers of dogs. It practically eliminates wastage, since refused or spilled food is almost non-existent. In cooler climates and in non-heated winter quarters, self-feeding provides an automatic adjustment to the caloric needs made by day-to-day weather changes. It is similarly effective where dogs do varied amounts of work or perform varying activities from day-to-day. Finally, it is proving to be an excellent way to provide a lactating bitch with all the food she needs, as she needs it.

The use of a self-feeding program also can provide fringe benefits. It helps to reduce *coprophagy*, the condition in which dogs eat their own feces, because most dogs prefer to eat food rather than feces. It tends to break down the social hierarchy, or peck-order of feeding, and eliminates bullying dogs from driving the more timid ones away from the feed container. All of the dogs are more content with a full belly, and that usually keeps them quieter. Self-feeding also helps keep the kennel quiet by eliminating noisy feeding times. Finally, it allows a kennel operator a day's relief from his feeding chores once in a while without having to fast his dogs.

There is one precaution which must be urged upon those about to embark on self-feeding programs. Alterations in a dog's feeding behavior are one of the major ways most dog feeders recognize illness in a dog. This is usually done unconsciously, the minute a dog stops eating. When a group of dogs are eating from the same self feeder it is almost an impossible task to determine whether an individual dog is eating or not. For this reason dogs that are on self-feeding programs must be kept under closer observation. This will help prevent those diseases that would ordinarily be recognized immediately, because of a loss of appetite, from going unnoticed. Bitches that have recently whelped should be watched especially until all possibility of pregnancy and parturition problems have been eliminated.

Artificial Alimentation

Another name for artificial alimentation is "force feeding." It is

177

the method of feeding to which a dog feeder must resort when a dog refuses to eat its food in the normal manner. Any procedure whereby food or water is placed into a dog's alimentary canal by a means other than the normal eating or drinking behavior is *artificial* alimentation.

There are numerous reasons why a dog refuses to eat all of the food it needs. The most common are disease, emotional upset, unacceptable food and injury. Disease is always the first thing a dog feeder should consider when a dog stops eating because over 90 percent of the diseases of the dog produce a loss of appetite. A loss of appetite is also called *anorexia*. Anorexia is discussed at some length in Chapter 19 on feeding sick dogs.

In addition to using artificial alimentation to furnish a dog with food it does not want, the dog feeder should also be working diligently to find out the cause of the food refusal. Once discovered, it should be eliminated and measures instituted to restore the dog's normal feeding behavior. Artificial alimenation should always be used as a substitute for normal eating behavior, never as a replacement for it.

Administering unwanted food or water to a dog can be done by two methods, spoon-feeding and intragastric intubation.

Spoon feeding is the first, and most often thought of, method of artificially feeding a dog. Spoon feeding is the most convenient form of artificial alimentation, requiring the least amount of preparation, skill or equipment. Furthermore, it probably has been responsible for saving more dogs' lives than any other form of artificial feeding. Dog feeders continue to use spoon-feeding because it is easy, even if it doesn't always produce acceptable results. Unfortunately, spoon feeders are a tiny minority, because many dog feeders won't bother to try to feed a dog the first few days it won't eat. Even spoon-feeding is better than allowing a fasting dog to remain unfed for more than 48 hours.

Even when done by an experienced dog feeder, spoon feeding can be less than successful. The results will range from getting most of the food into the dog to getting most of it on yourself and the table and floor, the odds being a little in favor of the latter results. In addition to the obvious disadvantages of having food all over yourself and the floor, another disadvantage of spoon-feeding is the inability to determine, with any degree of accuracy, how much food the dog actually ate. Most dogs spill or spit out as much as they swallow, and there is no suitable way to measure this wastage.

The method, as it is usually employed, uses a canned or similar soft food which is formed into little, bite-sized balls and fed with a spoon or the fingers, Figures 79-82. To perform the feeding, open the dog's mouth and drop the food onto the dog's tongue. Then, with the spoon or your finger, push the food as far back as possible. Quickly slip the spoon or finger out of the dog's mouth and hold it shut. With your thumb and forefinger gently stroke the dog's throat a couple of times, to provoke the dog into swallowing. When you see or feel the dog swallow, take another ball, place it on the tip of your spoon handle or fingers, and repeat the procedure. Continue until all of the food prepared for feeding has been fed and swallowed.

There is always the occasional dog that resents being force fed and refuses to cooperate in any efforts to have food balls crammed down its throat. When such a dog is encountered, the most sensible approach is not to fight either the dog or your patience. Instead, discard spoon-feeding and use another method of artificial feeding.

Intragastric intubation is the other form of artificial alimentation. It is usually referred to as "stomach tubing" by the few dog feeders who use it. The use of intragastric intubation is fairly common among veterinarians and trained animal technicians, but almost nonexistent among other groups of dog feeders. There are a number of reasons why the method has been of limited value to the average dog feeder. Foremost among these is the ever-present chance that a tube may be inserted into the lungs instead of the stomach, and the dog feeder will drown the dog as he administers the food. Another drawback is the fact that special equipment is necessary for the procedure. Still another is the specialized skill required, which can be gained only through experience. A final item is the fact that, of necessity, the only food that can be used must be in liquid form. This means the food must either be obtained in liquid form, or run through a blender with enough water to convert the mixture into a liquid.

With a little practice most dog feeders can become reasonably proficient at passing a stomach tube into the stomach of a dog. When done correctly, there is little danger associated with the procedure for either the dog or the dog feeder.

179

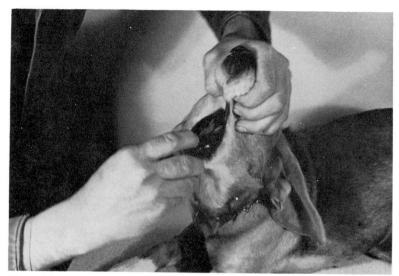

Figure 79. To force feed a dog, open its mouth by grasping its muzzle with one hand, as shown, and prying the jaw open with the other hand. As the mouth opens, roll the upper lips over the teeth with your thumb and forefinger and press them into the roof of the mouth. A firm, steady pressure into the roof of the mouth with your thumb will help to dissuade the dog from closing its mouth.

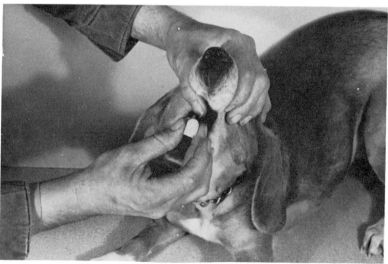

Figure 80. Once the mouth is open and being held by the top hand, drop the rolled ball of food into the dog's mouth with the other hand. Drop the food as far back into the mouth as you can get it.

180

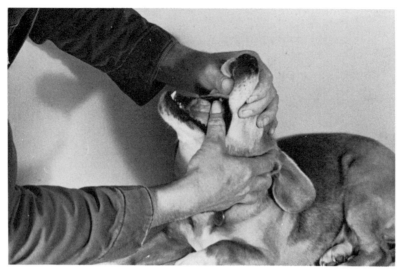

Figure 81. Quickly follow the ball of food with your thumb or forefinger, as shown, and poke the ball of food as far down the dog's throat as you can reach. Don't worry about hurting the dog. The farther back you can push the food, the more likely it will cause a swallowing reflex.

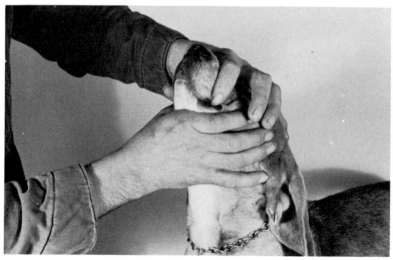

Figure 82. If the dog does not swallow the food as you poke it down, pull your finger out of the dog's mouth, snap it shut, and stroke the dog's throat gently with the thumb and forefinger of your free hand. Once the dog has swallowed the food, repeat the procedure until all food is eaten.

181

Single vs. Multiple-food Diets

Each of the four feeding methods can be sub-divided by whether the diet is composed of a single food or a combination of foods.

Single-food diets are almost always made up of a single commercial food. In the strictest sense, even these foods are usually composed of more than one ingredient. During processing these ingredients are combined into a single, uniform food in which the integrity of the individual ingredients is all but lost.

It is essential that the food of a single-food diet be complete and balanced. Since it will be the only nutrient source the dog will receive, it must be capable of supplying all of the nutrients a dog needs in balanced and adequate amounts.

Single-food diets have certain advantages. Dog feeders are able to learn more quickly, and predict with more accuracy, what their dietary program will or will not do. The effect its diet has on a dog's performance can be more easily watched when only one food is responsible for those effects.

Multiple-food diets are usually home-made diets, containing combinations of natural foods or combinations of two or more commercial foods with or without natural foods added. Unless the feeder knows the exact amounts of nutrients contained in the natural foods used, and has the capability of measuring those foods accurately, home-made diets are usually more imbalanced than they are anything else. Those made from a mixture of commercial foods and/or natural ingredients, if done properly, can be satisfactory multiple-food diets. Even balanced multiple-food diets produce a variable response. For this reason they are inferior to single-food diets where predictable performance (e.g. exact weight maintenance; constant, lustrous, full-bodied haircoat or prolonged endurance) is important.

Multiple-food diets are excellent means of utilizing inexpensive food ingredients that contain valuable nutrients, but are not balanced food by themselves. While the dog feeder may wish to incorporate these foods into a diet he is feeding, to improve its quality or energy levels, he must do so carefully. He must make absolutely certain that his diet remains balanced after including the food. One way of doing this is to adopt the practice of never adding anything to a balanced diet in excess of 25 percent of the total being fed. Another, more accurate method, is to follow the directions for compounding an adequate diet found in Appendix A.

Chapter 12

Determining How Much to Feed

THE proper quantity of food to feed a dog each day is that amount which will maintain the dog at its optimum body weight. Determining what that quantity should be for a given dog becomes a difficult task for some dog feeders.

As long as a food is balanced and adequate, the quantity of it which must be fed daily depends on two things. One is the food's caloric density, the other is the total number of calories the dog needs every day to maintain its weight. Once these two figures are known, the quantity of food that should be fed becomes a simple matter of calculation. By dividing the total number of calories the dog needs by the caloric density of the food, the quantity of the food needed will be the result.

Caloric Density

The term caloric density refers to the number of calories a given quantity of food contains. The caloric density most commonly used by dog feeders is the number of calories in a pound of food, but the number of calories per 100 grams or per ounce is also used from time to time.

The quantity of calories in a dog food can be determined by several methods.

The simplest method is to use a hypothetical figure for each type

183

of food. The hypothetical figures most frequently used for the various commercial dog foods are:

Canned ration-type ....500 calories per pound
Canned all-animal-tissue ....600 calories per pound
Soft-moist type ....1350 calories per pound
Dry, expanded ....1500 calories per pound
Dry, kibbled biscuit ....1400 calories per pound

These figures are arbitrary figures derived from an average of many of the more commonly sold foods. While using these figures is the most convenient way of arriving at a caloric density for a food, it is also the least accurate. Such arbitrary figures are satisfactory as a rule-of-thumb, or as a rapid screening to be sure there are adequate calories in a diet. Such figures are unsatisfactory where accurate amounts are needed to predict food performance or regulate weight control.

A slightly more accurate method of determining how many calories are in a food is to calculate them directly from the guaranteed analysis on the food's label. The accuracy of this method is limited by the accuracy of the guaranteed analysis.

Probably the most accurate method of determining the caloric density of a food available to the average dog feeder is by calculating it from the proximate analysis of the food. The biggest problem with this method is the fact that the proximate analyses of many dog foods are not immediately available. To get a proximate analysis of most of the food you will feed it will be necessary for you to write the manufacturer of the food for it. Unfortunately, not all the dog food makers will supply this information. This is not because they are afraid of giving away any trade secrets. It is because, in many instances, the food makers do not have the information themselves! But, from reputable manufacturers of quality dog foods, manufacturers who are proud of the food they take your money for, the analytical contents of their food is willingly supplied. Moreover, any food that claims to be "complete" or "balanced" will have to have such analytical data available to back up their claims.

Another means of obtaining an analysis is to have the food analyzed yourself. The only disadvantage to this method of obtaining the analysis of a food is that it is expensive.

Whether the figures used are from the guaranteed analysis or the proximate analysis, the method of determining the number of calories in the food is the same. Nutritionists use a rather complex formula to calculate caloric density, but I have reduced the calculations to simple addition by including Table XV. The information in Table XV is a list of the common percentages that the three major calorie-producing nutrients normally contribute to a dog food, and the number of calories each percentage of the nutrient will contribute to the food. With Table XV, you can determine the caloric density of any food by following these steps:

TABLE XV

The numbers of calories contributed by various percentages of the three major calorie-producing nutrients in a diet.

	Fat		
percent in diet	cals/100 gms	cals/lb	cals/oz
1%	9	40.5	2.5
2%	18	81.0	5.0
3%	27	121.5	7.5
4%	36	162.0	10.0
5%	45	202.5	12.5
6%	54	243.0	15.0
7%	63	283.5	17.5
8%	72	324.0	20.0
9%	81	364.5	22.5
10%	90	405.0	25.0
11%	99	445.5	27.5
12%	108	486.0	30.0

185

Protein

percent in diet	cals/100 gms	cals/lb	cals/oz
5%	20	90.0	5.6
6%	24	108	6.7
7%	28	126	7.9
8%	32	144	9.0
9%	36	162	10.1
10%	40	180	11.2
11%	44	198	12.3
12%	48	216	13.5
13%	52	234	14.6
14%	56	252	15.7
15%	60	270	16.9
16%	64	288	18.0
17%	68	306	19.1
18%	72	324	20.2
19%	76	332	21.3
20%	80	350	22.5
21%	84	368	23.6
22%	88	386	24.7
23%	92	404	25.9
24%	96	422	27.0
25%	100	440	28.2

Carbohydrate

percent in diet	cals/100 gms	cals/lb	cals/oz
2%	8.5	38.2	2.4
3%	12.7	57.1	3.6
4%	17.0	76.5	4.8
5%	21.2	95.4	6.0
6%	25.5	114.7	7.2
7%		133.8	8.4
8%	34.0	153.8	9.6
9%		172.1	10.8
10%	42.5	191.2	12.0
11%		210.3	13.2
12%	51.0	229.4	14.4
13%		248.5	15.6
14%	59.5	267.6	16.8
15%		286.7	18.0
16%	68.0	305.8	19.2
17%		324.9	20.4
18%	76.5	344.0	21.6
19%		363.1	22.8
20%	85.0	382.2	24.0
22%	93.5	420.4	26.4
24%		458.6	28.8
26%		496.8	31.2
28%		535.0	33.6
30%		573.2	36.0
32%		611.4	38.4
34%		649.6	40.8
36%		687.8	43.2
38%		726.0	45.6
40%		764.2	48.0
42%		802.4	50.4
44%		840.6	53.8
46%		878.8	55.2
48%		917.0	57.6
50%		955.2	60.0

187

STEP 1. List the three major nutrients and their percentage in the food, obtained from either the guaranteed analysis on the label, or a proximate analysis from the food's maker or your lab report. Most labels and many lab reports will not list the carbohydrate in a food. To obtain a percentage figure for carbohydrate add the figures for moisture, protein, fat, ash and fiber together and subtract their total from 100. The difference will be the percentage of carbohydrate in the food.

Example:

The following is a calculation of the carbohydrate content of a canned food, using both the figures taken from its label and from a lab report of its actual contents.

	Guaranteed Analysis	*Proximate Analysis*
Crude protein,	not less than 10.0%	10.41%
Crude fat,	not less than 3.5%	4.93%
Crude fiber,	not more than 1.0%	0.55%
Ash,	not more than 4.0%	3.32%
Moisture,	not more than 74.0%	73.84%
Total	92.5%	93.05%

Carbohydrate $\quad 100-92.5\% = 7.5\%$ Or $-93.05\% = 6.95\%$

STEP 2. From Table XV copy the number of calories contributed by the percentage of each nutrient listed. The table lists calorie contributions for 100 grams, for a pound and for an ounce. Be sure and use the same unit of measurement for all three nutrient percentages.

STEP 3. Add the figures for the three nutrients' contributions. The total will be the caloric density of the food measured in calories per 100 grams, per pound or per ounce, depending on which unit of measurement you chose to use.

Example:

The following is a calculation of the caloric density of the food used above to determine the carbohydrate content. The calculation has been made in calories per pound.

nutrient	guaranteed analysis	calories/lb	proximate analysis	calories/lb
Protein	10.0%	180	10.4%	187
Fat	3.5%	142	4.9%	198
Carbohydrate	7.5%	144	7.0%	134
		466		519

188

The following is a calculation of the caloric density of a typical dry food, but using calories per ounce instead of calories per pound.

nutrient	guaranteed analysis	calories/oz	proximate analysis	calories/oz
Protein	23.0%	25.9	23.8%	26.7
Fat	8.0%	20.0	9.0%	22.5
Carbohydrate	45.5%	55.6	47.5%	58.0
		101.5		107.2

You can see from these examples that there may be some variation in the results obtained using the guaranteed versus the proximate analysis when calculating caloric density. Whenever it is available, the one calculated from the proximate analysis should be used in preference to any others.

A final method of arriving at a caloric density for a food is to obtain it directly from the food's manufacturer. Like the proximate analysis, however, this may prove to be quite a challenge at times. Those food makers who have done adequate testing of their food to insure its nutritional adequacy will be more than happy to supply a figure for caloric density. It will be one of the first tests they will have made on their food. If you can obtain this figure from the food maker it will probably be the most accurate of all, since they probably arrived at the figure by actually burning the food and measuring the calories it produced.

If you are a conscientious dog feeder you will make it a practice to obtain from the makers of any food you use as much information as possible regarding their food. This, in fact, is one of the better methods of screening out undesirable foods. Any food maker who is willing to take your money for his food, but is too ashamed of its quality to inform you of its chemical content or caloric density, is probably not producing the kind of food you want to feed your dog. There are enough good-quality food makers around who *are* willing to share with you this information for you not to waste your money or time on a food maker who isn't. A few dog food manufacturers are proud enough of their food to actually have an analysis printed on the label. If more food makers would follow the example set by these few, a dog feeder's job would be made a lot easier and a dog's life a lot healthier.

Caloric Requirement

The quantity of calories a dog will need every day will depend on the dog's optimum weight and its activity.

Optimum body weight: Every dog has an optimum body weight. The optimum body weight is that weight at which a dog performs most efficiently. For most dogs, their optimum weight is identical to that point at which their body weight levels off at maturity.

One of the primary objectives of a good feeding program is to maintain a dog at its optimum body weight. This must be done in spite of such external forces as environment, work, play, emotional stress, and others, that constantly work at changing a dog's weight. To be able to accomplish this objective, the first requirement is to establish, for every dog being fed, the correct optimum weight to be maintained.

Establishing the optimum weight for a dog you have raised from a puppy is easy—if you have been keeping adequate weight records. By plotting the puppy's weights on a graph, its optimum weight can be determined by that point at which the weight curve becomes level, Figure 83.

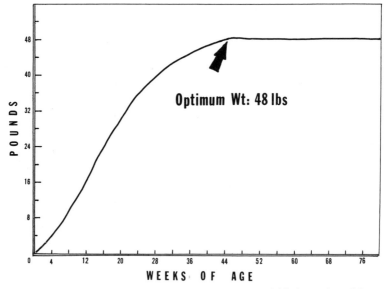

Figure 83. A dog's optimum weight is that point at which it attains ultimate growth and begins to hold that weight constant.

190

For the dog that has reached maturity before you have an occasion to establish its optimum body weight, the procedure may become a little more complex. The dog's breed, physical characteristics and parental heritage must be used to establish an arbitrary optimum weight for an adult dog. For example, if an optimum weight is to be assigned to a young-adult, male, Standard Poodle that is at the upper end of the size range for Standards, and whose parents are both on the large side, the weight chosen would probably be between 55 to 65 pounds. On the other hand, if the Poodle is a wiry little Standard whose sire is just $15\frac{1}{2}$ inches high, and whose dam is moderate in size but frail of bone, the weight chosen would more likely be in the 35 to 40-pound range.

There is a 20-pound difference between these two dogs' body weights, even though the dogs are both adult male Poodles, and of approximately the same age. To maintain such a weight difference the heavier Poodle must eat more calories every day. This is because every dog requires a certain number of calories every day to maintain each pound of its body weight. The more it weighs, therefore, the more calories a dog needs to eat each day to maintain its body at the same weight. While the larger Poodle weighs 40 percent more than the smaller one, it is unlikely that the larger dog will eat 40 percent more food than the smaller one. This is because the larger a dog becomes the fewer calories per pound it needs to eat to maintain each pound of its body weight.

Table XVI is a standard calorie chart for dogs. It lists the average number of calories required daily by dogs of different weights. In a *standard* calorie chart such as Table XVI the values are for dogs being subjected to a moderate environmental stress and engaging in only that amount of activity needed by an average housedog to carry on its life functions.

There actually is no such thing as an average dog, of course. Some are easy keepers, some are hard keepers, and the rest are somewhere in between. In short, all dogs, like all people, are individuals and must be treated as such. The greatest amount of success in feeding dogs is always enjoyed by the dog feeder who provides for his dog's individual needs. Standard calorie charts, like those listed in Table XVI, serve merely as convenient guides to be used for determining a starting place when feeding a dog. The same is true of all the "suggested feeding amounts" charts on dog food labels. Neither were ever meant to be absolute or inflexible directives. On the contrary,

191

all such tables are only starting points from which you must begin a trial and error program to tailor your dog's feeding program to meet its individual needs.

TABLE XVI

A standard calorie chart for dogs, giving the calories per pound and the total daily calories needed by dogs of different weights.

Dog's weight	Cals/lb/day	Total daily Cals.	Dog's weight	Cals/lb/day	Total daily Cals.
2.2	64	141	18.0	36	648
4.4	53	233	20.0	35	700
5.0	50	250	22.0	34	748
5.5	49	269	25.0	33	825
6.0	48	288	28.5	32	912
6.5	47	305	30.0	31	930
7.0	46	322	32.0	31	992
7.5	45	337	36.0	30	1080
8.0	44	352	40.0	29	1160
9.0	43	387	44.0	28	1232
10.0	42	420	50.0	27	1350
11.0	41	451	57.0	26	1482
12.0	40	480	66.0	25	1650
13.5	39	526	88.0	24	2112
15.0	38	570	118.0	24	2832
16.5	37	610	150.0	24	3600

Simple maintenance: The procedure for adjusting a dog's food intake to maintain its optimum weight is a straight-forward, trial and error approach, requiring only suitable record keeping and patience to be successful. Any dog can have its food intake adjusted to the correct quantity necessary to maintain its optimum body weight by following these steps.

STEP 1. Establish an optimum body weight for the dog if you have not already done so. Weigh the dog to see if there is any difference between what the dog should weigh and what it does weigh.

STEP 2. Determine from Table XVI the number of calories needed daily by the dog to maintain its optimum weight. Remember that this is only the starting point, not the final results.

STEP 3. Feed the quantity calculated to maintain the established optimum weight for about two weeks, then weigh the dog again. If the dog's weight at that time is closer to the optimum weight than the initial weight was, continue to feed the quantity you are feeding. If the second weight is farther away from the optimum weight than the first was, adjust the food in the proper direction by about 10 percent. (ie: Increase food 10 percent if weight is too low, decrease food 10 percent if weight is too much.) Weigh the dog again after a week of feeding the adjustment you made. Based on a comparison of the second and third weights, make any adjustment needed by a five percent change. With this five percent change, the quantity of food should be about as close as you can get to the correct amount for maintaining that particular dog's optimum weight during a maintenance situation. If the two adjustments do not provide a quantity of food that maintains the established optimum weight a re-evaluation of the optimum weight should be made to be sure it is not the optimum weight that needs adjusting.

When a dog's situation changes from maintenance to one producing an increase in the dog's need for nutrients or energy, the feeding program must continue to be tailored to maintain the dog's optimum weight. This means that the increase in the need for energy, nutrients, or both, must be met by a change in the dog's diet. What these changes are, for the different situations in which a dog may find itself, and how they can be met, are covered in the next seven chapters about the individual life cycle phases. A different table of caloric requirements is contained in each one of these chapters. It should be used in place of the standard table given in this chapter when determining how much to feed a dog when its life cycle is in the phase described in that chapter.

Determining quantity for more than one dog: Sometimes, when a number of dogs are being fed, as in kennel or boarding operations, the total quantity needed for a daily feeding must be determined as well as that for each dog. It can be determined as follows:

STEP 1. Determine the *total weight* (TW) of all dogs to be fed. This can be done by adding up the optimum body weights of all the dogs to be fed. If you are feeding your own dogs you should have records on each one giving its actual and its optimum weight. If you are feeding someone else's dogs you should have recorded the dog's actual weight when they were taken in, and jotted down on their record what you thought their optimum weight should be.

When necessary, TW can be calculated by estimating each dog's optimum weight and totaling these figures. An alternate method is

193

to estimate an average optimum weight and multiply that number by the total number of dogs to be fed. This last method works best when all the dogs being fed are about the same size.

STEP 2. Determine the *total number of calories* (TC) needed by multiplying the TW by the average calorie-per-pound requirement for a single dog (C). C is usually given the value of 30. The choice of the number 30 is arbitrary and was made because it hits at about the median caloric requirement for the largest number of dogs. With dogs kept outdoors, C can be changed to 45 during the coldest months of the winter. Both of these arbitrary values serve as a satisfactory rule of thumb when you are dealing with a number of dogs of the same breed or size.

Where dogs are of different breeds or of varying sizes a more accurate estimate of C can be obtained by using the figures from Table XVI under the "calories per pound per day" column.

STEP 3. Determine the *total pounds of food* needed (TF) to supply the TC by dividing the *caloric density* (CD) in pounds, into the TC. If the actual CD of the food you are feeding is unknown, it should be calculated following the procedure already described in this chapter.

If the diet being fed is a combination of several types of foods, calculate an average from the various amounts being used. For example, if you are feeding a mixture of 30 pounds of dry food and five pounds of canned all-animal-tissue, the caloric density of a pound of the mixture would be:

$$\frac{30 \times 1500 + 5 \times 600}{35} = \frac{45{,}000 + 3000}{35} = \frac{48{,}000}{35} =$$

1,370 calories per pound. (The arbitrary figures for caloric density of dry food and canned all-animal-tissue foods were used to make these calculations.)

The above three steps can be reduced to a set of formulas for those who are more mathematically inclined. The symbols for these formulas are:

> W —weight of any one individual dog
> TW —total weight of all dogs being fed
> C —calories required per pound body weight
> CI —calories required by individual dog daily
> TC —total calories required by all dogs fed

194

CD—caloric density of food being fed (cals/lb)
F—pounds of food required by individual dog daily
TF—total pounds of food needed by all dogs fed

The examples that follow assume a kennel of 10 dogs weighing between 36 and 44 pounds, with an average of 40 pounds. The TW is then 400 pounds (10 x 40). The food being fed is the 30:5 mixture used above having a caloric density of 1370 calories per pound.

To compute the total calories required, substitute the appropriate figures into the following formula like this:

$$TC = TW \times C$$
$$TC = 400 \times 30$$
$$TC = 12,000 \text{ calories}$$

To determine the total pounds of food required:

$$TF = \frac{TC}{CD} \text{ (in lbs)}$$
$$TF = \frac{12,000}{1370}$$
$$TF = 8.75 \text{ or about 9 lbs. daily.}$$

To determine the caloric requirements of a 44-pound dog:

$$CI = W \times C$$
$$CI = 44 \times 28$$
$$CI = 1232 \text{ calories.}$$

To determine the feeding for a single 44-pound dog:

$$F = \frac{CI}{CD}$$
$$F = \frac{1232}{1370}$$
$$F = 0.899 \text{ lbs (approx. 0.9 lbs)}$$

For any dog whose weight is not maintained by feeding the amounts calculated by these formulas, proceed as follows:

If the weight is substandard:

1) following five consecutive days during which the dog eats all the food offered, increase the total amount fed by about 10 per-

195

cent. Continue this adjustment until the dog's weight reaches optimum.

2) and the dog refuses to eat all of its food for five consecutive days but remains below optimum weight, the dog should be checked by a veterinarian. If the dog is healthy, the caloric density of the diet should be increased. This reduces the quantity of food needed to supply the same sumber of calories. For each 270 calories the dogs refuse to eat the diet can be increased that much in density by adding one ounce of corn oil. This rule remains accurate within 10 to 12 calories as long as no more than three ounces of oil is added. When replacement exceeds about 20 percent of the total calories in a diet there is a rapid rise in the amount of diarrhea it produces.

If the weight exceeds the optimum:

1) following five consecutive days during which the dog either eats all of the food or allows some to remain, reduce the quantity offered by 10 percent or greater if indicated. Continue this adjustment until the dog reaches and holds its optimum weight from the amount of food being fed.

PART IV

FEEDING PROGRAMS

Chapter 13

The Growing Dog

THE logical place to begin a discussion of feeding programs is with the puppy.

The usual time for the dog feeder to assume the responsibility of feeding a dog is at weaning. On occasion this responsibility begins at birth or shortly thereafter. In those unfortunate instances where a puppy is orphaned, or in cases where a bitch whelps so many puppies that she cannot feed them all, the dog feeder may have to begin his feeding chores while the puppy is still only hours old.

Whether the puppy is six hours, six weeks or six months old, the first step in any puppy feeding program is to weigh each puppy. A record of this weight and the date it was taken should be kept on a separate record for each individual. The second and third steps are fundamental to all feeding programs, determining the diet to be fed, and determining the quantity of food needed to start the program. The type of diet will depend on what stage of growth the puppy has attained. The quantity of food will depend upon the puppy's age, weight and the caloric density of the food.

The Newborn Puppy

Much has been written about hand-rearing newborn pups. Indeed, there is probably more written about hand-rearing than there is about the natural method of raising puppies. The development of successful hand-rearing techniques has made raising orphaned puppies today almost as effortless as raising puppies still

199

having their own mother. Dog feeders who enjoy a high degree of success raising newborn pups pay careful attention to the following basic principles:

1. Provide a suitable environment.
2. Feed a nutritionally complete formula.
3. Institute a satisfactory feeding schedule.

Regulating the environment: For this discussion, temperature, humidity, and keeping the puppy quiet and undisturbed are the three most important requirements for a puppy's proper environment.

Formulating the diet: The ideal food to feed to newborn puppies is bitch's milk. Any replacement for bitch's milk should approximate it as closely as possible. A comparison between the contents of bitch's milk and some of the substitutes often used for it is given in Table XVII.

TABLE XVII

A comparison of the composition of bitch's milk with some of the products commonly used to substitute for it.

nutrient	bitch's milk	cow's milk	evap. milk*	Esbilac**	Orpha-lac
Protein (%)	7.5	3.5	5.6	7.6	5.5
Fat (%)	8.3	3.9	6.4	8.2	6.1
Lactose (%)	3.7	4.9	8.2	2.9	3.7
Calcium (mg/100ml)	280.0	118.0	271.0	168.0	130.0
Phosphorus (mg/100ml)	240.0	93.0	216.0	141.0	130.0
Total solids	22.6	13.0	20.0	21.0	16.2
Calories/cc	1.2	0.68	1.15	1.3	1.1

* 20% solids (add one part water to three parts milk)
** reconstituted as per directions.

From this table it becomes readily apparent that cow's milk is too dilute for puppies. Cow's milk should only be used as an emergency food for puppies. Every effort should be made to replace it with a more suitable substitute as quickly as possible. A much more suitable emergency formula can be made from evaporated canned milk. By mixing three parts of evaporated milk, as it comes from the can, with one part of warm water, a milk with 20 percent solids will be formed. This mixture will have a distribution of nutrients much closer to that of bitch's milk. In fact, by adding $\frac{1}{4}$th teaspoonful of

200

powdered dicalcium phosphate to each cup of the evaporated milk mixture a formula that has actually raised puppies can be made.

Much more convenient are the commercial formulas designed to be used for feeding orphaned puppies. These products closely resemble bitch's milk in content. When one considers the trouble involved in mixing, boiling, and storing a homemade formula, the slight extra expense of commercial products is worthwhile for those who can afford them.

However closely a formula resembles bitch's milk, there is one ingredient that the dog feeder cannot provide—colostrum. Colostrum is found in the first few days of a bitch's milk and protects her puppies from disease while their tiny bodies are learning to protect themselves. There is no substitute for colostrum. Whenever possible, every newborn puppy should nurse a newly freshened dam, even if the dam is not the puppy's own, for at least 24 hours. The losses among hand-fed puppies that fail to get colostrum during that first 24 hours are amazingly higher than among those that do.

The reason bottle-fed human babies do not need to nurse at least 24 hours is because the human mother can pass these protective substances from her bloodstream into that of her baby. A human baby is born with them already in its body. In the bitch there is a barrier that prevents these protective substances from being transferred, and the puppy must absorb them from the bitch's milk.

Even colostrum cannot protect newborn puppies against the more dangerous bacteria. Nor can it protect the puppy against *overwhelming* numbers of the less dangerous ones, such as numbers that come with unclean utensils and feeding equipment. It has always worried me how many young mothers, who were sterilizing bottles and formulas for their own infants, were amazed that such precautions were necessary for newborn puppies. I have always wondered if those mothers actually knew why they were doing all that sterilizing, or if they did it just because their own mothers did.

When colostrum-filled milk is not available, the necessity for cleanliness and proper handling of all items used to house and feed the newborn puppies is increased ten-fold. The slightest break in proper procedure, where newborn pups without colostrum are concerned, invariably spells disaster.

Feeding schedules: If their formula resembles bitch's milk closely enough, newborn puppies of small and medium-size breeds do not need to be fed more than four times daily. For larger breeds this

201

number may need to be increased to six. To determine the daily quantity to feed each puppy, the following calorie intakes for pre-weaning puppies should be used:

weeks of age	Cals/lb body wt.	Cals/ounce body wt.
1st	60	3.7
2nd	70	4.4
3rd	80 to 90	5.0 to 5.6
4th	90+	5.6+

Using these figures with a formula of proper content, the total daily quantity required will divide into four to six equal feedings that will leave the puppy with a moderately distended stomach following each feeding. The exact quantity to be fed must always be left to the discretion of the person feeding the puppy. Common sense is still one of the most important aspects of successfully raising infant pups. Just remember, *it is better to underfeed than to overfeed.* Start with the figure given, as a guide to estimate the quantity needed, then let the puppy tell you how much it really needs.

A puppy tells a dog feeder whether it is receiving too much or too little food in several ways. Crying is one of the most often recognized, but least likely to be always accurate. Hungry puppies do cry, but so do cold puppies, hot puppies, puppies just disturbed from a nap, lost puppies, unhappy puppies, etc., etc. Crying is simply nature's way of giving a puppy a means for telling everybody that it is unhappy. Anything that makes a puppy unhappy will probably also make him cry, even having his tummy too full.

I seldom use any of a puppy's behavioral patterns as an indicator of its hunger. To say that because a puppy is crying, it is hungry requires a judgment on my part. And, since I can't think like a puppy, my judgments are very likely to be wrong.

Instead, I use the reactions of the puppy's system to determine whether or not it is getting enough to eat. Every time you feed a puppy, two things should happen. The puppy should have a bowel movement and it should urinate. Sometimes a puppy may need a little encouragement by rubbing its anal area, but it should always perform both acts if everything is going right.

The character and amount of a pup's feces and urine are important clues that tell you how well you are doing as its mother.

A puppy's stool should be formed as it is expelled, but its consistency should be soft and pasty. Its color will depend to some extent on what you are feeding the pup. But in every case, it should not vary from a pale tan to a mahogany brown. The inside of the stool may be yellow-brown in many cases, but this is not objectionable. Stools that are green, bluish-white or clear signal trouble. Even tan or brownish stools that are watery, lumpy, hard or curdled may indicate something is wrong. Whenever either off-color or off-form stools occur, stop feeding immediately and skip the next feeding entirely. Begin the following feeding with a formula that has been diluted one-half with boiled water. Continue to feed the same quantity as you did the undiluted food. If this fails to produce an improvement in the stool, cut the quantity you are feeding by 25 percent at each feeding. If stools continue to be off-color or off-form, call your veterinarian.

A puppy's urination is an indicator of its water balance. The quantity should be about the same each time the puppy urinates. It might be pale yellow to almost clear, but should never be deep yellow or orange. It should always be like water and never like syrup. It should smell like urine. Urine that is scanty, dark in color, or syrupy, indicates that the pup is not receiving enough water. Additional water should be supplied, either added to the formula or fed separately. If the urine seems excessive in amount, unduly clear, or thin, the water concentration of the formula should be re-examined to make certain that too much water is not being given. If urine production stops altogether for longer than four feedings, take the puppy to a veterinarian promptly.

Feeding procedures: There are two methods of feeding nursing puppies in common use—the bottle and the stomach tube.

Bottle feeding. Bottles and nipples have been used for feeding newborn puppies for many years. The form most often used today is the toy doll's bottle. Most of these are now made from plastic and some have real rubber nipples, made in the same shape and form as the larger baby nipples, Figure 84. For larger breeds the "premie" bottles and nipples, designed for feeding premature babies, work well, Figure 85.

Bottle feeding newborn pups is not much different from bottle feeding any other newborn mammal. First of all, everything should be impeccably clean. The bottles and nipples should be sterilized, the formula boiled, and the hands and utensils washed in hot soapy water.

The procedure for feeding a newborn pup is not difficult. Begin

203

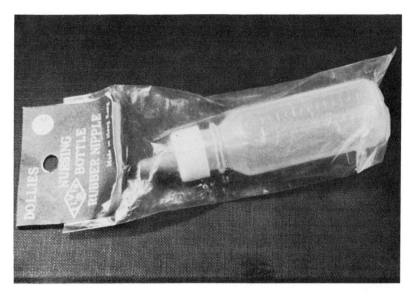

Figure 84. Doll bottles come in all styles. The most satisfactory one for feeding orphaned puppies is the one with a nipple that is a miniature model of those found on real baby bottles.

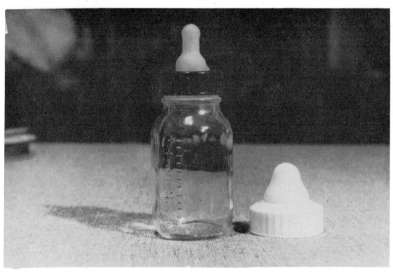

Figure 85. For larger breeds, doll bottles are not large enough, but baby bottles are too large. For these pups the "premie" bottles and nipples made for premature babies should be used.

204

by filling the bottles with water, putting on their nipples and inverting them to see if they leak. By squeezing the bottle slightly the increased internal pressure aids in discovering leaks. Discard any bottles that leak. If the stream of water from the hole in the nipple is less than the diameter of a straight pin, heat a needle and enlarge the hole slightly. Wash all the bottles and nipples to be used in hot, soapy water. If they can be boiled, they should be.

To feed the puppy, pour just enough formula into a bottle that will provide a single feeding and warm it to room temperature. This can be done by holding it under hot tap water, while turning the bottle. Another method is to let it stand in a pan of hot water for a few minutes. Do not use a boiling water bath because it overheats the tiny quantity of milk.

Once the milk is warmed, hold the puppy in a normal upright position and poke the nipple into its mouth. Some pups will get the hang of it immediately. Others are less perceptive. Squeezing a little drop of milk on to the tip of the nipple before putting it into the pup's mouth may encourage some pups to start sucking on the nipple.

Never squeeze milk out of the bottle while the nipple is in the puppy's mouth! This is one of the quickest ways to strangle a tiny puppy with milk.

If the milk drop, a little in-and-out movement of the nipple, or any other means of encouragement fails to get the puppy to suck and swallow voluntarily, put the pup back and try another.

Use a separate bottle for each pup. There are three good reasons for doing this. First, you know precisely how much you are feeding to each pup and can measure precisely how much that pup drinks. Second, if you get a disease outbreak you reduce greatly the chance of spreading it from puppy to puppy with an unclean nipple. And, third, if you need to go back and try to get a pup to drink a little more, you don't need to keep close track of how much it already has eaten. The amount it still needs is what's left in its own bottle.

While the puppy is nursing it should have a bowel movement and should urinate. The importance of these eliminations has already been discussed. If either fails to occur it usually can be provoked by a little stimulation. This stimulation can take the form of gentle rubbing of the anal area or sponging the groin and buttocks with a little warm water. Some feeders place their pups on a warmed, folded, terry-cloth towel while they feed them. The roughness of the

205

towel helps stimulate the elimination. The towel can be washed and dried between feedings, and provides a clean surface to place the pup for each feeding.

Sucking and swallowing reflexes never develop as strongly for the nipple as for the teat. As a consequence, the occurrence of gagging and choking is increased in bottle feeding. The greatest danger lies in the ever-present possibility that a puppy will suck some of the milk down its windpipe and strangle. If enough is sucked down, the pup will drown outright. Even if the amount sucked in is too little to drown the puppy, it will still injure the pup's sensitive lungs. When the lungs are injured, pneumonia is almost always the result. In 12 to 24 hours after strangulation the puppy will refuse food, begin to breathe with difficulty, produce bubbling and gurgling sounds as it breathes and very shortly, die.

Little can be done to save pups that develop strangulation pneumonia. The only thing to do is to prevent its occurrence by every means possible.

When a puppy gags or strangles and milk starts coming out of its mouth and nose, take the bottle away immediately. Place the pup between your palms, head outward, and use your fingers to hold its head and backbone in a straight line. Figure 86 illustrates how the pup should be held. Place the pup between your legs, at arm's

Figure 86. When swinging a strangled puppy it should be held between the hands so that the head faces out and the pup's back is nearest the ground. The index fingers are used to support the pup's head and neck if necessary.

206

Figure 87. a. The pup is held at arm's length, slightly above the head and, b. swung downward between the legs while still being held at arm's length. The rate and force of the swing should be sufficient to sling the milk out of the dog's throat, but not the dog out of the feeder's hands.

207

length, and swing it up and down, Figure 87. The centrifugal force produced by this will sling the milk out of the puppy's mouth and nose and, with luck, out of the windpipe as well.

Tube feeding. An even better means of preventing strangulation is to not feed puppies with a bottle and nipple at all. Instead a feeding tube can be used. With the proper equipment and experience, a pup's entire feeding can be placed into its stomach without getting the milk anywhere near the trachea or the lungs.

Once the dog feeder has mastered the technique of feeding the newborn puppy with a stomach tube it is unlikely that he will ever again feed a puppy with a bottle and nipple. The feeding tube eliminates bottles and nipples that have to be cleaned after each feeding and sterilized before the next. The danger of inhaled milk or vomitus, which readily occurs with bottle feeding, is greatly reduced. The feeding time is shortened by 75 percent.

The equipment needed to feed an orphaned puppy is quite simple, Figure 88. It consists of nothing more than a #8 or #10 French infant feeding tube, a hypodermic syringe, and a substitute for bitch's milk. The tube and syringe shown are disposable and can

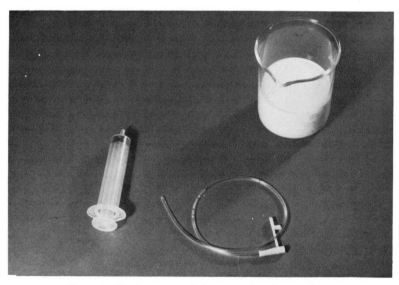

Figure 88. Equipment needed to stomach-tube puppies.

208

be thrown away after use. Reusable equipment, such as glass barrel syringes and rubber feeding tubes, are available but must be thoroughly cleaned after use.

For dog feeders with friends at a hospital for humans it is quite likely that an excellent supply of tubes and syringes are available to them. All OB rooms now pass an infant catheter on every newborn baby to check for clearance. This tube, once used, is immediately discarded. With a little persuasion, most OB nurses can be induced to save these tubes and, after a quick soap and water rinse, they are perfectly suitable to be used for feeding puppies. Another advantage of these feeding tubes is that they can be placed in water and boiled, along with any other equipment, when sterilization is required.

Once the proper equipment has been accumulated, the feeding of a puppy with a stomach tube is performed as follows:

Fill the syringe about half-full of the warmed bitch's milk substitute and lay it aside for future use. Then:

STEP 1, Figure 89. Determine the proper depth to which the tube should be inserted by measuring, with the tube, the distance

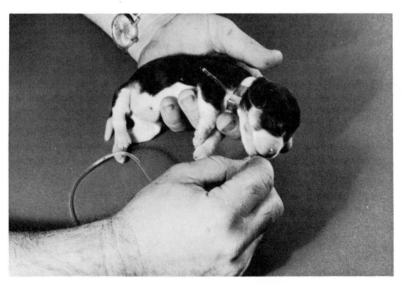

Figure 89. Step 1. Measuring the tube.

209

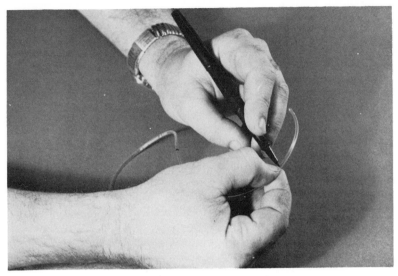

Figure 90. Step 2. Marking the tube.

between the puppy's nose and a point just behind the elbow or just in front of the last rib. This is approximately where the stomach of a puppy lies. Continue to hold the tube by your thumb and forefinger, and . . .

STEP 2, Figure 90. Mark the tube at the correct depth measured in Step 1. This can be done using a marking pen, or with a tiny piece of tape. With this marked tube still held between the thumb and forefinger. . .

STEP 3, Figure 91. Grasp the puppy with the opposite hand, placing the thumb and forefinger on the cheeks, one on each side of the puppy's mouth. Use the remaining three fingers of that hand to grasp the puppy. The middle finger is placed around the puppy's neck, in front of the forelegs. The fourth finger grasps the rib cage just behind the front legs. The little finger is placed in front of the hind legs, either in the groin or around the abdomen, depending on the puppy's length. Once the puppy is held firmly in hand, pry its jaw open with the little finger of the hand holding the tube. Gentle pressure is placed on the sides of the mouth at the same time. By maintaining this light pressure, the mouth can be held agape once it is opened. Into the open mouth . . .

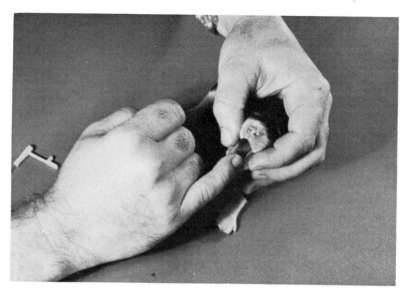

Figure 91. Step 3. Opening the pup's mouth.

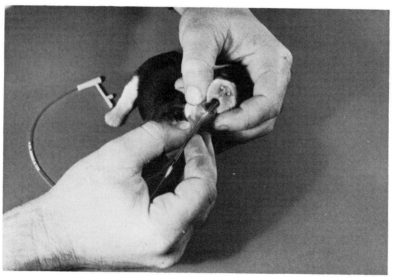

Figure 92. Step 4. Inserting the stomach tube.

211

STEP 4, Figure 92. Insert the end of the tube into the groove formed by the top of the tongue. Cautiously push the tube back into the pharynx. Push the tube straight in, to the depth of the pre-determined mark. If it does not go down smoothly to the depth of the mark, it is not where it should be. If it is accidentally inserted into the trachea, healthy puppies will cough and struggle violently. Should even this reaction fail, a tube that is inserted into the trachea will usually stop about half-way to the mark where it encounters the division of the trachea. Once the tube is successfully inserted to the depth of the mark, slip your thumb and forefinger from the cheeks to the tube, and hold it firmly in the mouth at the level of the mark. Slide your other fingers up and around the puppy's head, leaving the little finger behind the front legs to steady the hold. With the tube thus held firmly in place . . .

STEP 5, Figure 93. Stick the open end of the tube into a small jar of water. If a series of bubbles are produced in the water, it is likely indication that the tube has slipped into the trachea. It may also indicate that the puppy has a little gas on its stomach. In any event, the tube should be removed and blown clear of water, then rein-

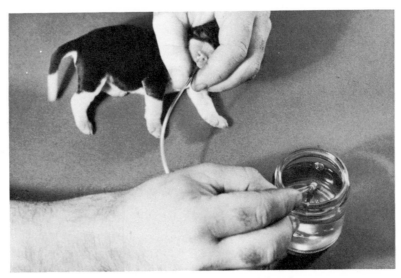

Figure 93. Step 5. Testing the tube's location.

212

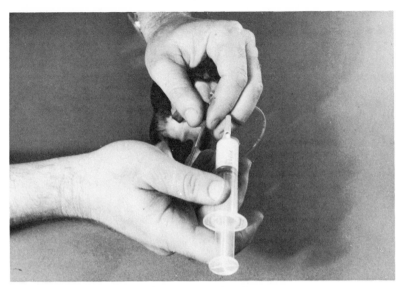

Figure 94. Step 6. Inserting the syringe.

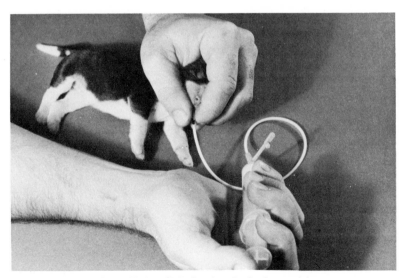

Figure 95. Step 7. Delivering the food material.

213

serted until no air bubbles appear in the water. Once the tube is safely in the stomach . . .

STEP 6, Figure 94. Continue to hold the tube firmly in the puppy's mouth with the thumb and forefinger. With the other hand, place the open end of the tube between the forefinger and middle finger of the hand that holds the tube in the puppy's mouth, as shown in the photo. Once again, with the opposite hand, pick up the previously filled syringe and insert it snugly into the open end of the tube. With the syringe firmly attached . . .

STEP 7, Figure 95. Slowly apply pressure with the thumb to the syringe plunger and deliver the substitute bitch's milk. Continue to deliver the food until the correct amount has been administered. Draw back slightly on the plunger and gently slip the tube out, still attached to the syringe.

The Weanling

Whether a newborn puppy is fed by its own mother or by you, it must eventually be taught to depend upon something besides milk for its food. This learning process is called "weaning", and constitutes the changing of a puppy's diet from liquid to solid.

At about three to four weeks of age, as soon as their eyes open and they are able to move about with some ease, most puppies will begin to experiment with the solid foods being fed their mother. When this happens it is time to begin to teach the puppies to eat from the pan.

Instituting such an early feeding procedure accomplishes four important things. First, it allows you to feed the puppies a food more satisfactory for them than the food you are feeding their mother. Second, it hastens the weaning process because the puppies will learn to eat solid food at an earlier age. Third, it begins the social interaction between puppy and man. Finally, it allows you to reduce the bitch's intake of food at the same rate you increase that of her puppies. The latter prevents the bitch from overeating as the early feeding of her pups promotes reduced lactation.

Weaning is a *true* learning process, in which the pups' digestive system is trained to eat solid foods. Before the puppy is born it is fed by its mother with pre-digested nutrients. When it is whelped the puppy drinks the mother's milk. Bitch's milk contains some of the most digestible nutrients that a dog can eat. At weaning the

214

puppy's digestive system must learn to handle each new food in turn, as it comes to it. Like all learning processes, the weaning process cannot be hurried faster than the puppy's ability to learn.

Formulating the diet: The ingredients that make up the food fed to a weanling puppy must be highly digestible. They should also be relatively non-irritating.

An excellent weaning diet can be made easily by preparing a slurry using the specialized dietary animal foods designed to be fed to patients with gastro-intestinal disorders, mixed into equal parts of the bitch's milk substitutes. "Half and half" coffee cream can also be used. Top-quality ration-type commercial foods also make satisfactory solid foods to mix with the liquid part of the diet. In all cases, 1/4 to 1/2 tablespoonful of grated, raw liver should be added to each can of food just before it is mixed. The slurry can be either beaten with a fork or mixed in a blender. For the larger breeds it may become economically necessary to use the higher quality, expanded dry foods in combination with the canned foods to blend with the liquids. Addition of dry foods may also assist these larger, faster-growing pups to get sufficient nutrients in the quantity of food they are able to consume in a day's time.

Whatever the mixture used, the quantity of milk substitute in it is gradually reduced, so that when the puppy is about six or seven weeks old it is eating only solid food.

The weaning procedure: Most dog feeders allow their pups to eat directly from the mother's bowl as soon as they are able. This enables the pups to learn, by observation, how to eat. Continuing this practice for more than a few days after the pups begin to eat has several objectionable features, however. First, the mother usually is not eating the same diet that her puppies should be eating. Second, on occasion a mother resents her pups eating from her bowl and will snarl and snap at puppies that investigate or experiment with her food. Such conduct is hardly conducive to an atmosphere for teaching little puppies that the food pan is one of the best places they know. Finally, feeding containers for bitches are seldom satisfactory for tiny pups, and *vice versa.*

If the suckling puppy's diet has contained some solid food beginning three to four weeks after it was whelped, it will be weaned by six to seven weeks of age. If the pup has been orphaned and hand-fed, it will have to be trained by hand to eat solid foods. Likewise, if

215

the pup is abruptly snatched from its mother at six or seven weeks of age and has had little or no solid food beforehand, it too will need to be taught to eat solid foods.

Teaching the young puppy to eat can be a hilarious experience. To some dog feeders it may also seem like a time-wasting step in rearing a dog. By individually hand-training each pup, however, you can assure yourself that no pup will fall behind nutritionally simply because it doesn't know how to eat food from a pan.

Infant puppies should get their first lesson in pan-eating on an individual basis, without the distraction of a littermate's shenanigans. Place the pup up to the pan of food and stick his muzzle in. Try not to get his nose in too, if that's possible. I've never strangled a puppy this way, but some of them really splatter and fuss when milk hits them in the face for the first time! Repeat the dunking several times, and if the puppy gets the idea, let him have his own way to explore and experiment with the panful of food.

Some puppies get the hang of pan-feeding almost instantly. One lick of their tongues and they are after the milk mixture as if it was their first meal in a week. Other pups may appear to miss the idea entirely, and would rather bathe in the pan than drink from it. After a few minutes, or before your patience has become exhausted, pick the puppy up, wipe off the surplus milk with a damp cloth, dry the dampened hair and put the pup back with its litter mates. Then try another, until every pup in the litter has had a turn.

Once you have succeeded in training one or two pups to become proficient eaters it may help to put a slow-witted pup up to the bowl with one of the good eaters. Puppies learn by example, and since an empty stomach is one of the greatest motivating forces known to animaldom, the "see and do" method often turns the trick.

The Rapidly Growing Puppy

Once weaned, the puppy does not stop learning how to handle and digest different new foods. Indeed, it is only beginning. During the next 12 to 18 months of its life the puppy will continue to learn how to cope with the new and different foods it eats. For the first six to eight months of that period the puppy will be both growing and using nutrients and energy at a fantastic rate. If a food is fed containing ingredients to which a puppy is unaccustomed or nutrients that are indigestible, the puppy may be unable to obtain sufficient

216

Figure 96. The effects of not receiving enough nutrients during growth is stunting. The puppy on the left is actually three days older than the puppy on the right! Because it has not received adequate nourishment the pup on the left has had its growth rate slowed to keep with the reduced nutrient intake.

nutrients and energy to sustain its rapid growth. In such cases the puppies are usually stunted, Figure 96.

Foods containing too many ingredients which the puppy has not yet learned to digest can cause another problem, too. That problem is called "hurry diarrhea". When a dog feeder gets in too big a hurry to feed adult food to a puppy, excessive amounts of indigestible materials are usually introduced into the puppy's digestive tract. These materials irritate the sensitive intestine of the inexperienced puppy and produce a diarrhea. A more detailed discussion of "hurry diarrhea" is given in the chapter on feeding a sick dog.

Diet formulation: Formulating the correct diet for a puppy is one of the most important steps in starting a dog's life. The only source of nourishment a rapidly growing puppy receives comes exclusively from what its owner puts down for it to eat. The puppy's health and growth will be a reflection of how well the job is done. What the dog feeder puts down before his puppy is what that puppy will use to build the house in which it will live the rest of its life. Many of the parts of that house become permanent and are never replaced. If you provide your dog with poor materials during this

217

building period your dog will be condemned to carry inferior parts for the rest of its life.

The rapidly growing puppy needs twice as much energy and nutrients as an adult dog. Merely feeding the rapidly growing pup twice as much as an adult dog's food is not enough, however. The energy and nutrients must be in a form that is digestible by the puppy's inexperienced digestive tract. As the puppy grows older, the diet can include foods that are more and more difficult for a dog to digest.

Continue to feed the rapidly growing puppy the same food that was used to wean it, but gradually add additional foods to train the puppy's inexperienced digestive system. Just as the food fed to an adult is not suitable for a puppy, the food fed to a puppy is not suitable for an adult. By the time the pup has reached maturity its digestive system should be thoroughly trained to handle all of the foods it will be fed during its adult life.

Canned and soft-moist foods will, as a group, contain ingredients of higher digestibility than dry foods. As a general rule, canned foods are more suitable to feed to rapidly growing puppies than soft-moist foods are. There are exceptions, of course, and a few dry foods containing easily digestible nutrients are much better for feeding rapidly growing puppies than numerous canned foods containing poorly digestible nutrients.

One thing every diet for a growing pup should contain is liver. Chopped, raw or slightly braised, liver adds something to a puppy's diet that cannot be had from any other source. The only problem a dog feeder may encounter when feeding liver to a puppy is diarrhea. Because rapidly growing puppies are highly subject to diarrheas anyway, they should be trained slowly to eat liver and should not be fed amounts so great that their quantity, alone, produces a loose stool. A good rule of thumb is to never add more than 10 percent of the total diet as liver.

If commercial foods are used to feed rapidly growing puppies, such foods should be improved by the addition of a tablespoonful of liver and a tablespoonsful of corn oil per pound of dry matter. This is equivalent to approximately $1/4$th tablespoonful per can of canned food and $2/3$ tablespoonful per 16 ounces of soft-moist.

The amount of good-quality protein may also need to be increased in some commercial foods fed to puppies. This can be done by adding two ounces of any one of the following to each

218

pound of canned food: cottage cheese, hard-boiled egg, processed American cheese, ground chuck, fried or baked fish or chipped roast beef. Four tablespoonsful of dried, skimmed milk also adds a satisfactory amount of extra protein to a dry food being used to feed a rapidly growing puppy.

The feeding procedure: The growing puppy should be weighed weekly for the first six months of its life. The weekly growth rate, from weanling to six months, should be so constant that it forms a straight line when plotted on a graph, Figure 2. The quantity of food eaten by a rapidly growing puppy increases at almost the same rate as the puppy's growth, Figure 97. The only way to make sure this increase in food consumption occurs at the proper rate is to feed a puppy *ad libitum* or from a self-feeder. Whenever a puppy eats everything it is fed, add a little more, so that you are always offering the puppy just a little more than it will eat.

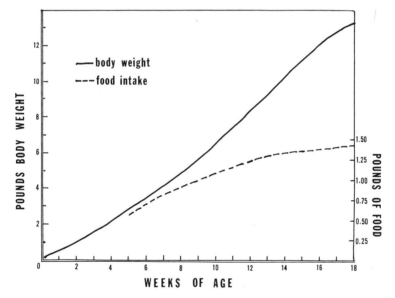

Figure 97. During the first months of a dog's life its food intake increases just like its body weight does. Rapidly growing puppies should always be offered all they will eat to insure that they are getting all that they need.

219

Puppies obtained after weaning already will have been exposed to a feeding program by the previous owner. Make every effort to find out everything you can about that feeding program from the old owner. This should include what the food and feeding times have been, and the amounts fed, so that you can duplicate them for at least a few days until the pup has become accustomed to its new surroundings.

Do not be afraid to change the old routine, however. Such a change is one of those that are considered acceptable in dog feeding. Never be misled into feeding a new puppy what and how its previous owner fed it, just because you feel that owner is an experienced dog feeder. Some of the most false, and potentially harmful, information about dog feeding I ever heard was perpetuated by experienced dog owners. Most, in their innocent ignorance, felt they were doing one of their puppies and its new owner a favor by passing their misinformation along.

If you feel there is a need to change your new puppy's diet or feeding method, do so. Once the puppy is accustomed to its new home and the people that go with it, you can begin. Remember to do it gradually, one step at a time.

To determine the quantity of food to begin with when you start feeding any rapidly growing puppy, proceed as follows:

STEP 1. From Table XVIII determine the number of calories per pound of body weight your puppy should have for his age. For example, a 7-week-old pup weighing five pounds needs 400 calories every day.

STEP 2. Divide the number of calories contained in a pound of the food you are feeding into the number of calories your puppy needs every day to find out how much food you should offer initially. For example, If the 7-week-old pup is being fed a food containing 600 calories per pound, then it needs 400/600 cals per lb. or .66 pounds of food each day.

STEP 3. Divide the amount of food needed each day into the appropriate number of daily feedings, according to the following arbitrary rule:

If the pup is from six weeks to four months of age feed it four times daily, morning, noon, evening and before bedtime.

If the pup is from four months to 12 months, feed it three times daily, morning, noon and evening.

220

When the pup is over 12 months feed it twice daily for the rest of its life, 1/3rd in the morning, 2/3rds in the evening.

Contrary to what you may have heard or read, puppies do not need to be fed six to eight times daily. While such frequent feedings may improve slightly the efficiency with which the puppy uses the food, it is to such a small degree that the extra time spent in preparing and feeding so many meals is not worth the effort. Puppies have been raised successfully with only two or three daily feedings immediately from weaning, but four seems to be the number that provides the best growth for the least effort by the dog feeder.

If a puppy cleans up every bit of food offered for three days in a row, add five percent more food to the daily feeding. If it continues to eat everything it is offered for three more days, add five percent more food again. Continue to add food at this rate until the puppy leaves a tiny bit at each meal. It is entirely possible, in a rapidly growing puppy, that you may never reach a point at which it will leave any food, until it is almost grown. There is no need to be disturbed by this, as long as the puppy gains about the same amount of weight each week as it did the week before.

Between 10 and 12 months of age the rate at which a puppy grows begins to slow down. At the same time the dog's food consumption also begins to drop noticeably. This is a normal occurrence, brought about by the reduction in the dog's need for extra nutrients and energy required for growth. The reduction is merely an indication that the puppy is reaching maturity.

Novice dog feeders may mistake this reduction in food consumption as an indication of illness. This fear becomes even more pronounced when the maturing process makes the dog less active, as well. Inexperienced dog feeders usually forget that human adolescents go through the same steps on their way to becoming human adults. Other dog feeders may forget the fact that the maturing process in the dog requires only about 12 months to complete, while in humans it usually takes 20 years! This telescopes, somewhat, the signs of maturing.

The alert, experienced dog feeder knows that when maturity brings about this reduction in food intake and activity, it is time to stop feeding a puppy a growth diet, and to start feeding it a maintenance ration.

221

TABLE XVIII
Daily Caloric Needs Of Puppies

Weeks	1	2	3	4	5	10	15	20	25	30	40	50	60	70
5	100	200	300	400	500	1000	1500							
6	90	180	270	360	450	900	1350							
7	80	160	240	320	400	800	1200							
8	75	150	225	300	375	750	1125	1500						
9	70	140	210	280	350	700	1050	1400						
10		130	195	260	325	650	975	1300	1625					
11			180	240	300	600	900	1200	1500					
12				224	280	560	840	1128	1400	1680				
13				208	260	520	780	1040	1300	1560				
14					240	480	720	960	1200	1440	1920			
15						450	675	900	1125	1350	1800			
16						420	630	840	1050	1260	1680	2100		
17							585	780	975	1170	1560	1950		
18								720	900	1080	1440	1800	2160	
19									825	990	1320	1650	1980	
										900	1280	1500	1800	2100

To determine the number of calories needed by a particular puppy, find the dog's weight in the top row of numbers and move downard until you come to the line corresponding to the dog's age. The figure in the spot where the two lines intersect is the number of calories that puppy needs during a 24-hour period.

222

Chapter 14

The Reproducing Bitch

MOST nutritionists agree that reproduction is the most critical stress encountered by a bitch. While the healthy male dog can sire hundreds of puppies without any stress whatever, the bitch is called upon to use tremendous amounts of energy and nutrients during pregnancy and lactation. If her feeding program does not adequately supply these nutrients and energy she will obtain them by using up her own body tissues. If neither dietary nor body sources of nutrients and energy are available, a multitude of problems will result.

The manifestation of an inadequate diet during early phases of reproduction may take on several forms. Those most likely to be recognized are:

1. An "out of condition" appearance of the bitch. This may not become apparent until after the pups are born. An actual loss in body weight throughout gestation can occur, but is unusual in most instances.

2. An uncontrollable diarrhea in the bitch following whelping and throughout much of lactation. This is most often seen when the bitch must increase her food intake excessively to meet increased lactational demands because the food she has been eating is poorly digestible or low in calories.

3. The "fading puppy" syndrome. The puppy may appear normal at birth, but several hours to several days later it is found crying or whimpering and chilled. It is off by itself, obviously disowned by the

bitch. Attempts to reunite the two are usually met with failure. The puppy's stomach will be empty and its body will be dehydrated. When weighed, it will weigh the same or less than the day before. A more detailed discussion of the causes and corrections of the fading puppy will be found in the chapter on feeding sick dogs.

4. Anemias. When an anemia occurs as the result of a dietary deficiency during reproduction, it will be present in both the dam and pup. When both mother and pup are anemic, the first place to look for its cause is the diet.

Once pregnancy is terminated by the whelping of the pups, an inadequate diet during lactation is most likely to appear as:

1. Lactation failure (agalactia). This is a complete failure of the mammary glands. The bitch produces no milk at all from which the pups can be nourished. These pups cry continuously, fail to gain weight, and unless immediate remedial feeding is started, the pups will die.

2. Lactation depression (dysgalactia). While the mammary glands are functional, they are unable to produce adequate amounts of milk to fully support the pups' complete nutrient needs. The pups are restricted in growth rate and may become stunted, Figure 96.

3. Deficient milk. The milk, although it may be produced in adequate amounts, is deficient in one or more nutrients.

When gestation or lactation failures occur, they can usually be traced back to one or both of the following dietary deficiences:

1. *Feeding an imbalanced diet.* Marginal deficiencies in a diet, which may be masked under maintenance situations, may become painfully obvious during demands of gestation, whelping and, in particular, during lactation.

2. *Feeding insufficient nutrients and energy to the bitch.* One of the most frequent causes of lactation failure is the refusal of a dog feeder to provide adequate quantities of food for the bitch. Another common cause is feeding a diet intended for maintenance use. This becomes especially disastrous if the maintenance diet is marginal to start with. Even with adequate maintenance diets, gestation produces depletion, lactation produces deficiency. Reproductive failures may also be caused by foods containing nutrients of poor digestibility, even when they are fed in increased amounts. In both of these cases the bitch often is incapable of consuming enough food to obtain all of the nutrients and energy she needs.

Formulating the Diet: The ideal reproduction diet is one that can be fed both during pregnancy and lactation. This poses certain problems, however. An adequate diet for a healthy bitch during pregnancy does not need to exceed that of a high-quality maintenance diet. Such a diet used during lactation, however, may fail completely. This failure is due to the fact that even high-quality maintenance diets are not concentrated enough. The lactating bitch will require three times more nutrients and energy at the peak of lactation than she required during maintenance. But, many lactating females cannot, physically, consume three times as much food. Even when they can, eating such large quantities reduces the digestibility of what they do eat to such an extent that they are still unable to obtain all the nutrients and energy they need.

A satisfactory diet for lactating bitches should contain about one and one-half to two times as much energy and nutrients as a good-quality maintenance diet. This means that a diet suitable for raising rapidly growing puppies is also suitable for feeding lactating bitches. It also means that lactating bitches that are properly fed will need to eat only about one-half as much as they would if being fed a maintenance diet.

If ordinary commercial dog foods are used for a reproduction program, certain modifications will probably be necessary. During pregnancy the commercial food may be entirely satisfactory if it is balanced and contains sufficient calories to maintain the bitch's weight. During lactation the addition of three tablespoonsful of corn oil to each pound of dry food, or one tablespoonful to each pound of canned food, will improve the caloric density of the food. A similar quantity of chopped, raw liver should also be added when the food is being fed to a lactating bitch.

The Feeding Procedure: Correctly feeding a pregnant bitch begins long before she is bred. It begins when she is a puppy herself. Potential brood bitches should be given special dietary attention from the moment they are whelped. While she is a rapidly growing puppy, the potential breeder should be fed a diet containing high levels of usable protein and energy. The amount she is fed should be sufficient to bring her to her optimum size and weight, but never in an attempt to push her to her maximum weight potential. Once she has reached sexual maturity she should be kept in an optimal nutritional state by feeding her a diet that is known to support maintenance.

Not all bitches enjoy the feeding program just described. Every

225

new bitch should be made ready by reviewing her diet for any nutritional deficiencies, and by correcting any that are present. Bitches that are too fat may not ovulate, or if they do, will produce very few ova. Generally pups whelped by fat bitches are few in number, but large in size—so large in fact that they may lead to a difficulty at birth. Overweight bitches should have their food restricted in order to reduce their weight to optimum before they come into heat. Underweight bitches should be fed a diet suitable for a lactating bitch. If either over- or underweight bitches have not reached their optimum weight and condition by the time their breeding date arrives, they should not be bred until their next heat.

Once bred, the bitch should be fed the lactation diet during gestation as well as lactation. During the last three weeks of pregnancy the bitch's food intake should be increased by about 25 percent of her usual consumption. Figure 7 illustrates this increase graphically.

No supplements should be added at any time during gestation. For some dog feeders, supplementation has become such a way of life that they place more emphasis on the supplement they use than on the food they feed. As with any other phase of a dog's life cycle, the ill-advised use of food supplements during pregnancy can cause great harm.

Many bitches will consume little or no food for the first 24 hours after whelping. If a bitch remains inappetant longer than 48 hours after whelping, consult your veterinarian. Between the two of you, you should be able to determine the cause of the lack of appetite. Persistent anorexia following whelping usually signals serious complications of pregnancy or parturition—complications that can lead to grave consequences unless attended to early.

Under healthy circumstances, the bitch's appetite will increase sharply following whelping. This increase will continue until the puppies are weaned, or unless supplemental feeding is begun. By the fourth week of lactation the bitch's intake will have doubled over the amount eaten during gestation, Figure 7. By this time it usually becomes necessary to increase the number of daily feedings to reduce the quantity of food the bitch must eat at any one meal. Smaller meals at more frequent intervals help to avoid the discomfort and loss of nutrient digestibility caused by larger meals. By the sixth week of lactation it is not unusual for the bitch to be eating three times what she was eating during gestation.

As soon as the puppies begin to show an interest in the bitch's

226

food, she should be separated from them when she is fed. This allows her to eat in comfort, without the help of a half-dozen puppies tramping and tumbling through her food. It may also save a puppy from injury if the bitch happens to resent her puppies sharing her food with her.

In all fairness to the bitch, and in the interest of her good mental health, a bitch should never be scolded for snapping at her puppies when they attempt to eat her food. It is not unusual for wild canines to make their pups wait until last to eat. Your bitch may be acting out of instinct. Instead of scolding her for what appears to you to be the behavior of a poor mother, you may actually be punishing her for a behavior that reflects what a good mother she really is. Remember, she's not raising baby humans, but baby dogs, and *one of the biggest mistakes a dog feeder can make is to forget that fact.*

When you separate the mother dog and her pan of food from the puppies, replace her pan with one containing a specially prepared food for the puppies. Measure the amount you feed the puppies each time, and how much food they eat. Subtract the amount of solid food the puppies eat (do not include the milk portion) from the amount you feed the bitch at her next feeding. In this manner you can reduce the bitch's intake at the same time you are increasing the puppies', and at about the same rate.

On the day of weaning return the bitch to her maintenance diet and feed her only one-half of her normal maintenance quantity. Be sure she has plenty of water during the weaning procedure. On the second day after the pups have been permanently removed, feed her three-fourths of her usual maintenance quantity. Beginning with the third day she can be fed a full maintenance portion from then on. By reducing the quantity of food for a few days, the bitch will dry up more quickly and with less problems.

The ideal goal for a reproducing bitch is to have her weigh within 10 percent of her pre-pregnancy weight after her puppies have been weaned and she has completely stopped lactating. This occurs only rarely, unfortunately. Even when recommended feeding practices are followed during pregnancy and lactation, many bitches will deplete some of the reserves in their bodies. Nursing bitches are invariably depleted of calcium, and usually other nutrients as well. For this reason, bitches should be observed closely after weaning for several months. Only by taking such precautions can you

227

make certain their weight is re-established at optimum and they return to the point of optimum nutrition and condition they enjoyed before being bred.

Bitches that are to be self-fed during pregnancy and lactation, and that are not already on self-feeding programs, should be placed on such a program well in advance of breeding. Doing so will not only accustom the bitch to self-feeding, but will allow you to make sure she is not a glutton. Bitches on self-feeding programs adjust their own food intakes satisfactorily as long as the dog feeder makes certain food is in the feeder at all times.

The amount of water she drinks will be in direct proportion to the amount of food she eats. Consequently, a careful and frequent check to be sure the pregnant or lactating bitch on a self-feeding program has plenty of clean, fresh water is essential to the success of that program.

Chapter 15

The Housepet

ONCE upon a time the poorest fed dog in America was the farm dog left to fend for itself for food. These dogs, undernourished bags of bones, were once so common they almost became symbolic of impoverished rural America, Figure 98. Today vast numbers of those small farms have vanished. With them have gone the gaunt, hollow-eyed hounds that greeted every farm visitor with a hungry, ill-tempered bark.

The farmer has moved to the city, gotten a job, and become the suburbanite. With him have come his companion dogs. And, the suburbanite housepet has replaced the farm dog as the poorest fed dog in America. Probably 75 percent of all dogs in the United States owned by private individuals are household pets. Most of these dogs are anywhere from 10 percent to 50 percent overweight because the most frequent error made by feeders of housepets is overfeeding. Unlike their predecessors, today's poorest fed dogs are not underfed, but overfed, Figure 99. The irony of it all is the fact that, while they may be overfed and overweight, they may also be undernourished!

Unfortunately, there is a widespread misconception among dog feeders that any dog food that comes out of a can or box they bought at the grocery store is adequate and nourishing for a dog. This belief has led politicians, sociologists, and even some nutritionists to express the opinion that most American housepets are better fed than most Americans. While these statements may grab sensational headlines, the accuracy of such a proposition does not stand

229

Figure 98. Once so common as to be symbolic of rural America, the malnourished farm dog has all but disappeared, even from the rural scene.

Figure 99. To replace the malnourished dog, as the most common example of improper feeding, the dog feeder has invented the fat dog. Encouraged by his own impulsiveness to overfeed his dog, and supported by some equally guilty pet food manufacturers. America's modern dog feeder robbed the dog of his built-in protection against obesity.

up under critical examination. While it certainly is true that *some* housepets receive far better nourishment than some people, it is also true that many dogs in this country are woefully malnourished. Some of the dogs suffering from the greatest malnourishment are those eating the very item to which the politicians and sociologists attribute such grandiose performance—commercial dog food.

Not all, probably not even most, of the canned dog foods in this country are guilty of malnourishing a dog, but some do exist, and they are being fed. Nowhere does a dog feeder need to evaluate the food he feeds more than he does when he is feeding canned foods to a housepet. Yet, the number of pet owners who actually feed their dogs based on their evaluation of the foods available to them is practically nil. Unfortunately most feeders of house dogs consider it an inconvenience to evaluate a dog food. They usually feed only one or two dogs, never weigh them, and rarely keep any records on them at all. Many base their selection of a dog food solely on how well their dog eats it, not on what the food does for their dog nutritionally. Moreover, the shopper for the house dog's food is the same individual who shops for the rest of the family's food, the housewife. From the early morning news to the final night-time talk show, the housewife is bombarded with TV commercials, and newspaper and magazine ads, extolling the virtues of one brand of dog food over another.

Food chosen for the house dog should always be made by the evaluation procedure outlined in Chapters 7 and 8, never on the claims of some TV commercial. Stop and consider for a moment that TV commercials and magazine ads are designed to sell *you* the food. So is the food's packaging and other promotions. After all, your dog can't read and doesn't understand a word the ad man pitches. Just remember your dog *does* have to eat the food you buy and feed it. Simply because *you* like your food with gravy is no reason to believe that your dog does. Just because some people *say* all your dog needs is meat won't stop your dog from dying from the calcium deficiency produced when it is fed an all-meat diet. *You* may prefer that hickory-smoked flavor, but your dog prefers the essence of rotten rabbit.

And, if a food maker tosses in a little essence of rotten rabbit to make sure your dog gobbles up his food without pausing for a breath, remember that how fast your dog eats a food has little to do with the nutritional value of that food. The mere fact that your dog eats a food every time it is fed is no indication whatever that the

231

food is good for your dog. Most dogs love the all-animal-tissue foods, but an exclusive diet of nothing but meat will prove fatal.

Diet formulation: While dogs kept as pets may fall into any number of categories, only three are important where feeding is concerned. These three categories are related to where the dog lives— exclusively outdoors, outdoors-indoors or exclusively indoors. There are, naturally, some areas of overlap, but these three categories are generally easy enough to separate. Most dog owners can place their dogs into the correct category without too much difficulty.

The pet dog has the same nutritional needs as any other dog. The only difference is the reduced number of calories it uses because of the type of life a dog leads as a household pet.

The house dog living exclusively indoors is probably one of the least active animals in the world. More inactive, even, than its owner. Most of a house dog's time is spent sleeping. Its greatest effort, in many instances, consists of a 50-foot jaunt from the back door three times a day for eliminations, and a 10-foot walk from the family room couch to its food bowl in the kitchen. As a consequence the house dog is the most overfed and suffers from the greatest overweight problems of all the housepets.

The dog that spends most of its daylight activities outdoors, but comes in at night, has a higher energy need than the pet kept indoors constantly. Not only does it get more exercise, but it requires extra energy to maintain its body temperature during cooler weather outdoors. Even with such additional requirements it is not uncommon to find indoor-outdoor pets that are fed too much and are borderline overweights.

The dog that stays outdoors all of the time is the pet least likely to develop obesity. As an outdoor dog it enjoys the same, or more exercise as the indoors-outdoors dog. In addition, outdoor dogs have a considerably increased need for energy to maintain body heat. This need for extra energy for body heat becomes especially high at night and in colder weather. In fact, there are occasional instances where outdoor dogs, when improperly fed, begin to appear just like the undernourished farm hounds of a past era of dog feeding.

The quantity of food a house dog needs is determined by the same things that determine the amount of food any other dog eats —its optimum body weight and the caloric density of the food it eats. The amount is calculated in the same manner as for other dogs. A different calorie chart is needed for the three categories of house dogs. Table XIX lists the number of calories needed by dogs of different weights when they are sedentary housepets, house and yard pets, or backyard-only pets. The method for calculating the quantity of food from these charts is identical to that already described. Determine the number of calories a dog needs daily to maintain its optimum weight. Divide that number by the number of calories in a pound of food you are feeding. The results will be the quantity of food you should feed, measured in pounds.

TABLE XIX

A Calorie Chart for Dogs Kept As Household Pets

if dog weighs this many lbs . . .	it needs this many calories each day:			if dog weighs this many lbs . . .	it needs this many calories each day:		
	indoors	*both*	*outdoors*		*indoors*	*both*	*outdoors*
2.2	130	141	*	18.0	558	648	828
4.4	211	233	*	20.0	600	700	900
5.0	225	250	*	22.0	638	748	968
5.5	242	269	*	25.0	700	825	1075
6.0	258	288	*	28.5	770	912	1197
6.5	273	305	*	32.0	832	992	1312
7.0	287	322	*	36.0	900	1080	1440
7.5	300	337	*	40.0	1000	1160	1560
8.0	312	352	432	44.0	1100	1232	1672
9.0	342	387	477	50.0	1250	1350	1850
10.0	370	420	520	57.0	**	1482	2052
11.0	396	451	561	66.0	**	1650	2310
12.0	420	480	600	88.0	**	2112	2992
13.5	459	526	661	118.0	**	2832	3894
15.0	495	570	720	150.0	**	3600	4800
16.5	528	610	775				

* Dogs under 8 pounds should not be kept outdoors.
** Dogs over 50 pounds should not be kept indoors only.

Feeding procedure: If household pets are fed a canned food, it should always be fed on a portion controlled basis. There are several reasons for this, but one stands out over all the rest. Canned foods are among the most palatable foods offered to a dog. The palatability of canned foods does not exist by accident. If there is one thing every dog food canner wants his food to be, it's palatable, palatable, palatable! Only with a food that is eagerly eaten by a dog can the food maker depend on the re-purchase of his product. In the dog food business, re-purchase is the name of the game. Palatability is so

233

important in commercial foods that the test for palatability is the first test to be run on a new food by makers with plenty of research funds, the only test to be run by makers with limited research funds, and the test most wanted by those makers with no research program.

The obsession by dog food makers for having every dog devour their food as if it were the dog's last meal defeats completely the built-in mechanism each dog has for preventing obesity. That mechanism is the instinct for eating only enough food to meet its caloric needs. Housepets offered these highly palatable canned foods quickly learn to eat to satisfy their palates. And, like their owners with the same problem, they become more and more gluttonous as long as more and more food is made available to them.

If this reason were not enough to feed the house dog by portion control, there are also the problems of boredom, habit, and indulgent masters to encourage gluttonous activities by a house dog.

Another serious mistake made by many house dog feeders is the insidious practice of "treating" or "tidbitting." The feeding of tidbits can be a major contribution to the excessive weight of a housepet. Most tidbits are even more highly palatable than canned food. This feature is often attributable to their high fat content. A few highly palatable tidbits, on top of a normal quantity of food, quickly leads to an excessive intake of energy that is stored by the dog's body as fat.

An excellent example of a treat is ice cream, the most common treat fed to the house dog. Five rounded tablespoonsful of plain ice cream will add over 150 calories to a dog's diet. Five tablespoonsful of ice cream can be put away by a 20-pound Dachshund with ease, even after a full meal. If it is allowed to do so, that Dachshund will be increasing its daily caloric intake by 20 percent!

Of course, part of the pleasure of owning a dog is being able to indulge yourself by spoiling it a little. A tidbit now and then does no harm. But, killing your dog with kindness is ridiculous. It also is preventable.

Most tidbits and treats are fed to a housepet at the same time its owner is eating them. Every time the owner eats a spoonful of ice cream or a potato chip he gives his dog one. What that dog feeder fails to realize is that he may weigh five times what his dog weighs and therefore can tolerate five times more calories. By feeding his dog a tidbit every time he eats one himself the dog feeder is actually

234

feeding his dog five times more calories, by proportion, than he is feeding himself.

By putting this knowledge to work it is possible to develop a little habit for tidbitting that will prevent you from overdoing it. Make it a rule never to feed your dog a tidbit until you have eaten five of them yourself. Then every time your dog eats five tablespoonsful of ice cream (150 calories), you will have to have eaten 25 tablespoonful (750 calories)! If you follow the rule to eat five times as much of every treat as you feed your dog, then you can feed your dog all the treats you wish. When you become alarmed about your own weight, you will realize how much you have really been feeding your poor pet all these years. As soon as you become so fat you can't waddle to the icebox for more ice cream, your dog's diet will also be curtailed . . . by the same amount of ice cream that *you* stop eating.

The housepet that is kept outdoors all of the time, or that is fed an exclusive diet of dry food, does not need to be restricted to portion control feeding. These dogs will do quite well, as a rule, even when self-fed. One precaution should be pointed out about outdoor pets that are put on self-feeding programs. If they have not been eating dry food, their water consumption will jump perceptibly when they begin to eat it. A special effort should be made to keep plenty of cool, fresh, potable water before these dogs at all times. Outdoor dogs require even more water during the summer because a dog's body-cooling processes depend on water.

When outdoor pets are individually fed they can be fed by either *ad libitum* or portion control. The feeding location should be under some kind of shelter. This will keep the direct sunlight, dust and dirt to a minimum.

Outdoor feeding locations should also be well away from garbage cans. A back porch, back steps or corner of the garage may be convenient, but if there are garbage cans nearby such places are unsuitable as dog feeding locations. First, such places allow flies of all descriptions to contaminate the food. Flies are not particularly objectionable, esthetically, to a dog. Most outdoor dogs go through life snapping up and swallowing a fly now and then. Ordinarily this is no cause for alarm, but around garbage cans flies become so numerous in a dog's food that they constitute a disease danger. A second danger associated with feeding near garbage cans is the fact that a dog may, once it starts eating, not want to stop. A nearby garbage can makes a convenient source of all the wrong things for a dog to eat.

With dogs fed outdoors, it is of particular importance to pick up any food remaining uneaten after 20 or 30 minutes. Food served at room temperature, then allowed to stand outdoors, quickly warms to temperatures at which contaminating bacteria rapidly multiply. Most dogs do not find the odor of over-ripe dog food unpleasant. Many, in fact, consider the smell quite desirable. The toxins and other waste products produced by bacteria, at the same time they are creating that smell, may have a distinctly detrimental effect on the dog, however.

There is another, and perhaps more important, reason for feeding an outdoor housepet at the same time and place every day and allowing the food to remain before the dog only 20 or 30 minutes. It is to train your dog to eat only at that time and at that place. If the dog does not, it learns quickly that it must wait until the next feeding before it gets anything more to eat. Your dog will soon become accustomed to eating at only a specified time, and will come to the specified place every day about that time anticipating its food.

Once trained into this pattern, a dog is far less likely to get food from garbage cans or other undesirable sources. If he should decide to take a few hours away from home one day he will be less likely to eat another dog's meal, or something left around for another animal. It also reduces the likelihood that he will eat any poisonous substances fed to him intentionally, or unintentionally, by person or persons unknown.

Whether fed by portion control, *ad libitum* or self-feeder, all dogs housed outdoors year-round must have seasonal adjustments made in their food. The colder the weather, the more calories are needed to produce heat to keep the dog warm. Dogs living in the northern-most states may double their food intake during the coldest months. This increased intake is not as dramatic in the south, but is every bit as important.

236

Table XX lists the percentage by which the quantity of a dog's food should be increased each month to compensate for seasonal demands.

TABLE XX

The percent increase which should be made each month to the quantity of food fed to a dog living outdoors the year-round. The southern tier lies between the 25th and 35th parallels, the middle between the 35th and 45th parallels and the northern tier is every state above the 45th parallel.

month	northern tier % increase	middle tier % increase	southern tier % increase
August	0	0	0
September	0	0	0
October	10	5	0
November	40	15	10
December	70	30	15
January	100	60	30
February	100	60	30
March	70	30	15
April	40	15	10
May	10	5	0
June	0	0	0
July	0	0	0

Chapter 16

Show Dogs

SHOW dogs may be purchased for their pedigree, but they win points for their conformation, condition and haircoat. The most important factor in the development of all three of these is not a dog's genetic background, but its feeding program.

A dog's conformation *is* influenced by its heredity. A dog *will* follow the template nature has cut out for it, *as long as adequate nutrients and energy are available for it to do so.* Not even double dominance can overpower the results of a dietary deficiency! No matter how straight a dog's leg might have been, once a twist or bend occurs because of poor mineralization or excessive vitamin D supplementation, there is *absolutely nothing* that can be done to correct it. Not by the dog, not by the dog feeder, not by the veterinarian, and not by all of those genes from the dozen champions in its pedigree.

The conditioning of show dogs has often had an aura of magic about it. Most of those who claim to have just the right combination for properly conditioning a show dog for the ring jealously guard the secret. As often as not, these close-kept formulas of success fail as many times as they succeed, but the failures are an even more closely guarded secret!

All the while, professional handlers, who consistently win, have no such secrets. (Although many fanciers attribute to them powers bordering on sorcery.) All the professional handlers have is experience, a practical outlook and lots of common sense. They have fed and shown enough dogs to know that one thing consistently and repeatedly keeps their dogs healthy and in the peak of condition. That something is an adequate, well-balanced diet—a diet unspoiled by the addition of all those miracle hair conditioners; coat replenishers; and high-protein, fatty acid, vitamin or mineral supplements.

The technique of merely feeding a dog an adequate and balanced diet *sounds* so simple and uncomplicated that most novices and many experienced exhibitors cannot believe there is no more to it . . . until they try to do it. They quickly learn that the job does not consist of a crash feeding program of the right diet a few weeks before a show, but is a lifelong process. Nowhere in all of the world of dogs is proper nutrition more important than in the dog destined to compete with other dogs in a contest of "general appearance, carriage, expression and condition". The excellence of each one of these characteristics relies as much upon what a dog was fed when it was a 10-week-old pup as it does on what is fed 10 days before competition. In fact, what was fed when it was a 10-week-old puppy is probably more important!

The procedures for properly feeding the bitch during gestation and lactation, and the growing pup from weaning to adulthood, have been covered in earlier chapters. The dog feeder who successfully masters these phases of dog feeding will be rewarded with the finest conformation and carriage his dog is genetically capable of giving. The remainder of this chapter is devoted to how you can bring the condition and expression of your show dog to their peak and maintain them while the judge compares your dog's attributes with those of the other entrants.

The bloom in a dog's show coat begins, as a bud, the day that dog is conceived. Unless you begin conditioning your show dog from the time it's nothing more than a four-cell blob, you will never be able to obtain the show coat your dog could have produced. By starting your conditioning program with the pregnant bitch the bud matures, through growth, until, as a young adult, it blossoms into the beautiful, lustrous covering so indicative of health and vitality. Without nutritional health and vitality, no haircoat will ever reach its full bloom, however many pounds of hair conditioner or hundreds of dollars are spent in attempts to make it do so.

Each time the developing haircoat is short-changed nutritionally, it dulls the bloom a little. Unless you nourish and care for a dog's haircoat when it is a developing bud, you will never compete with

239

those who care for the bud from the moment it is formed to the hour of its bloom. A dog feeder who waits until only a few weeks before a show to start thinking about good condition or beautiful showcoats may discover that all he has left is a dull, lifeless bud where a beautiful blossom could have been. Politicians and press agents may be able to make silk purses from sow's ears, but dog feeders will never make Bests in Show winners out of malnourished mutts!

Diet Formulation: The diet for show dogs between shows does not need to differ from that of any other dog being kept under similar conditions. It should contain adequate energy to maintain the dog's weight, and be balanced.

There are a few nutrients in a show dog's diet that should receive particular attention. By attention I do not mean they should be added to the diet in increased amounts! I mean only that the diet should be checked periodically to make certain that there are adequate amounts of these particular nutrients always present in the diet. These nutrients are:

linolenic and linoleic acid
essential amino acids
fat
B-complex vitamins, in particular thiamine,
   riboflavin and pyridoxine
Vitamin A and Vitamin D.

Once again I must warn that those who misconstrue my inclusion of a discussion of these nutrients as a justification to begin adding large quantities to their diet are flirting with disaster! These nutrients are not just needed. They are needed in exact amounts and in precise ratios and the indiscriminate use of the many supplements containing them leads to more harm than help. Whenever any of the nutrients mentioned are found to be marginal in a diet, that diet should be discarded and a completely new diet substituted for it. Attempts to add or balance particular nutrients by any means other than critical chemical analysis and precise measurement of ingredients will only lead to deficiencies and imbalances greater than those already present.

Determining how much to feed a show dog during the off season can be calculated from the "both" section of the calorie chart on housepets in Chapter 15. As with all such calculations, the quantity

240

is only a starting point and should be adjusted using changes in the dog's weight as a guide.

With some show dogs, the maintenance of peak condition and weight is no more difficult than opening a bag or cutting the top out of a can. Many show dogs tend to be difficult keepers, however, and ordinary maintenance foods are not always satisfactory for them. In those instances where only a slight increase in caloric density is needed to maintain the weight of these hard keepers it can be accomplished by adding corn oil to the diet. The amount added will depend on how many extra calories are needed to maintain the dog at its optimum body weight. The addition of corn oil should never increase the number of calories in a diet by more than 10 percent. If a diet needs more calories than that, it should be replaced with a more concentrated diet.

If you still feel you *must* add something to your show dog's diet besides a balanced food, chop a hard-boiled egg (shell and all) into your dog's food at the rate of one egg to every can of food or two to three in every pound of dry food. That single hard-boiled egg will contain, in one package, most of the fatty acids, protein and vitamins and minerals contained in many of the supplements peddled to produce a lustrous haircoat or top condition. Furthermore, that egg will cost only one-half as much as most supplements, and 10 times less than a few.

The diet used for a show dog on the road should be as uncomplicated as possible. A single-food diet is best. With a single-food diet, all you need to do to add a little weight is to feed a little more food. Convenience is also a factor with a single-food diet, and the longer the circuit, the more important a convenient food becomes.

If you choose a canned food as your campaign diet make certain that the food you have chosen will be available everywhere along the circuit. Only a few of the many brands of canned food sold in this country are sold on a national basis. Most are local and regional. A change in food along the route could precipitate a reduction in food intake. A food reduction almost always produces a loss of condition. The same problem can occur with dry foods, but considerably more dry food can be taken on the road than canned food. The soft-moist foods incorporate both the convenience and the keeping qualities of the canned foods, along with the storage qualities and shipping weight of the dry foods. Soft-moist foods usually

241

do not sacrifice any great amount of nutritional quality because many of the ingredients that are used in canned foods are incorporated in the soft-moist foods as well. Soft-moist foods are the most expensive of the three, but for those willing to spend the money they probably offer as satisfactory a single-food campaign diet as any marketed.

Feeding Procedures: During the off season, show dogs can be fed by either portion control, *ad libitum* or self-feeding, whichever is most convenient. The main objective during this period is to maintain not only the show dog's body weight, but also its condition. The latter consideration is necessary in show dogs because haircoat, gums, teeth, eyes and muscle tone are vitally important in ring competition.

For many show dogs it is no problem maintaining their weight and condition when they are not on show circuit. For others, they seem to continuously remain about five percent to 10 percent below their optimum weight and top condition all during the off season. As long as off season weight loss does not exceed 10 percent of a dog's optimum weight, this situation can usually be handled by the addition of one or two teaspoonsful of corn oil to each day's diet. Once the weight loss has been regained and the dog's condition improved a re-evaluation of the dog's optimum weight should be made. If the corn oil is going to be continued, the quantity of food being fed should also be re-calculated using a corrected figure for the caloric density of the food after the corn oil is added. This corrected figure will be the old caloric density to which has been added 36 calories for every teaspoonful of corn oil. Unless this calculation is made, the dog may begin to gain weight.

Occasionally dogs may consistently remain 10 percent or more below their optimum body weight, yet still refuse to eat all they are fed every day. In these cases the first thing to do is to re-evaluate the dog's optimum weight. It may be set too high. If the optimum weight has been established correctly, then the dog should be taken to a veterinarian to make sure the underweight condition is not due to some organic disease. Once disease has been ruled out then a more concentrated diet, or one having a higher acceptability should be fed. Either will raise the dog's energy intake and increase its body weight. Increasing the quality of the food from one capable of supporting maintenance to one capable of supporting growing puppies or lactating bitches is often all that is needed to restore the weight on the underweight show dog.

242

To add any more corn oil than the quantities already suggested will be unsatisfactory. When corn oil is added in quantities that supply more than five percent of the calories in the total diet, the increased caloric density reduces the quantity of food eaten. When this happens, the dog's intake of all nutrients is reduced in proportion to the reduction of food intake. Such a reduction creates the potential for a marginal or actual deficiency to occur.

Several weeks prior to the beginning of the show circuit all dogs that are to be shown should be started on a pre-show diet program. The food used for this program should be identical to that which will be carried and fed while on the road. Doing this not only accustoms the dog to eating the food (if it is different from the dog's current food) but also allows you to adjust the quantity to be fed to maintain optimum weight while on the road.

It is a good idea to weigh the dog daily during the last couple of weeks before the season begins. This will provide you with an accurate weight baseline and reveal any corrections that need to be made before show time. Major corrections should never be attempted close to a show. Minor adjustments are not dangerous and are probably desirable.

Everyone who has taken a peak-conditioned dog on a show campaign knows that only half the battle is delivering a prime animal to the first show ring. The other half is keeping the dog at peak while it is traveling from ring to ring.

Once on the circuit a dog is expending energy at about the same rate that a house dog living outdoors expends. In fact, that part of the calorie chart for housepets that relates to outdoor dogs, Table XIX, can be used with excellent results when calculating an approximate quantity of food to feed a show dog on circuit. Some dogs may require much greater amounts than those calculated from the table, a few may require less. Each dog you have on campaign should have its diet tailored to meet its own individual needs. Every dog not fed adequate amounts of food to meet such needs will draw from the stores within its body. The stores that are maintaining the dog's condition will be the first to go.

A show dog's energy need will be increased by stresses due to strange dogs, strange and sometimes unhospitable environments, tense owners and handlers and large crowds. Additional food must be supplied to provide that energy. The only way a dog feeder can tell how much stress a dog has been subjected to is by weighing him frequently while on the road. Most dogs will eat just a little more

243

food when they are stressed, but some will refuse to eat altogether. When this happens body fats are broken down to meet the energy needs, and weight loss is the result. More important to the exhibitor in the middle of a circuit, a refusal to eat is followed almost immediately by a loss of condition in even the best conditioned dogs.

Having the dog a little overweight at the beginning of the circuit is not a satisfactory answer. Such a practice penalizes the dog both at the beginning and at the end of a campaign. There are only a few days in the middle—as the dog goes from overweight to underweight—when the dog is at optimum weight and top condition.

There are some show dogs, the true "hams," which present no difficulty in maintaining their weight or condition, even on the most trying campaigns. These dogs love to compete in a show ring. The excitement of travel, new faces, and new experiences overcome their inborn need for consistency. Of course, a bitch in her first day of heat right in the next crate may constitute more than even the best campaigner can take. But, at the next show, a good campaigner will be back to eating and acting normal again.

Unfortunately, all show dogs are not endowed with such a constitution, and it takes much, much less to disturb their psyche and disrupt their eating habits. On occasion an upsetting situation may prove severe enough to cause a dog to stop eating completely. When this happens it is called *anorexia*. Nothing can destroy a dog's condition more rapidly than anorexia. From a medical standpoint, dogs do not constitute a real medical problem until they have refused food for about 48 hours. Anorexias of medical importance are discussed in the chapter on feeding sick dogs. From the handler's viewpoint anorexia is considered a problem as soon as a dog has missed its first meal. If the dog refuses the second meal as well, it is frequently fed artificially. The longer one waits and the more meals the dog misses, the greater will be the loss of condition—and the longer it will take to restore it to peak.

Artificial feeding: The practice of artificially feeding dogs when they stop eating on a show campaign is highly controversial. My purpose in the following discussion is not to advocate a position on the ethical or moral issues of artificial feeding, but simply to describe some of the methods by which artificial feeding may be accomplished.

The most often used practice of artificial feeding, whether on the show circuit or with a sick dog at home, is spoon-feeding. This is the

244

procedure in which little balls of food are placed, forcibly if necessary, far down into the dog's mouth to initiate a swallowing reflex. Some dogs have no objection to this whatever. Others resent it violently. At one extreme, attempts at spoon-feeding wind up with more food on the dog feeder and floor than in the dog. At the other extreme, some dogs become so habituated to hand-feeding that they refuse to eat normally and insist on being fed everything by spoon. This is particularly objectionable, and should not be encouraged, even if it means a dog must miss a campaign because its condition cannot be maintained by normal eating.

Dogs that are being spoon fed to supplement a *reduced* food intake may benefit from artificial feeding enough to maintain their condition. Dogs that are being spoon fed to replace their entire dietary intake may fail to maintain any resemblance of peak condition. The reason is simple. It is almost impossible to replace a dog's total dietary intake by feeding it with a spoon.

A far more efficient method, but one requiring considerably more skill, is that of intragastric intubation. This is, simply described, the passing of a hollow tube through the dog's mouth and, by way of the esophagus, into its stomach. Through the tube, then, is passed whatever type of nourishment the dog needs, and in the precise quantities necessary to replace whatever amount of the daily diet is desired. Once the technique is mastered, it becomes a simple matter for two people to feed artificially a dozen dogs in a half-hour.

Intragastric intubation: The equipment needed for feeding a dog with a stomach tube is simple and inexpensive. The mechanics of the procedure are not difficult, but do require a certain degree of skill. This skill can only be obtained by "on the job" practice, and persistence if initial attempts are not 100 percent successful.

To pass a stomach tube on a dog . . .

STEP 1, Figure 100. Collect the necessary equipment for feeding a dog by intragastric intubation. This includes (1) a 2½-inch rubber funnel, (2) a hard plastic adapter to go between the funnel and tube, (3) a thick-walled rubber tubing section about 24 inches long and 3/8ths inch in diameter, (4) a one-direction, double-action squeeze bulb, and (5) a 30- to 36-inch long, #22 French, urinary catheter or the equivalent. In addition to the items shown, a liquid food and a container to hold it in are also needed.

Once the necessary equipment has been accumulated . . .

Step 2, Figure 101. Using the catheter as a ruler, measure the

245

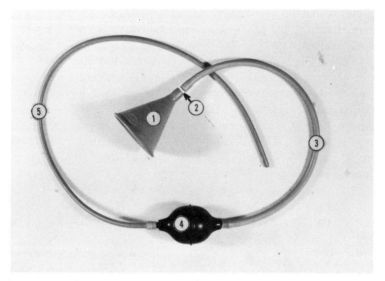

Figure 100. The equipment necessary for feeding a dog via stomach tube,

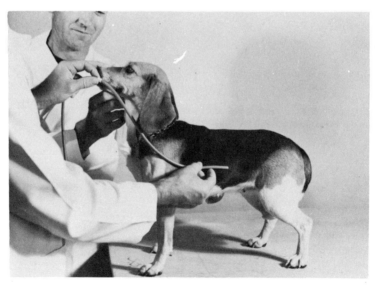

Figure 101. Measuring the stomach tube.

246

mouth to stomach distance as shown. The tip of the catheter should extend to the 10th or 11th rib. Once measured, the tube should be marked with a felt pen or small piece of tape. Before inserting the marked tube ...

STEP 3, Figure 102. Lubricate the first four to six inches of the tube with white petrolatum or some similar lubricant. Then ...

STEP 4, Figure 103. Restrain the animal's head by grasping it with the free hand. Insert the index finger of that hand into the mouth while at the same time folding the lip inward over the teeth. In this manner the index finger acts as a spacer to establish the proper gap between the jaws so that the tube can be passed between them. The other three fingers are used to hold the lower jaw shut against the index finger. This prevents the dog from opening the jaw too wide or chewing on the tube or the index finger.

With the dog so restrained, the catheter is passed over the tongue and into the *pharynx.* The pharynx is the back portion of the dog's mouth. When the dog swallows, which he invariably does when something is pushed into his pharynx, the tube is pushed progres-

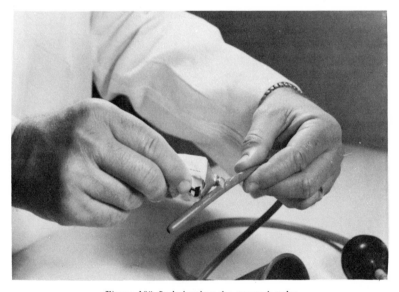

Figure 102. Lubricating the stomach tube.

247

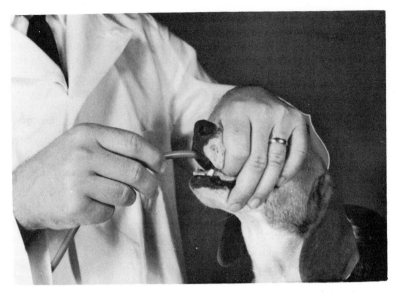

Figure 103. Restraining the dog's head and inserting the stomach tube.

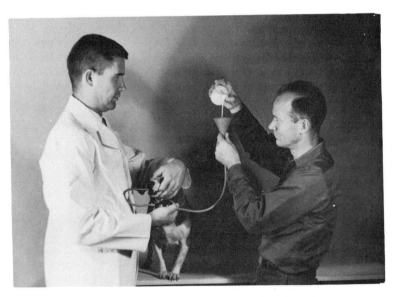

Figure 104. Delivering the food by use of the funnel.

248

sively inward into the esophagus until it reaches the premeasured mark.

If the tube is pushed into the dog's windpipe by mistake it will cough violently. Continued efforts to push the tube will be met with violent attempts to escape by the dog until it is removed from the windpipe.

Once the tube is safely in the stomach . . .

STEP 5, Figure 104. Pour the premeasured liquid food into the funnel, which has been raised above the working level, and deliver the material to the stomach by squeezing the bulb. When all of the food has been pumped into the dog's stomach, it should be followed by a small amount of water, administered the same way.

Before removing the tube, a small quantity of air should be forced through it to clear the tube of any materials that might spill into the pharynx and cause strangulation or pneumonia. A single squeeze of the empty bulb is usually sufficient for this purpose.

STEP 6, not illustrated. To avoid both discomfort and possible injury to the dog, the tube should be removed by a slow, steady pull rather than a quick jerk.

STEP 7, not illustrated. All intubation equipment should be thoroughly washed after use. Between dogs a vigorous cold-water rinse is satisfactory, as long as none of them has any contagious disease. Between feedings the equipment should be given a hot, soapy water scrubbing, and be hung to drain and air dry.

Chapter 17

Sporting Dogs

THE HUNTERS

THE stables of hunting dogs across this country resemble, somewhat, the teams of college athletes that play football each fall. Their season starts about the same time that cold weather arrives. They spend most of the year in relative inactivity. And they are expected to perform at the peak of their abilites during the season.

No one would ever consider suiting-up 11 football players and sending them onto the field without some preparation. The players are put through training sessions, exercise sessions and skull sessions. To be sure they are equipped for the rigorous activity ahead, the football players are fed from a training table where specially prepared meals are served.

Unlike football players, few hunting dogs receive either pre-training or pre-feeding. Instead, since hunting dogs are unproductive during the off season, they are fed a minimal diet for reasons of economy. But when hunting season starts, nothing is too good or too expensive for a good hunting dog. As a result, they are often fed an unbalanced mish-mash of expensive, but useless, items, thrown together in a haphazard manner. Finally, to make matters worse, these dogs are then hunted in a fasting state to make sure they "work harder"!

The results of such a feeding program can lead to total disappointment. The dogs, eager to hunt, will work like trojans for an hour or two. Then, usually without warning, they begin to "poop out." Some may even become dazed and begin to stagger. They act afraid, and in extreme cases, may even collapse into epileptic-like seizures. This strange behavior is due to a critical lowering of the level of sugar in the blood. The sudden drop in blood sugar is the result of the inadequate feeding program.

In a few instances, disappointment in a dog's performance turns to frustration and anger, and a good hunting dog is left behind because it won't keep up. In most of these cases the truth is, the dog *can't* keep up. Ironically, the person most responsible for the dog's inability to perform, the dog feeder himself, is the one who is first to blame his own mistakes on his dog. And, the saddest part of all is that it could all be avoided.

Correctly feeding a stable of hunting dogs on a year-round basis is neither expensive nor elaborate. When done properly, it is not a difficult procedure, either.

The Off Season
A hunting dog's needs, during most of the year, are no different from those of any other dog living in similar circumstances. During the off season hunting dogs should be fed just like any other dog of comparable size.

Diet Formulation: The Pointer living outdoors during the off season varies little in its food requirements from that of a housepet kept outdoors. The outdoor dog section of the calorie chart for housepets in Chapter 15 can be used as a guide for estimating how much food to feed a hunting dog during the off season.

The food fed to hunting dogs during the off season can be the same as that used for any other dog for maintenance. It must be balanced and adequate, contain sufficient calories to maintain the dog's weight and be acceptable enough so the dog will eat enough to obtain all of the nutrients and energy it needs. The food can be dry, soft-moist, or canned. Where cost is a factor, dry foods usually prove to be most economical.

A good-quality, expanded dry food, fed unsupplemented, will maintain off season hunting dogs as well as anything available. When small numbers of hunting dogs are kept, canned foods may find more advantage and make up for their extra expense through convenience and time saved.

251

Feeding Procedures: Self-feeding is an excellent method of maintaining adult hunting dogs during the off-season. Most Pointers, hounds or retrievers will eat anything put before them. A few will overeat, and get fat. Once these have been separated a self-feeding program is the most economical and convenient method of feeding hunters during the off season. When self-feeding is not used, off-season hunting dogs should be fed *ad libitum.*

Preparing for the Hunting Season

Dogs that will be housed somewhere other than the kennel where they spend their off season should be converted to the food and type of feeding program they will be fed during the hunting season. This should be done two or three weeks before the season begins. Hunting dogs on a self-feeding program must be converted to individual feeding. Where more than two dogs are being kept in the same pen, it is advisable to separate the dogs at feeding time while making the conversion. The quantity of each individual's portion should be based on that dog's optimum weight and the caloric density of the food being fed.

For those dogs returning each night to the same pen in which they spend their off season, no change in the method of feeding is necessary.

Feeding During the Hunting Season

All dogs that hunt need increased energy intakes. The harder they work, and the longer they work, the more energy they will need. At the same time they will need additional B-complex vitamins to be able to utilize the additional energy. Because of the duration of sustained work that a hunting dog experiences, it also develops an increased need for protein and blood-forming minerals and vitamins. As long as a balanced diet is fed, these increased needs will be met by the increased quantities of food eaten to meet the increased energy needs.

Diet Formulation: Which foods are best, and how much of each constitutes the best diet, will depend entirely on the circumstances of the moment. For this reason, dietary formulation will be discussed part and parcel with feeding procedures.

Feeding Procedures: In general, all hunting dogs, whether on self-feeding or fed individually, should be fed an additional small, high-protein meal each morning on the days they will be hunting.

This should supply about 180 to 190 calories for every 25 pounds of dog. The meal can consist of a meat and meat by-product commercial food, hamburger, hard boiled eggs, or even venison strips or squirrel loins—whatever is handy. In no case, should it ever be overlooked or forgotten. *You* may be able to get by with no more than a cigarette or a cup of coffee for breakfast, but your dogs positively cannot!

Once in the field, the dogs should not be allowed to hunt continuously for longer than two hours at a time. At the end of each two-hour period there should be a 10-minute rest break. During this break each dog of Pointer size or larger should be fed at least one ounce (approximately 1/3rd patty) of a soft-moist food, or a handful of dog biscuits, or a handful of expanded dry food. All three should be given with a drink of water. Any of these three foods can be stuck into the pocket of a hunting vest and carried with ease. If the dog is hunted for longer than six hours, a full 30 to 60 minute lunch break should be taken at the end of the first six hours of hunting. During this lunch stop, a midday meal of 2 ounces of soft-moist or expanded dry food per 40 pounds of body weight should be fed each dog, along with a full drink of water.

These frequent feedings, of small amounts of food high in carbohydrate, maintain the efficiency of the dog's performance at a peak during the time the dog is working. The water improves the dog's endurance. Endurance depends on the dog's ability to mobilize and burn the fat stored in its body. And, to do this, the dog must have water. Always have clean, drinkable water available for your dog at each rest stop. Just because you don't get thirsty every two hours doesn't mean your dog doesn't. Remember, you may weigh 180 pounds, and 12 gallons of you is water. Your 40-pound Pointer contains slightly less than three gallons of water, yet he's burning energy a lot faster than you are.

At the end of the day give each dog a drink and cool them all for at least 30 minutes to an hour. Resting the dogs before feeding them their main meal helps to avoid such problems as bloat, torsion or intussusception. After cooling off, those being fed individually can be given their main meal. Provision will have to be made somewhere to rest those dogs on self-feeders before they are allowed to return to their pens. Once cooled off these dogs, too, can be returned to their pens with the feeders.

For dogs being individually fed, Table XXI should be used as a guide for calculating the quantity of food to be fed at the main meal. Obtain from the table the correct number of daily calories required, according to how long the dog has been hunted and what it weighs. Subtract 185 calories for each 1/4th pound of hamburger, 1/4th can of meat and meat by-product food or four eggs fed at the morning meal from the total number of daily calories required. Subtract 100 calories for each two-hour rest feeding and 200 calories for the lunch break. After all of these corrections have been made, the balance remaining from the original figure obtained from Table XXI should be used to calculate how much food to feed at the main meal.

Example: Assume a 50-pound Pointer hunts for seven hours and is being fed a basic ration of dry food that contains 1600 calories per pound.

50-pound dog needs	2100 calories
1/2 pound breakfast	—375 calories
	1725 calories balance
Two rest stops	—200 calories
	1525 calories balance
Lunch break	—200 calories
	1325 calories

TABLE XXI

A calorie chart for hunting dogs, giving total daily calories needed by various weight hunting dogs that are hunted for less than, and more than, two hours.

Dog's weight (pounds)	two hours (cals)	over two hours (cals)	Dog's weight (pounds)	two hours (cals)	over two hours (cals)
15.0	720	795	36.0	1440	1620
16.5	775	858	40.0	1560	1760
18.0	828	918	44.0	1672	1892
20.0	900	1000	50.0	1850	2100
22.0	968	1078	57.0	2052	2337
25.0	1075	1200	66.0	2310	2640
28.5	1197	1339	88.0	2992	3432
30.0	1230	1380	118.0	3894	4602
32.0	1312	1472	150.0	4800	5850

TABLE XXII

The percentage adjustment to be used in adjusting a dog's diet to meet the increased energy needs during cold weather. The figure on the left is the average temperature of the day, the figure on the right is the percentage by which the dog's daily caloric intake should be increased for a day with that average temperature.

Air Temperature	Percent increase
0° F.	70%
10° F.	50%
20° F.	35%
30° F.	20%
40° F.	10%
50° F.	0
60° F.	0
70° F.	0
80° F.	10%
100° F.	20%
120° F.	30%

1325 calories balance to be fed as the evening meal.

$1325 \text{ cals} \div 1600 \text{ cals/lb.} = .83$ pound or 13 ounces of dry food fed as the evening meal.

Remember that seasonal adjustments have not been made in these calculations, and if a cold-weather increase is needed the amount should be calculated using Table XX by adding the results to the total amount fed. An even more accurate guide to seasonal adjustment can be made on a daily basis by using Table XXII, which gives adjustment percentages based on average daily temperatures. This table is particularly useful for dogs that are hunted one day and not the next, or hunted during the day and housed indoors at night.

THE RACERS

Another type of sporting dog is the racer, which includes the Greyhounds and the Whippets. The racer's energy needs are quite different from the hunter's. Instead of a continuous moderate level of energy expenditure for extended periods, the Greyhound expends tremendous amounts of energy over rather limited spans of time. The Greyhound's needs are not those of maximum endurance, but of instant peak performance sustained for only a brief period.

Complicating the Greyhound feeder's problems is the matter of racing weights. A Pointer can hunt whether he's overweight or under. The racing Greyhound will be disqualified from any race in which its body weight varies more than one and one-half pounds, up or down, from its original racing weight. This means the calculation of the quantity of food to maintain the weight of a Greyhound must be highly accurate.

Non-racing Racers

Non-racing dogs usually fall into four categories, 1) reproducing bitches during pregnancy and lactation, 2) growing pups, 3) dogs in their training program and 4) racing dogs during the off season. Whether they are Greyhounds or "pothounds", feeding reproducing bitches and growing puppies is handled in the same manner. That manner has already been discussed. The information contained in Chapters 13 and 14 is entirely applicable to Greyhounds and Whippets. The feeding of off-season racers and young dogs in training will be discussed in this section.

Off-season Racers. The primary objective of feeding a racing dog during the off-season should be to maintain the dog's body weight within its tolerable racing limits while providing it enough energy to support its exercise program. The maintenance of the off-season racer requires a little more planning and control than most simple maintenance situations because of the need to control the dog's weight within specified limits.

Diet formulation: For a Greyhound, its optimum body weight is the weight at which it will qualify to race. The caloric intake should be regulated to maintain that weight exactly. For off-season racers this can best be done by adjusting the quantity fed to that amount needed to keep the dog at its optimum weight. The adjustment must be made for each dog individually. When a new food is fed, or first season racers need to have their off-season food adjusted, use the "outdoor" section of Table XIX to estimate the daily caloric need of the dog and then make your adjustment in the following manner:

Weigh each dog and record the weight. Feed each dog the quantity of food calculated to supply the number of calories estimated from Table XIX. Weigh each dog weekly for three weeks. Then, evaluate the effects produced by the quantity of food being fed and make any adjustments as follows:

256

a.) If the dog's body weight is in excess of racing weight by at least one pound and each new weekly weight is greater than the previous weight, reduce the quantity fed by 10 percent.

b.) If the dog's body weight is in excess of racing weight by at least one pound, but each weekly weight is about the same, reduce the quantity fed by about five percent.

c.) If the dog's weekly weights are no more than one pound over or under the racing weight the quantity of food being fed is correct.

d.) If the dog's body weight is under the racing weight by at least a pound but each weekly weight is about the same, add five percent to the quantity of food fed each day.

e.) If the dog's body weight is under the racing weight by at least a pound and each weekly weight is smaller than the week preceding it, add 10 percent to the quantity of food being fed each day.

In situations a, b, d and e make the necessary adjustments and feed for another two or three weeks, again weighing the dog each week. Then re-evaluate the quantities being fed, using the guidelines already given, and make any further adjustments needed. If, by the sixth week there are still a few dogs that are not maintaining optimum weight, continue to adjust their food intake. Use the procedure described until all dogs are being fed the correct amount of food needed to maintain their weight within one pound of their racing weight.

Racing dogs may need to have a seasonal adjustment made in their food intake if they remain outdoors. The best way to handle such seasonal adjustments is to post somewhere in the diet kitchen or on the feeding cart the percentage adjustment figure for each month of the year. The figures listed in Table XX should be used.

Feeding procedures: Once the exact amount of food needed to maintain a dog's weight has been determined, each dog should have its own feeding container identified and the quantity it eats put on the container. A list of dogs and their food needs should also be made and posted in the diet kitchen or on the feeding cart, for the feeder to use in the event a food pan is lost or the figures become obscured.

Portion control feeding is used almost exclusively with racing dogs, in season and out. This is because it is the only successful way of maintaining, with any precision, a dog's weight at a desired level. The only exceptions to this will be pregnant and lactating bitches, growing pups and in-training dogs. All but the in-training dogs are most appropriately fed *ad libitum* or from a self-feeder. In-training dogs require their own special handling.

In-training Racers. Dogs that are in training are young, active animals, many of which will still be growing. They are frequently trained every day, or at least five days each week. During the training sessions these dogs are called upon to expend extreme amounts of energy during brief periods, and moderate amounts for extended periods. This pattern is similar to adult dogs, during actual racing conditions, but lasts for the in-training dogs somewhat longer each day.

Diet formulation and feeding procedure: The dog in training is subjected to a varied schedule, depending on the stage of training and degree of development. Because of this, the daily energy requirements of dogs in a training program never remain the same. Consequently, the most satisfactory program that can be used for young racers in training is a combination of *ad libitum* and portion control feeding. Use the figures in Table XXI under the "two hours" part to estimate the quantity of food to feed dogs in training. If the dog eats everything offered, adjust the quantity slowly upward until the dog is leaving a little food after each meal. If a dog leaves more than a small quantity of its food at each feeding reduce the quantity fed until only a small amount is left after each feeding. Dogs on training programs should be weighed weekly to make certain that growing dogs continue to gain weight, but that grown ones don't. When a dog begins to gain weight above its optimum switch to portion control feeding to hold the dog at its optimum weight.

The food used during the training of racing dogs should be the same food that is going to be fed during the racing season. This accustoms the dog, during training, to the diet it will be eating when it is actually racing. It also enables you to adjust the quantity of racing diet needed to maintain each individual dog's racing weight. Finally, it allows you to determine whether or not each individual will be able to perform satisfactorily on the racing program and food you plan to use. If a racer is not going to perform at peak on a given diet, the time to discover it is during training, not during the first racing meet.

Racing Dogs. If a racing dog does not weigh the correct amount it cannot race. A common practice among Greyhound owners is to weigh all dogs scheduled to race on the evening before they are to

258

race and for each pound that a dog is overweight, $\frac{1}{4}$ to $\frac{1}{2}$ pound of food is reduced from its evening meal. Those that are underweight are offered more food, at about the same rate. Sometimes this works and sometimes it doesn't. As often as not, when it doesn't work it's because the food being fed is not uniform in ingredients or mixing, and it fails to perform the same way this time as it did the last. When a dog food varies from 100 to 500 calories per pound within the same brand it becomes a very difficult task to try to maintain a dog's weight at a reasonably constant level. But, by using the proper food and program the Greyhound feeder can maintain his dog's weight to within a few ounces of where he desires.

Diet formulation: It goes without saying that a racing dog's diet must be balanced, adequate and contain enough energy to support racing. The secret to a winning racing diet, however, is its uniformity. Because of the body weight limitations, and short, maximum performance energy demands, a food that varies to any extent at all will not perform the same from feeding to feeding. As a consequence, the dog will not perform the same from race to race. A dog may win one time and not the next because its diet fails to supply it with the same energy and spark from one feeding to the next.

Adjusting the quantity of food to feed an adult racing dog has already been discussed under the section on off-season racers. To obtain an estimate of how much to feed a racing dog on racing days add five calories per pound of body weight to his total daily calorie need. This starting quantity is then adjusted up or down until the precise amount of food is found that will maintain that particular dog's weight on racing days.

Feeding procedures: All racing dogs must be fed by strict portion control during the racing season. Only by carefully regulating the quantity fed to each dog can a racing-dog feeder control his dog's weights.

All dogs that are to be raced should be fed twice on the day of the race if they are going to be able to put out maximum performance. The first feeding should be at least two hours before racetime, but not more than about four to six hours before. This pre-race meal should consist of mostly highly digestible carbohydrates and a little fat. This can be obtained from two slices of white bread soaked in two tablespoonsful of half and half coffee cream or two tablespoonsful of honey for every 25 pounds of dog. Any comparable mixture, supplying digestible carbohydrates and fats, will be satisfactory.

259

The pre-race meal should provide between 15 and 25 percent of the total daily calories. The amount of the calories actually provided by the pre-race meal should be subtracted from the dog's total daily need, and this balance used to determine the quantity of food to be fed at the after-race meal. Each dog should be relaxed for at least two hours after the race before feeding it this meal.

Example: Assume a 50-pound racing male requires 2100 calories per day on racing days (1850 + 5cal x 50 lbs = 2100), and is being fed a dry food that contains 1550 calories per pound. If we feed four slices of bread and coffee cream as a pre-race meal it will supply 372 calories. (Use 63 cals/slice and 30 cals/tblsp.) 372 calories is 17.5 percent of the daily total of 2100, well within the range of 15 to 25 percent.

$$
\begin{aligned}
\text{daily need} &= 2100 \text{ calories} \\
\text{pre-race meal} &= -372 \text{ calories} \\
\text{balance needed} &= \overline{1728} \text{ calories, to be fed as} \\
& \quad \text{the after-race meal.} \\
1728 \text{ cals} \div 1550 \text{ cals/lb.} &= 1.1 \text{ pounds or 18 ounces} \\
& \quad \text{of food as after-race meal.}
\end{aligned}
$$

Racing dogs may be fed only one meal on those days they are not racing. In fact, because of the time required by portion control feeding, most Greyhound feeders customarily feed all of their dogs only once daily under current practices. There is a possibility, however, that a twice-a-day feeding program for all dogs might eliminate some of the staling-off seen during the later meets of the season.

Remember that seasonal adjustments have not been considered in the above example. If a cold-weather increase is needed, it should be calculated by choosing the proper figure from Table XXII and adding a sufficient amount of food to the daily diet to supply the additional calories needed.

Chapter 18

Working Dogs

WHILE the first dogs were undoubtedly only companions, it probably did not take man long to realize the utility value of his newly-made friend. Before recorded history, dogs were helping man to hunt for food. In those days, hunting was not a sport, but deadly serious work. Today the dog still helps man in his quest for food, but the nature of the job has taken on a different form. The dog still helps man to hunt, too, but for a different reason.

Whatever the purpose or nature of the job, the performance of work always requires the expenditure of energy. As a consequence, every working dog's primary dietary need is increased energy. Whenever dietary energy is increased, those B-complex vitamins, minerals and the water necessary for burning the energy must also be increased.

Except for this increased need for energy and the nutrients to burn it, working dogs require most nutrients at no greater levels than non-working dogs (i.e.: their MDR). As a result, when working dogs eat large quantities of ordinary maintenance dog foods to obtain all of the energy they need, they frequently consume some of the nutrients in excessive amounts. Paradoxically, they may also eat such large quantities that the digestibility of all the nutrients in the diet are adversely affected, and some nutrients may actually be obtained in inadequate amounts.

In other cases, a working dog simply cannot, physically, eat all of a food needed to supply its energy needs. In these instances the dog

261

suffers from the lack of total digestible energy, and loses weight. If the condition is allowed to continue, the dog will reduce its activities in order to reduce its caloric demands. If the dog is forced to continue working at the same pace, it will lose weight faster and faster, and eventually work itself to death.

The working dogs fed in the United States usually fit into one of three groups: the herd dogs, the guide dogs, and the guard dogs.

Herd Dogs

Dogs that watch or protect animals use the least amount of extra energy of any of the working dogs. They seldom are required to expend energy in excess of normal activity for any duration of time. Even their short-term expenditures of energy are not very great. The only time herd dogs ever utilize large amounts of energy are when they are rounding up strays, lost or semi-wild animals running at large.

Diet formulation: When not participating in round-ups, most herd dogs expend about the same amount of energy as any other dog that lives outdoors and engages in only modest physical activity. Most herd dogs do well when fed amounts of food calculated to supply the "Outdoor only" section of Table XIX. In those few cases where a herd dog is left a little lean on such a diet, an additional five to 10 percent usually corrects the situation. Care must be taken to avoid adding too much food because excess weight reduces the herd dog's efficiency and over-taxes the heart, lungs and liver of any working dog.

Dogs engaged in round-up activities are a different matter. Like hunting dogs, round-up dogs are consistently on the go. Unlike hunting dogs, however, round-up dogs seldom get a chance to rest every couple of hours. They work continuously, until they have recovered all the strays, brought in the last maverick, or are called off by their owners. As a consequence, round-up dogs burn tremendous amounts of energy every day they are working. Many of them are performing at the upper limits of a dog's capabilities and endurance. When dogs are used for round-ups they should be fed a quantity of food that has been estimated from Table XXIII.

Feeding procedures: Both self-feeding and *ad libitum* feeding are satisfactory for herd dogs, and either are more desirable than portion control. By allowing the dog to establish its own daily intake it

TABLE XXIII

A calorie chart for herd dogs during round-up activities.

If dog weighs this many pounds,	it needs this many calories each day:
20.0	990
22.0	1065
25.0	1182
28.5	1317
32.0	1443
36.0	1584
40.0	1716
44.0	1839
50.0	2035
57.0	2257
66.0	2541
88.0	3291
118.0	4283
150.0	5280

will do a far better job of determining how much it needs, in relation to how hard it is working, than you could ever do.

Dogs that are on ordinary herd duty can be fed any time that is convenient to the herdsman. Like all working dogs, they should be fed twice daily, if at all possible. For herd dogs, about half of the daily needs should be fed at each meal. Round-up dogs should be fed their morning meal at least an hour before they begin, if that's possible, and should always be allowed to rest an hour or so at the end of the day before being fed their evening meal.

Like all dogs, herd dogs should always have water available. This is particularly important in herd dogs that are on round-ups. These animals depend on their endurance, as well as their performance, to accomplish their jobs. Without water no dog will have much endurance.

Guide Dogs

These are the dogs that act as a blind person's eyes. Much of their expenditure of energy depends on the activity of their masters. Active persons will have active dogs. In addition, psychological stress and tension play a role in the requirements for energy in guide dogs. Consequently, even guide dogs with owners who are reasonably inactive have a greater need for energy than dogs of the same breed that live as house pets.

263

Diet formulation: Most guide dogs can be fed satisfactorily using the figures for "outdoors" from Table XIX as a guide. They, like any other dog, must have their food intake adjusted to maintain their individual body weight.

The convenience of the food is almost as important as its quality where guide dogs are concerned. Elaborate mixing of ingredients, or even moderate combinations, become impossible tasks for people who cannot see to read a scales or level a tablespoonful. A single-food diet is most desirable for guide dogs, and the foods of higher caloric density (1600 to 2000 calories per pound) give the least trouble for the greatest performance.

Feeding procedure: Feeding guide dogs is best done by using portion control. It poses the least problem for a blind owner to simply measure out a fixed amount of food at each meal and throw away any food remaining uneaten. By having a sighted person weigh his dog at regular intervals, a blind master can make a judgment as to whether or not his dog's food should be increased or decreased for the next interval.

Guard Dogs

Engaged in military as well as civilian occupations, guard dogs serve on sentry duty, patrol duty, shore watch, riot control, store and warehouse security and many similar missions.

Whatever the nature of their mission, all guard dogs have one thing in common, their high degree of training. Every guard dog is trained to maintain a peak performance for the entire time it is on duty. Ordinarily this is for extended periods of time. Such sustained performance requires huge amounts of energy. The guard dog also needs large amounts of energy to cope with the extreme emotional stress that occurs while the dog is on duty. Often, during periods of sustained performance, a guard dog's energy need exceeds that of a bitch during lactation.

Because of this greatly increased consumption of energy, not even the dry foods, with their 1500 to 1600 calories per pound, have a caloric density high enough to satisfactorily provide all the energy needs of a guard dog. Because they are customarily fed only once daily, guard dogs must eat great quantities of even these foods to meet their energy needs. Available energy within the food is thereby even further reduced.

264

To adequately supply a guard dog with enough energy it must be fed a diet that is more concentrated than ordinary maintenance diets. Such a diet must contain a large amount of energy in a relatively small quantity of food. At the same time, it must contain *all* of the necessary nutrients, balanced to the increased caloric density.

One of the major problems with civilian guard dogs that patrol within a building or shopping center mall all night is the stool that they produce. Not only do these stools present a clean-up problem, but their odor often lingers several additional hours after the stools are gone. Most customers and employees do not enjoy smelling the odor of dog stools during their donuts and coffee every morning! Some guard dogs may leave as many as two or three, voluminous, odoriferous stools, at different locations throughout the building, each night they patrol.

To reduce this stool problem to the barest minimum, a food containing large amounts of energy, in the least quantity of dry matter possible, must be fed. This can be accomplished by increasing the digestibility of the ingredients put into the food, or by reducing the amount of indigestible dry matter. When either is done, most of the food will be digested and absorbed to be used for energy, while only a small amount will remain to become stool. What's more, when the digestibility of the proteins and carbohydrates is improved, the odor of the small quantity of stool that is produced will be considerably less.

Diet formulation: Most dogs used as guard dogs are German Shepherds, with an occasional Doberman Pinscher, Boxer or Labrador Retriever thrown in. The average weight of an adult, male guard dog is about 70 pounds. None should weigh less than 50 pounds. The quantity of energy necessary to maintain these weights can be estimated from Table XXIV.

To satisfactorily provide a guard dog with adequate amounts of energy and nutrients every day, its food should have the following three characteristics: 1) It should contain approximately 2000 calories in each pound. 2) It should have the nutrients balanced to be fed at about 40 available calories per pound of body weight. 3) The overall digestibility of the food should not be less than 80 percent.

No food exists, in normal commercial food channels, that will satisfy the characteristics just listed. While a few canned foods meet the digestibility requirements, no dry foods do. Neither type meets the

265

caloric density or nutrient balance requirements. Soft-moist foods meet the digestibility requirements, but have even lower caloric densities than the dry foods.

The addition of fresh, or canned, meat and meat by-products to a dry food usually improves the digestibility of the protein and fat in the diet. But, because of the high water content of meat foods, their addition actually reduces the caloric density of the final diet combination.

Caloric density can be increased by the addition of corn oil. This procedure works well only when increased energy needs are minimal. With a guard dog's energy requirements, however, so much corn oil is needed that it, too, will dilute the food and nutrient deficiencies are apt to occur.

Recently a food was developed specifically for guard dogs. It was designed to meet the extreme needs of military dogs in southeast Asia. This area is considered by the military to be one of the most stressing duty stations of their guard dogs. The new food exceeds the qualifications already mentioned. It is available for feeding to civilian guard dogs on a limited basis. The food can be purchased through almost any veterinarian or scientific research institution, or can be ordered direct* if the shipment is 1000 pounds or more.

TABLE XXIV

A calorie chart for guard dogs for a 24-hour period.

If dog weighs this many pounds,	feed this many calories daily:
40.0	1960
44.0	2112
50.0	2350
57.0	2622
66.0	2970
88.0	3872
118.0	5074
150.0	6300

Feeding procedures: All guard dogs should be fed by strict portion control. How each dog's weight, general condition and performance are affected by its diet can be much more accurately compared when feeding by portion control. Guard dogs fed *ad libitum,* or from a self-feeder, are apt to become overweight, sluggish or unre-

* Hill's Div. of Riviana Foods, 520 Harrison, Topeka, Ks. 66601.

266

sponsive. The last two are particularly fatal to a guard dog and its mission.

Guard dogs should be fed no less than three hours, before or after, their tour of duty. To feed any closer to the tour is an invitation to bloat, torsion or other gastric distress. The danger of these diseases is further increased if the dogs are eating low-quality foods containing poorly-digested nutrients.

Feeding guard dogs is an exception to the rule that all dogs should be fed at the same hour every day. A guard dog's tour hours are subject to frequent change. Its meal hours must change also, because feeding three hours before duty tours is more important than regular feeding hours. Actually, once their feeding routine is learned, most guard dogs will become accustomed to being fed three hours before going on duty and will adapt their behavior to cue on their feeding time the same way any dog does that is fed at the same time every day.

Because of the highly responsive nature of the guard dog, each should always be fed separately. Each dog should be housed in a pen designed so that it cannot see other dogs while it eats. The ideal situation is to have the pens built away from all outside activity and distractions, allowing the dogs to relax, eat and rest, undisturbed.

A guard dog should be fed by the same person every day, and should be trained never to accept food from anyone else. Where dogs are assigned to individual handlers, they should be the individuals who feed (and do everything for) the dog. When the dogs work alone, as in warehouses, department stores or shopping center malls, their feeder should be the person who is responsible for transporting them to and from their guard stations and their quarters.

Chapter 19

Feeding the Sick Dog

SICK dogs must eat, the same as healthy dogs, and for the same reasons—to feed 100-million tiny fires; to supply energy and nutrients for growth, replacement and repair; and to meet an ever changing need. A sick dog's *nutritional requirements* usually do not differ greatly from those of a healthy dog. A sick dog's *dietary needs,* however, can become substantially different from those of a healthy dog.

Diseases in which a dog's diet will need to be changed fall into two broad groups. The first is that group in which the diet, itself, is responsible for the disease. These are the true *nutritional diseases.* The second group is made up of those diseases in which one or more organs of the body cannot handle food or nutrients in a normal manner and the diet being fed must be changed in order to compensate for the *altered organ function.*

TRUE NUTRITIONAL DISEASES

Most of the true nutritional diseases are *deficiency diseases.* That is, they are diseases caused by a diet that contains an insufficient amount of one or more needed nutrients. A few nutritional diseases are *diseases of excess.*

Deficiency Diseases

The first diseases recognized as being related to a dog's diet were deficiency diseases. Most of these diseases were the result of inadequate or improperly balanced home-made rations. As economical commercial food became more and more nourishing, most of these deficiency diseases gradually disappeared.

Vitamin or mineral deficiencies are rarely seen as a primary disease any more. Both vitamins and minerals are inexpensive, and are needed in such small amounts that, today, few commercial dog foods fail to contain them in adequate amounts. Tables XXV and XXVI list the minerals and vitamins required by a dog and give the primary signs seen when these nutrients are deficient in a dog's diet. These signs are given as a reference rather than as a guide to existing disease, since most vitamin and mineral deficiencies that do occur involve more than one nutrient at a time.

Although energy and protein continue to be a problem with some dog foods, the number of brands that still contain insufficient fat or poor quality, indigestible protein become less and less every year. When a deficiency of fat occurs, it most often appears as an insufficient amount of total energy in the diet. This results in weight loss, sluggishness, dry, dull haircoat, poor physical condition and, in extreme cases, emaciation and uncontrolled diarrhea.

A deficiency of essential fatty acids may also occur, but it is unlikely. The total amount of the fats most often used in commercial foods can drop to as low as one percent of the diet and that diet will still contain sufficient fatty acids. The only exception to this might be cases of dry foods where larger quantities of fat have turned rancid.

When a deficiency of fatty acids does occur, it appears as a loss of weight and condition, a dry, dull coat, but more specifically as eroded areas on the skin. These may take place on the pads of the feet, between the toes and over the bony protuberances of the body where pressure reduces the blood supply.

Although these erosions may superficially resemble "hot spots," Figures 105-108, they differ from them in four major aspects. 1) They do not respond to routine steroid therapy. 2) They appear on both short-haired as well as long-haired dogs. 3) They require not three days, but closer to three months to heal. 4) Adding fatty acids to the diet promotes their recovery, because a deficiency of fatty acids caused them.

A deficiency of total protein in the diet is still sometimes seen. This, too, causes weight loss and dull, dry haircoats. It may also pro-

269

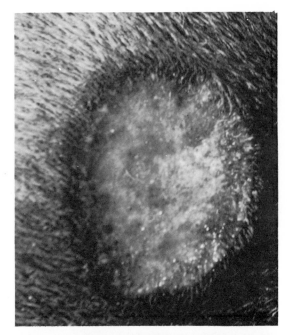

Figure 105. This is an eroded area on the hip of a Great Dane caused by a fatty acid deficiency in the dog's diet. While it looks much like a "hot spot", it is not. This wound did not respond at all to steroids, was found on a short-haired dog and took over a month to heal, all contrary to the reaction of a hot spot.

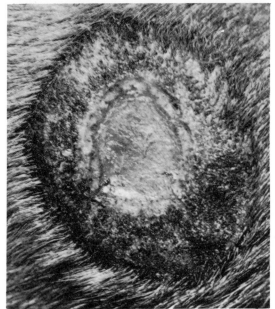

Figure 106. Here is the same wound as that in Figure 105, one week after the dog had been switched to a food containing an adequate amount of fatty acids.

270

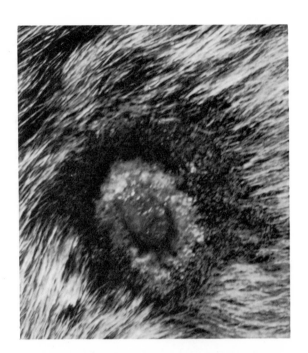

Figure 107. This is a picture of the wound shown in Figure 105 three weeks after the replacement of fatty acids.

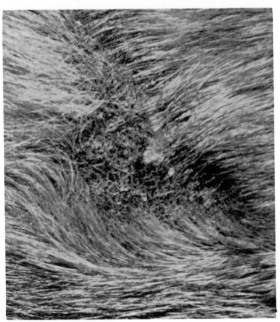

Figure 108. The same wound as shown in Fig. 105, six weeks after adequate fatty acids were fed. The healed wound left virtually no scar.

271

duce anemia, reduce the body's ability to cope with and recover from infections and, if uncorrected, will eventually lead to the dog's death.

TABLE XXV

The symptoms seen when vitamins are fed in too little and too large amounts.

Vitamin	Deficiency signs	Toxic signs
A	Poor growth, eye disease, weeping sores on the skin, impaired bone growth.	Loss of appetite, weight loss, decalcification of bone, joint ills.
D	Rickets in young and osteomalacia in adults. Swayback, chest deformities and poor tooth eruption.	Anorexia, nausea, fatigue, renal damage, calcium deposition, diarrhea, dehydration and death.
E	Reproductive failures, weak or dead pups, muscular dystrophy, steatitis.	None recorded.
K	Inability of blood to clot, free hemorrhage following injury.	None recorded, high levels thought dangerous.
C	Retarded healing, increased susceptibility to disease.	Non-toxic.
B_1 (thiamine)	Loss of appetite, arrested growth, muscular weakness, incoordination.	Non-toxic.
B_2 (riboflavin)	Dry scaly skin, redness of skin, muscular weakness in hindquarters, anemia.	Non-toxic.
Niacin	"Black tongue," anorexia, weight loss, diarrhea and anemia.	Dilation of blood vessels, itchy, burning skin.
B_6 (pyridoxine)	Anemia, atherosclerosis.	None reported.
Pantothenic acid	Anorexia, low blood sugar, gastritis, enteritis, convulsions, coma and death.	None reported.
Folic acid	Poor bone marrow growth, anemia, inflammation of tongue.	Non-toxic.

Continued on next page

272

Table XXV continued

Biotin	Tension, aimless movements, spastic paralysis of hind limbs.	Non-toxic.
B_{12} (Cobalamin)	Anemia.	Non-toxic.
Choline	Fatty liver, hypoproteinemia, poor blood clotting, anemia.	Persistent diarrhea.

TABLE XXVI

The symptoms seen when minerals are fed in too little amounts:

Mineral	Deficiency signs	Normal role
Calcium	Skeletal deformities,* lameness, milk fever (eclampsia), weak puppies.	Bone and tooth production, blood coagulation, nerve irritability, activator.
Phosphorus	Almost identical to calcium.*	Main energy transfer system (ATP), bone and tooth formation, fat and carbohydrate metabolism, buffer.
Magnesium	Retarded growth, skeletal deformities*, hyperirritability, tetany, death.	Bone and tooth formation, carbohydrate metabolism, nerve irritability.
Potassium	Rare. Ascending paralysis, depressed reflexes.	Acid-base balance, kidney integrity, body defense mechanism.
Sodium	Rare. Weight loss, hair loss, acidosis.	Fluid regulation, acid-base balance, osmotic pressures.
Chlorine	Same as sodium.	Same as sodium.
Iron	Anemia.	Component of hemoglobin, activator, oxygen transfer.
Copper	Anemia, skeletal deformities.*	Hemoglobin formation, function of bone-making cells, skin pigmentation and hardening.

Continued on page 274

273

Table XXVI, continued from page 273

Cobalt	Anemia.	Essential part of vitamin B_{12}.
Zinc	Rare, except in excess calcium supplementation. Retarded growth, delayed intestinal absorption.	Constituent of insulin, activator, protein synthesis.
Iodine	Sterility in adult dogs, still-born and goitrous pups, skin disease, hypothyroidism.	Thyroid function, skin integrity.
Manganese	Rare. Skeletal disease.*	Proper tissue respiration, activator in enzyme systems.

* Deficiency signs of calcium, phosphorus, magnesium, manganese, or copper, when manifest as a skeletal disease, many be indistinguishable.

Diet formulation: Regardless of the nutrient deficient, all deficiency diseases are managed in the same manner. *The deficient diet is replaced by an adequate one.* Any temptation to add supplemental nutrients, to correct the diet being fed, should be strenuously resisted. The only time supplementing a diet is acceptable is when the dog feeder knows *exactly* what nutrient is deficient and the *precise amount* of that nutrient needed to bring the diet into balance. Without a series of expensive and impractical laboratory studies, the latter question cannot possibly be answered. Even if it could, actual cases of deficiency disease most often involve more than one nutrient (multiple deficiency disease) and correcting for one deficiency alone only serves to antagonize another one.

Feeding procedure: The feeding procedure should remain the same, during the correction of a deficiency disease, as it would have been if the dog had no disease.

The "All-meat Syndrome." For awhile it looked as if commercial dog foods would make deficiency diseases a thing of the past. Then a new deficiency disease popped up. And, it was the direct result of feeding commercial dog foods. This disease is produced by the exclusive feeding of the so-called "all-meat" dog foods, and is referred to by many veterinarians as the "all-meat syndrome."

The "all-meat" syndrome is caused by a deficiency of dietary calcium and an upset in the balance between calcium and phosphorus in the diet.

The abrupt appearance of this disease was due to the aggressive

274

advertising of these foods, promoting the myth that, because dogs were carnivores, they were "meat" eaters. Many innocent dog feeders concluded that "all-meat" or "100% meat" foods were more desirable than those containing cereal and other ingredients.

When dogs are fed commercial all-animal-tissue food as their sole diet they will develop diarrhea, dull, dry coats, a loss of body weight, diseases of the joints. Figures 109 through 112, and thin, porous, fragile bones that break under the dog's own weight, Figure 113. If the later stages are not corrected, the dog will become progressively worse and quickly die. When the disease has progressed far enough, it will leave permanent injury, even if the diet is corrected.

The way to correct the "all-meat" syndrome is the same way to prevent it—don't feed your dog all-animal-tissue foods. Instead, feed an adequate diet containing calcium in sufficient amounts and in proper ratio to the phosphorus in the diet.

Anorexia. When a dog refuses to eat, or eats only a fraction of what it needs every day, this will also produce a deficiency. The term *anorexia* is used to describe the condition when a dog refuses

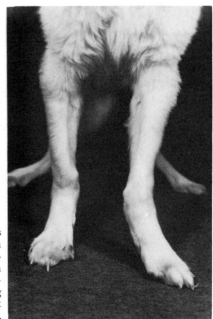

Figure 109. The forelimbs of a dog suffering from a multiple deficiency disease. This dog has been fed nothing but a commercial "all-meat" dog food since a week after it was weaned from its dam.

275

Figure 110. The forelimbs of a dog of similar size and age as the dog shown in Figure 109, but which has been fed a commercial dog food containing all of the nutrients needed by a dog, and in the proper amounts to nourish it.

Figure 111 (below left). A side view of one of the forelimbs of the dog shown in Figure 109. Notice the position of the paw and the condition of the toenails. The toenails are growing in such an abnormal position that they have not been worn down normally.

Figure 112 (below right). A side view of the forelimb of the healthy dog shown in Figure 110. Compare it to the forelimb shown in Figure 111.

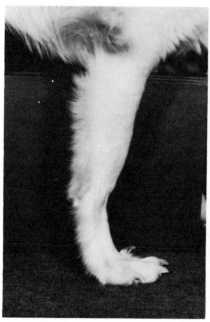

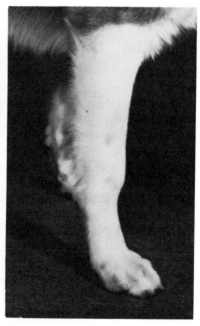

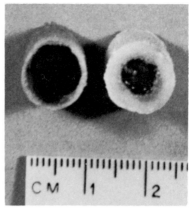

Figure 113. The dog shown in Figure 109 died about a week after the pictures were made. The bone from its femur was removed and a cross section of it is shown on the left in this photo. The cross section on the right is from an apparently healthy dog that was about the same size and age as the dog in Figures 109 and 111. This dog had died in the hospital the same day from an accident.

to eat. It can be contrasted to a *fasting* dog if you remember that a fasting animal does not have any food available to eat, while a dog with anorexia refuses to eat the food that is available.

Everyone takes a dog's eating for granted—until the dog stops eating. A dog's eating habits are normally controlled by hunger, appetite, and the satisfaction of these two. This control may be abnormally affected by emotions, sensations, or the food's palatability. Another thing that causes a disturbance of the dog's natural eating behavior is mechanical interruption. A broken jaw, a fish hook in the tongue or a rubber ball stuck in the throat are typical examples of *mechanical anorexia*.

Some dog feeders have the notion that all dogs miss a meal, now and then, and that a missed meal doesn't mean anything. A *healthy* dog is always hungry at meal time, just as a healthy dog feeder is. Any time a dog refuses to eat, it is a signal to you that something is awry. If the dog refuses two meals in a row, you can bet there's something wrong, either with your dog or with its food.

When a dog stops eating, it begins to lose weight. A 20-pound Beagle will lose 0.4 pound (six and one-half ounces) each day it refuses to eat, Figure 114. This weight loss occurs because the dog is breaking down and using up its own body. Since there are no nutrients coming in, a dog with anorexia must literally burn itself up to obtain the energy and nutrients needed for its essential life functions.

When extra demands from disease are piled on those of anorexia, the burn-up is even faster. A 20-pound Beagle cannot afford to lose a half pound of its body weight every day for very long!

277

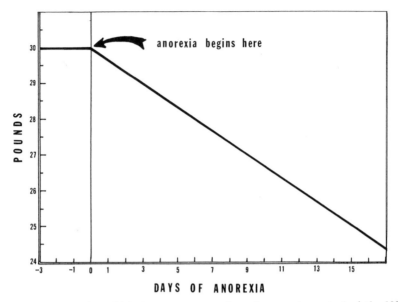

anorexia begins here

POUNDS

DAYS OF ANOREXIA

Figure 114. A dog which does not eat must burn its own tissues to feed the 100-million tiny fires of its body. When it does this, it loses weight. This graph illustrates the daily weight loss of a 30-pound dog who abruptly stops eating.

Included within the weight lost will be fats, carbohydrates and protein. The most important loss to a dog will be the protein. By the end of only two days of anorexia, that 20-pound Beagle will already have lost about three percent of its total body protein. This becomes increasingly important if one considers that protein is essential not only for normal metabolism, but for wound healing, tissue repair and combating infections as well.

Measures to replace the intake of anorectic dogs should be instituted immediately. Unwillingness or failure to overcome the deficiencies of calories and nutrients created by anorexia can mean the difference between recovery and death during an illness. And, anorexia is the most common symptom seen in almost every disease suffered by dogs.

Diet formulation: The same diet the dog was eating before anorexia is suitable, as long as the cause of the anorexia does not make it unsuitable. Since dogs become inactive with anorexia, their calorie need is somewhat less than for most dogs. If they have a fever, how-

278

ever, this rapidly increases their caloric requirements. Table XXVII
lists the energy requirements for anorectic dogs.

TABLE XXVII

*The caloric needs of dogs with anorexia
and fever.*

Dog's weight (lbs)	Anorexia	Anorexia with fever*
5	275	325
10	490	590
15	675	825
20	860	1060
25	1000	1250
30	1140	1440
35	1260	1610
40	1400	1800
45	1575	2025
50	1650	2150
55	1815	2365
60	1920	2520
65	1950	2600

* An average 10 calories per pound of body weight was used to calculate the figures in this column. If a more accurate figure is desired, the adjustment can be made by adding 2.5 calories per pound of body weight for each degree of fever.

Foods fed to anoretic dogs should be concentrated so that the daily quantity needed is low. A food satisfactory for feeding anorectic dogs should contain nutrients at the following levels:

Moisture = 50 to 70 percent
Protein = 5 to 7 percent
Fat* = 20 to 30 percent
Carbohydrate = 10 to 5 percent**
Energy level = 2.5 to 3.5 calories per
gram about 75 to 100
calories per ounce.

* Fat should be highly emulsified.
** As the fat content goes down, the carbohydrate content should go up.

The quantity of vitamins and minerals in an anorexia diet is not as important as the quantity of the nutrients listed above, since the diet is designed to be fed only a short time. Nevertheless, B-complex

279

vitamins—especially thiamine, riboflavin and pantothenic acid—and sodium, potassium and chloride levels should be correct to prevent energy loss and electrolyte imbalances.

Feeding procedure: Dogs with anorexia must be forcefed. This can be done either by spoon feeding or by intragastric intubation. Spoon feeding is described in Chapter 11, intragastric intubation in Chapter 16.

Anorexia diets should be fed only long enough to get a dog back to eating satisfactorily on its own. These diets should never become a substitute for actually determining the cause of the anorexia or for overcoming that cause.

Worms. Internal parasites are a constant threat to dogs because of the dog's natural habits and the fact that dogs are so numerous.

Moderate infestations with intestinal worms may go unnoticed unless the dog is eating a deficient diet. When puppies, infested with only moderate amounts of roundworms, are fed diets containing inadequate protein, the injury resulting from the worms is far greater than the injury would be in pups eating an adequate diet. This is because the protein deficiency favors the rapid growth and build-up of the parasites. Every new parasite further decreases the effective value of what little protein the dog does eat. Feeding the infested dog a diet adequate in protein stops the injuries and weight loss being caused by the worms, but will not reverse these effects until the dog is wormed.

Dogs fed adequate levels of energy and protein, on the other hand, show very little adverse effects from even heavy infestations with roundworms, except for being slightly underweight. This is immediately corrected when the dog is wormed.

Dietary considerations should be made from the viewpoint of prevention rather than from the viewpoint of treatment. Dogs fed a diet adequate in protein and energy have far less susceptibility to either roundworms or hookworms, and are much more capable of resisting potential infestations.

The "Fading Puppy". One of the most common causes of newborn puppy deaths is what has been termed the "fading puppy syndrome." Many of the unexplained puppy deaths thrown into this category would undoubtedly go elsewhere if only an accurate diagnosis could be made, Figure 115. Unfortunately, many of these poor little beasts die so radidly that no diagnosis, antemortem or postmortem, can be made.

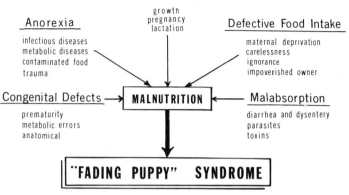

Figure 115. This is a schematic diagram of the things that lead to the so-called "Fading Puppy" syndrome. The complexity of the causes would indicate that many of the diagnoses are missed on these little fellows because they succumb so rapidly.

Whether or not the fading puppy syndrome is actually a distinct disease is questionable, in fact. More likely it is what happens to any puppy that is unprepared (for whatever the reason) to face the rigors of living in the world outside its mother's womb. Whether or not the failure in preparation occurs before or after the pup is born depends on the reason for the puppy's fading, Figure 115.

Successfully saving the fading puppy that can be saved depends on recognizing the condition early enough and instituting proper remedial action. The potential syndrome pup can be recognized early enough only by the *observant* dog feeder. Some of the things to be watched for are:

1. *An absence of the flight reaction.* Normal pups, when taken from their mother and released, will make every effort to scurry back to their mother. The syndrome puppy will not attempt to go anywhere.

2. *Abandonment by the bitch.* A normal puppy is licked and protected by its mother. The syndrome puppy is nosed out of the litter and left in the corner to die.

281

3. *"Slow-motion" activity.* A normal pup doesn't move slowly to do anything. The syndrome puppy makes slow, deliberate movements, almost like a slow-motion picture.

4. *Hypothermia.* Normal puppies in a litter feel warm. They have ample energy to keep their bodies warm. The syndrome puppy hasn't eaten and feels cold to the touch. Pups can survive considerable hypothermia. Never discard a cold, still puppy you think is dead until you drop it from two or three inches above the table onto its belly. A live puppy in deep hypothermia will extend its legs to full extension, either abruptly or gradually.

When you have recognized a puppy that is in the early stages of the fading puppy syndrome, take it away from its mother and littermates, and handle it just as if it were an orphan. Once it has been abandoned by its mother, it is, indeed, just that. The procedure for feeding orphan puppies is discussed in Chapter 13.

The "hurry diarrhea puppy". Every puppy must, eventually, be taught to depend upon something besides milk for its food. This process is called "weaning" and constitutes the changing of a pup's diet from liquid to solid.

Most dog feeders consider weaning to be that instant in time when one takes a pup from its mother. Weaning actually occurs both before and after a pup is separated from its mother. During that time the pup's digestive system is learning to digest the foods it will be eating for the remainder of its life. Like all learning experiences, the steps of weaning must be taken slowly or the pup's digestive system will rebel, and "hurry diarrhea" or dysentery will be the result.

An improperly weaned puppy often finds itself with nothing but strange food to eat, strange people pawing over it, and a strange environment surrounding it. As a result of this physical and psychological trauma, it develops anorexia. As the puppy adjusts emotionally to its new environment, anorexia is followed by ravenous hunger. The hunger becomes so great that the pup will even eat the strange food it hasn't learned to digest yet. If allowed to eat such a diet, the pup begins to suffer from alternating bouts of diarrhea and constipation.

These constant bouts with diarrhea and constipation lead to poor food absorption and injury to the lining of the intestines. Finally, the degenerative changes progress through the entire wall of the intestines. The intestines become sluggish and may stop their movement altogether. Ultimately, there is a disappearance of the intestinal lining. The intestinal wall may become as thin as tissue paper. The pup rapidly becomes emaciated and dehydrated. If the proper remedial actions are not taken instantly, the pup will die.

The secret to preventing hurry diarrhea is a full understanding of the name. The "hurry" is there because somebody tried to push the animal too fast with a food its intestinal tract was not yet ready for. Food, which might be perfectly suitable for an adult, was fed too soon to a weanling.

When *you* have gotten in too big a hurry, and hurry diarrhea is the result, back up and start all over again. Return to the bland, simply digested foods that should be fed to a pup just learning to eat solid food. Then train the pup's intestine to handle each new food in succession. At the same time, you must contend with an irritated, perhaps diseased intestine, which complicates your efforts considerably. There is no "hurry cure" for hurry diarrhea. There's been too much hurry already. What your puppy needs is a little "slow and easy" treatment.

Diseases of Excess

The opposite of a deficiency disease is a disease of excess. These diseases occur when too much of a certain nutrient is eaten by a dog. The most common cause of diseases of excess is simply feeding too much food. The disease produced when a dog eats too much food is called *obesity*.

Obesity. While some dog feeders may not think of obesity as a disease, it is. In fact, it is probably the most common nutritional disease in American dogs. Obesity is the result, pure and simple of eating more calories than are burned.

Dogs have a built-in protection against this disease—a control mechanism in their brains that satisfies their hunger after they have eaten enough calories to meet their daily energy needs. Unfortunately, for the dog anyway, it is possible to upset this control mechanism. By feeding a dog a food that is highly palatable, the dog will eat to satisfy its appetite (which like all appetites is insatiable), and not its hunger.

The only way to remove the excessive fat from a dog's body is by reversing the way it was put on—feeding the dog fewer calories than it will burn for energy. When this is done the dog's body will burn up energy stored in its body to obtain what it needs. Fat is the most

283

efficient source of energy and will be used in the greatest amount whenever energy is needed.

A reduction in caloric intake cannot be accomplished by simply cutting down the quantity of food you feed your dog. Drastic cuts in the quantity of food fed will only lead to deficiencies that pose an even greater threat to the dog than the obesity does . . . deficiencies of proteins, vitamins and minerals. It will also make your dog ravenously hungry! Instead, the fats and carbohydrates, those nutrients that contain the most calories, should be replaced by ingredients that are less digestible and lower in calories.

Dietary formulation: The diet of a dog that is overweight should not contain more than 1400 calories per pound of dry matter. This is approximately 1250 to 1300 calories per pound of dry food or 330 to 350 calories per pound of canned food. Since an average dry commercial food contains approximately 1500 calories per pound, and a ration-type canned food has about 500 to 550, neither will serve as a reducing diet unless they are diluted with a few low-calorie expanders.

Corn grits, farina or rice, when boiled and drained, serve as satisfactory expanders for canned foods. These grains, when cooked, contain only about 270 calories per pound. By blending four cups of cooked grits, farina or rice into every can of food, the resulting mixture will contain about 350 calories per pound of food.

Dry foods can be diluted using a bread cooked from a standard cornbread recipe, but eliminating all the shortening from the recipe. Corn grits, farina or rice grits may be substituted for the corn meal. The batter can be baked in standard muffin tins. (A little shortening must be used to grease the tins to prevent sticking.) By adding 10 muffins to a pound of dry-type food, the caloric density of the new mixture will be approximately 1300 calories per pound.

A far more accurate and convenient way of obtaining a reducing diet is to use a dietary animal food specifically designed for that purpose. This food can be obtained from any veterinarian. It already contains 330 calories per pound and is balanced to provide the correct amount of other nutrients for the dog when fed at that caloric density.

Whatever the food used, the quantity of it that should be fed should be estimated from Table XXVIII. Obtain from the table the number of calories needed to maintain the dog's *optimum weight,*

284

not its actual weight. Using this figure, calculate the amount of the reducing diet required to supply that many calories.

TABLE XXVIII

A Calorie Chart For Overweight Dogs.

If dog's optimum weight is . . .	. . . feed it this many calories each day:	If dog's optimum weight is . . .	. . . feed it this many calories each day:
2.2 lbs	110	18.0 lbs	484
4.4	180	20.0	510
5.0	191	22.0	532
5.5	206	25.0	595
6.0	219	28.5	655
6.5	232	32.0	707
7.0	244	36.0	765
7.5	255	40.0	850
8.0	265	44.0	935
9.0	292	50.0	1063
10.0	315	57.0	1197
11.0	336	66.0	1386
12.0	357	88.0	1848
13.5	390	118.0	2478
15.0	421	150.0	3150
16.5	449		

Feeding procedure: Obviously, portion control is the only method of feeding that can be used during a weight reducing program. No food, treat or supplement, other than the reducing food, can be given during the reduction program. If a dog is more than 10 pounds overweight (i.e.: over its optimum body weight) begin your weight reducing program by feeding the dog only two-thirds the quantity calculated to maintain its optimum weight. Once a reduction in weight begins to occur, the full amount of food should be given. For dogs that are less than 10 pounds overweight begin with the full amount calculated. In dogs weighing under 10 pounds, use the two-thirds guide for any dog that is more than 33 percent of its optimum weight overweight.

It may require several months or longer before a dog reaches its optimum weight. *Do not be discouraged!* Remember, it took longer than a few months to put all that extra weight on. You can't expect to take it off in a few days. In fact, taking off weight too fast can be dangerous to a fat dog.

Once optimum weight has been attained, most dogs will have to be kept on portion-control feeding. Dogs that tend to get fat need to have their intake closely regulated to prevent them from regaining the lost weight.

Other Diseases of Excess. Another common cause of diseases of excess is the unwise use of vitamin and mineral supplements. A dog's cells use most vitamins and minerals at only so fast a rate. Once the cells are using them at the maximum rate, the cells cannot use these vitamins or minerals any faster, regardless of how much of them is present. Any excesses due to too much in the diet will either accumulate in the body or will be excreted by some organ. If the excess nutrients build up so rapidly that the organ cannot keep up, the same substances that are vital in small amounts, may become deadly in excess amounts.

A dog does not eat to meet its need for vitamins, minerals, protein or any other nutrient. It eats to meet its need for calories. If too much vitamins, minerals or protein are fed in relation to the number of calories in a diet, the dog will consume an excess of these nutrients. If too little is fed, the dog will develop a deficiency, yet will not seek out more of the deficient nutrient as long as its energy requirements are being met.

ORGANIC DISEASES

While most ailments do not change a dog's MDR for a nutrient, some diseases drastically reduce the ability of a dog's organs to digest, absorb or properly use the fuel and raw materials contained in the food the dog eats. This means that, since the need for nutrients continues even in a sick dog, the fires may slowly go out and the cells starve, even when the nutrient supply remains identical to what it was before the dog got sick. To avoid such a possibility, you must alter the food you feed a sick dog to enable every organ and cell to get all the energy and nutrients they need. This is much easier said than done!

Diarrhea

Diarrhea is one of the more common ailments seen in dogs. It can be caused by infections, parasites, allergenic foods, toxins, improper feeding, emotional disturbances, or a hundred and one other things.

Regardless of the cause, two things invariably occur in the dog

286

with diarrhea. First, the ability of its intestine to digest and absorb nutrients from the food is reduced. This reduction is in direct proportion to the amount of injury to the intestinal walls. Secondly, any irritation of the intestinal wall causes food to be moved through the gut so rapidly that the intestine doesn't have time to absorb much of the nutrients in the food, even if it were digested.

Diarrhea associated with feeding. In some dogs it is not unusual to notice a mild diarrhea following a change in food. This is particularly true in younger animals. (See section on "hurry diarrhea", earlier in this chapter.) In most instances it persists only until the dog's intestinal tract adjusts to the new food. In rare instances the diarrhea resulting from a change in diet lasts longer and may precipitate more serious forms of diarrhea.

To prevent diarrhea from developing during a dietary change, make the change gradually. (See section on changing the diet in Chapter 10.) A gradual change allows the intestinal tract to make a slow transition from the ingredients and physical characteristics of one food to those of the other. Should diarrhea develop despite the precautions taken, reduce the amount of food being fed by one-half for a day or two. If this fails to correct the upset return to feeding the old food until the stool is normal again. Should the addition of the new food a second time also precipitate diarrhea, it is probable that the new food does not agree with your dog. If a third food is available it may be best to try this alternative rather than to continue to subject your dog to a food that fails to agree with it.

Overfeeding. Another cause of profuse, and sometimes watery, stools is overeating. This happens most often with foods of low digestibility. Such foods usually have low caloric densities and dogs must eat enormous amounts to obtain the energy they need each day. The large amount of indigestible plant materials present in such foods attracts an equally large amount of water, preventing it from being reabsorbed by the intestine. The roughage also acts as a mechanical irritant to the intestine's tender walls, stimulating the walls to increase their movements. This combination of large amounts of indigestible roughage filled with water and the rubbing of an easily irritated intestinal wall can result in sudden, explosive bouts with diarrhea.

Eating non-foods. Garbage, carrion, buried bones, etc. are sometimes eaten by dogs. These items invariably cause a diarrhea because

287

they contain toxic substances, indigestible or irritating materials and, unless vomited shortly after being eaten, they move rapidly through the intestine.

Dogs that repeatedly eat these non-food items may be suffering from hunger. When provided with ample food, containing adequate energy, many of these dogs will stop eating foreign materials. This problem is particularly difficult to manage in puppies from weaning age to about one year. Dogs at this age have a critical need to keep their stomachs filled with food. Their attempts to do so often result in the ingestion of all manner of foreign materials. An additional problem, occurring about the same age, is the cutting of the teeth. This event prompts the dog to chew on almost anything that comes within range of its mouth. This "teething" can result in vast amounts of indigestible materials being swallowed.

Dietary formulation: The food fed during diarrhea should be the most easily digestible and bland food that you can find. For this reason, the large quantity of ingredients of low digestibility contained in dry foods precludes their use in cases of diarrhea. This same fault may be found with those canned foods containing large amounts of meat by-products of low digestibility (cartilage, lungs, udders, etc.). Muscle meat, in large quantity, should also be avoided in severe cases of diarrhea because of the fiber it contains. In such cases, animal protein can be supplied by low-fiber sources like cottage cheese, skim milk, whole eggs or fish. Two medium eggs or four ounces of cottage cheese will supply all of the protein a 20-pound dog needs for 24 hours.

As with any home-made food, a teaspoonful of raw liver should be mixed with every pound of food fed. Fats for energy should be vegetable fats in a highly emulsified form, and should not exceed five percent of the total diet as a general rule. Additional energy can be provided with dextrinized starches such as cornstarch or with simple sugars such as dextrose, lactose or fructose. Sucrose (table sugar) should be avoided since it tends to increase the retention of water and also serves as an energy source for putrefactive bacteria.

Feeding procedure: Any dog developing diarrhea should have all food witheld for at least 24 hours, to allow the dog's intestinal tract to rest. When feeding is resumed, begin with soft or liquid foods. Feedings should be divided into numerous small portions, fed throughout the day. When the frequency and appearance of the stool begins to improve, more-solid food can be offered, but still at frequent intervals through the day.

288

A bland, easily digestible food should be fed for at least 48 hours after normal stools have reappeared. After that, if no recurrence of loose stools follows, the dog's regular feeding schedule can be resumed.

For diarrheas caused by overeating, the obvious remedy is to reduce the amount of food the dog eats. Reducing the quantity of food eaten by simply not feeding as much food is likely to result in your dog not receiving enough energy. The correct method of reducing the food intake, in cases of diarrhea, is to reduce the amount of indigestible materials by replacing them with more digestible ingredients that will contain ample calories.

An immediate, but temporary, remedy, when diarrhea is produced by overeating, is to add three tablespoonsful of corn oil to each pound of dry food being fed. This should result in a rapid reduction in the quantity of food being consumed, a reduction in the quantity of undigested roughage in the intestine, and a consequent reduction in the volume of stool. The addition of corn oil should not be continued for long, however, since the reduction in food consumption may also result in a reduction of nutrient intake. Instead, the diet causing the diarrhea should be discontinued and a diet containing a greater caloric density, yet still balanced for the dog, should replace it.

Diarrhea caused by eating non-foods should be handled the same way as any other irritating or toxic diarrheas.

Vomiting

The dog vomits with ease, seemingly at will, and often without apparent cause. One thing that almost never causes a dog to vomit is eating too fast. Bolting food is the natural way for a dog (see Chapter 10). Eating too much, however, is another matter. The capacity of a pup's stomach to hold food is phenomenal. LIFE Magazine once ran a story about a five-pound puppy that ate a five-pound ham, all but the bone! Such examples, of course, are the ultra-extreme. Adult dogs, on the other hand, can hold only about one and one-half ounces of liquid for each pound the dog weighs. Some dogs may even hold as much as two ounces per pound of body weight, but any quantities above this almost always produce vomition.

Vomiting, like diarrhea, is often seen in puppies. Dogs at this age have the exasperating habit of eating such things as dirt, stones, sand, bedding, toys, foil, paper, socks or almost anything else they can get into their mouths. Vomiting also occurs in adults from eat-

289

ing bones, sour food, garbage, carrion or feces. In these cases, vomiting is a sign of *gastritis*, which is an inflamation of the stomach. Gastritis is rapidly produced by such things as garbage, carrion or caustic chemicals. Most older dogs eventually learn that the foreign materials will make them sick, and stop eating them. The same dogs never seem to realize that garbage, buried bones or sour food may do the same thing—and neither do many owners!

One of the most serious consequences of vomiting is that, once begun, vomiting can persist, even though the cause no longer exists. The usual course in such cases, if uncorrected, follows a characteristic pattern. The dog has a more or less violent seizure of vomition that ordinarily eliminates the causative substance or object. The vomition continues, but in a somewhat less violent nature, giving the appearance that the dog is improving. The loss of fluids and electrolytes in the vomitus causes an imbalance and a noticeable thirst develops. Mild depression develops as well as anorexia, and the vomition begins to become more severe. Thirst is exaggerated, loss of fluids and electrolytes is accelerated and depression becomes marked. The vomition becomes more and more violent and the continued loss of fluids and electrolytes creates a critical imbalance. If the situation is allowed to continue uninterrupted, the dog eventually dies from electrolyte imbalance and dehydration.

Diet formulation: Liquid foods should be fed first. Such things as beef and chicken broth not only supply a few calories, but are excellent for re-establishing many of the electrolyte balances that have been disturbed by vomiting. Within 48 hours it is usually possible to finely chop a little hard-boiled egg into the broth. If this does not cause a return of the vomiting, then a little cottage cheese, some vanilla ice cream or a little toast and milk can be offered. Resumption of the regular diet can commence as soon as the bland foods are tolerated for at least 24 hours.

Feeding procedure: When your dog begins to vomit, withhold all food and water immediately. Empty all water containers and pick them up so that your dog can drink no water voluntarily. Allow the dog to rest quietly. If the cause of the vomition is known to be toxic or caustic substances take your dog to a veterinarian at once. If the cause is unknown, but the attacks continue for longer than two hours, you should take your dog to the veterinarian then. While vomiting can be absolutely harmless, it can also be the sign of grave

290

sickness. Underlying causes may be nowhere near the stomach, but may reflect such dangerous conditions as a twisted bowel, malignant tumors, toxemia, intestinal obstruction, or infections.

Once vomiting has been stopped, you should allow your dog's stomach to rest for at least two to four hours before offering it anything, even water. After that you can place a few ice cubes in a water bowl for your dog to lick. This provides the dog the water it craves, but in amounts small enough to prevent vomiting starting again. When your dog has licked up the cubes, several more can be put down. Eventually the water from the ice cubes will replace the body's shortage lost during vomition and your dog's thirst will disappear. At about the same time you can begin to offer your dog a little liquid nourishment.

Fever

When a dog's temperature goes above normal it means its millions of tiny fires are burning faster. When fires burn faster, they need more fuel. Fuel for the body's fires can come from only two places, the food taken into the body, or from the body itself. Fevers ordinarily occur during illness. Illness is a time when every calorie of fuel is needed by the dog for recovery. Any increase in fuel consumption due to fever should always come from a dog's food rather than from its body.

When a dog has a fever, its fuel intake should be increased by three calories per pound of body weight for each degree of elevated temperature. This can be done quite easily by adding corn oil to the diet. Each teaspoonful of corn oil equals 45 calories. Corn oil also helps to improve the palatability of most foods to which it is added, a decided advantage in dogs with a fever, since their appetite is almost always poor.

Table XXIX provides a quick reference to the amount of corn oil that should be added each day to the food of a dog with a fever.

Fevers of prolonged duration result in a loss of body protein as well as energy consumption. The protein being lost can be replaced by adding three ounces of cottage cheese or one hard-boiled egg to every pound of canned food or every four ounces of dry food.

Feeding procedure: Except for the addition of corn oil, feed a dog with a fever the same as you would feed it when it has no fever. In cases where anorexia accompanies the fever, follow the feeding pro-

291

cedure described earlier in this chapter for dogs with anorexia. The extra calories needed should be taken into consideration when the quantity to be fed is calculated.

The addition of extra energy should begin as soon as the fever is noticed. Any time a fever persists for longer than three days, protein replacement should be started, too. As soon as your dog's temperature has returned to normal the extra energy and protein can be discontinued.

In most cases a fever is caused by an infection from some microorganism. When it is a bacteria, the routine treatment includes a course of antibiotics. The use of antibiotics, especially the oral forms, may also produce a need for a dietary change.

TABLE XXIX

The number of extra calories needed daily by different weight dogs with a fever, and the teaspoonfuls of corn oil that will supply that number of calories. The teaspoonfuls are listed in parenthesis.

weight (lbs)	102.5°	103.5°	104.5°	105.5°
5	15 ($\frac{1}{3}$)	30 ($\frac{2}{3}$)	45 (1)	60 ($1\frac{1}{3}$)
10	30 ($\frac{2}{3}$)	60 ($1\frac{1}{3}$)	90 (2)	120 ($2\frac{2}{3}$)
15	45 (1)	90 (2)	135 (3)	180 (4)
20	60 ($1\frac{1}{3}$)	120 ($2\frac{2}{3}$)	180 (4)	240 ($5\frac{1}{3}$)
25	75 ($1\frac{2}{3}$)	150 ($3\frac{1}{3}$)	225 (5)	300 ($6\frac{2}{3}$)
30	90 (2)	180 (4)	270 (6)	360 (8)
35	105 ($2\frac{1}{3}$)	210 ($4\frac{2}{3}$)	315 (7)	420 ($9\frac{1}{3}$)
40	120 ($2\frac{2}{3}$)	240 ($5\frac{1}{3}$)	360 (8)	480 ($10\frac{2}{3}$)
45	135 (3)	270 (6)	405 (9)	540 (12)
50	150 ($3\frac{1}{3}$)	300 ($6\frac{2}{3}$)	450 (10)	600 ($13\frac{1}{3}$)
55	165 ($3\frac{2}{3}$)	330 ($7\frac{1}{3}$)	495 (11)	660 ($14\frac{2}{3}$)
60	180 (4)	360 (8)	540 (12)	720 (16)
65	195 ($4\frac{1}{3}$)	390 ($8\frac{2}{3}$)	585 (13)	780 ($17\frac{1}{3}$)

Antibiotic Therapy

All of the bacteria in a dog are not harmful. Indeed, some of them are highly beneficial. Among this latter group are the bacteria normally living in a dog's intestines. These bacteria produce several vitamins essential to the dog. The most important of these are the B-complex vitamins. Large amounts of B-complex vitamins utilized by healthy dogs come from the bacteria living within those dog's intestines.

When antibiotic therapy is instituted to help your dog's body destroy a bacterium that is attacking it, many of the innocent, helpful bacteria may also fall victim. With a reduced population of normal bacteria, production of needed vitamins will fall, and vitamin deficiencies may be created. Such deficiencies are more serious during infections since many of the vitamins are essential to healing and tissue repair.

To insure that adequate amounts of vitamins are available to your dog during infections, the water-soluble vitamins should be added to your dog's diet at MDR levels.

Diet formulation: One gram of brewer's yeast for every ten pounds of a dog's weight will replace the B-complex vitamins and serve as an appetite stimulant, as well. Multi-vitamin preparations that contain the equivalent of an MDR for the B-complex vitamins and vitamin C can also be used.

Feeding procedure: The dog being treated with antibiotics is fed the same way it would be fed if it were not being treated with antibiotics.

Injuries

When a dog is injured, its most immediate need will not be food, but whatever emergency treatment is required. Once the business of closing wounds, stopping bleeding or immobilizing broken bones has been attended to, the dog will begin to repair itself almost immediately. How effective this beginning will be depends almost entirely on what the dog was fed *before* it was injured.

Any wound, no matter how small, constitutes a break in the body's defenses against disease. The body mobilizes all of its resources to close the break as rapidly as possible. The healing of a new wound has one of the highest priorities for nutrients of any of the body's activities. The body will provide the wound with large excesses of the raw materials needed for healing, even when the body may be starving for these raw materials. If a dog's diet has failed to provide it with adequate stores before it is injured, the dog's body will be unable to provide the raw materials needed for wound-healing after it is injured.

When broken bones are a part of the injury it is not only unnecessary, but often dangerous, to add calcium and phosphorus supplements or vitamin D. Raw materials for early bone healing do not come from recently-eaten nutrients circulating in the blood. They come from minerals already deposited in the surrounding bone. The use of supplements only threatens to cause an imbalance in the mineral equilibrium of the dog's blood. This may cause the mineral taken from the bone to be used to correct the upset mineral balance, which has an even higher priority than the wound has. To do this denies the healing bone its vitally needed raw materials.

When large amounts of blood are lost, as a result of injury, anemia may be the consequence. This is usually a quickly passing problem, for the dog's body is capable of making blood cells at six times the usual rate when it needs to. The only limitation on the increase of blood cell production is inadequate nutrients to the job.

Diet formulation: Should your dog ever suffer from an injury, the most satisfactory food to feed it is a food similar to that which you would use to feed growing pups. To this growth diet you should add those nutrients needed in extra amounts during wound healing. Ingredients that will supply the extra nutrients are: One hard-boiled egg (including shell) for every 10 pounds of weight, to provide the amino acids needed for wound healing. Two tablespoonsful of orange juice for each three pounds of weight, for vitamin C. One teaspoonful of corn oil for every ten pounds of weight, to supply energy. And, the addition of a half-dozen brewer's yeast tablets, crushed over the food every day, will add the extra B-complex vitamins and improve the dog's appetite enough to eat the other material you've added.

Feeding procedure: The feeding procedure used for an injured dog does not need to be changed as long as the injury does not interfere with the method being used. A dog with a broken leg, for example, probably should be changed from a self-feeder to *ad libitum* until it can get around well enough to walk to and from the feeder.

Feeding During Other Diseases

Prescribing the proper diet for a sick dog requires a veterinarian to make a correct diagnosis of the dog's illness. Once he has accurately determined what ails your dog, the veterinarian can determine if any changes are needed in your dog's diet. Choosing the proper food to feed the dog with a disease requires as much knowledge as choosing the correct drug to use for that disease. In fact, in many diseases, the food is as important as the medicines used.

As an example, suppose you have an older bitch who has won several Bests in Show, produced her share of pups, and now is retired to the leisure of barking at the postman and sitting on laps. You've allowed her to become just a little too fat because she loves sweets

294

and you love her. One morning you notice she seeems overtired when she returns from her morning constitutional. She has a little cough, too. At first you're not too worried. But, every day it seems to get a little worse. Finally you take her to your veterinarian for a check-up. After an examination he advises you that the old gal is developing congestive heart failure, a common disease among older dogs. Although ultimately fatal, he explains, with proper care your dog's life span can be extended by several years and she can remain comfortable the rest of her life—with the right food.

Just as with human beings, one of the most important steps in the management of congestive heart failure in dogs is a low-salt diet. The reason for the success of restricting salt in dogs with heart failure is due to the altered metabolism of sodium in dogs with the disease. Healthy dogs are able to excrete the sodium they do not need through their kidneys. Dogs with heart failure are unable to excrete this sodium, and it accumulates within their bodies. When sodium accumulates, water accumulates with it, and congestion and edema develop. By restricting sodium to the least amount that the dog needs, the accumulation of sodium is stopped and the sodium already accumulated will gradually be excreted. To prevent re-accumulation, the dog must be fed a diet low in sodium for the rest of its life.

Feeding a low-sodium diet to dogs with heart failure *does not cure* the disease. The only thing that will do that is to give the dog a new heart. Sodium restriction relieves some of the stress placed on the failing heart by the sodium and water that is accumulating in the body.

Numerous other diseases respond favorably to dietary management. Some of the more important of these are Chronic Interstitial Nephritis, hepatitis, Diabetes Mellitus, pancreatitis, food-induced allergy, chronic enteritis, acute enteritis and chronic colitis. Any time your veterinarian makes a diagnosis of disease you should discuss with him the proper dietary program he recommends for your dog's individual problem.

PART V

FACT AND FANCY

Chapter 20

Fact and Fancy

NOWHERE in the art of raising dogs has there grown a greater accumulation of mis-information than there has in the area of dog feeding. This mis-information has been perpetuated from one generation of dog feeders to the next. The more imaginative feeders have added their own fallacies along the way, until today there is almost as much fancy in print about dog feeding as there is fact. This chapter examines many of the old wives' tales that are always swapped between the novice dog feeder and the experienced one. It is hoped that this chapter will help *both* of these groups to correct any misconceptions they may currently hold about how to properly feed their dog.

"Raw meat causes a dog to be vicious."
Fancy! There is no basis in truth in the belief that raw meat will make a dog vicious. In fact, when meat is used in a dog's diet it is probably more desirable to feed it raw, since meat is more digestible in that form. A dog *is* more likely to be aggressive when defending a bone or chunk of raw meat it is eating. But this is related more to the palatability of the food the dog is defending than to the fact that it is raw. Most children are more possessive of a bowl of ice cream than they are a bowl of spinach, too!

"Raw meat causes worms."
Fact and Fancy. Most worms, like the roundworm and the hook-

299

worm, come from eggs passed in the stool. It is not likely that any of these eggs, or the larvae that hatch from them, will come into contact with raw meat. Tapeworms and thorny headed worms, however, can be obtained by eating wild animals raw. They can also be obtained from the raw viscera of home-killed sheep and cows.

"Starches cannot be digested by dogs."

Fancy! While raw starches are poorly digested by the dog, cooking the starch until it has dextrinized makes it readily available to the dog. Almost all commercial dog foods now contain cooked starches to insure that this nutrient is well utilized by a dog.

'Pork should never be fed to a dog."

Fancy. The nutritional value of the protein in pork is as good as that of beef and horsemeat. Pork fat (lard) is far better than beef fat (tallow) for supplying essential fatty acids to the dog. Beef tallow contains two percent linoleic, while lard contains 12 percent. Pork liver and kidney are both equal to, or better than, those of beef and horse. The only precaution a dog feeder should take when feeding pork or pork by-products is to be sure the muscle meat is well-cooked to prevent the possibility of infection with the disease parasite *Trichina spiralis*, which causes Trichinosis.

"Dogs need a variety of foods to keep them healthy and eating."

Fancy. Dogs thrive on monotony. They are creatures of habit by nature. Dogs can live their entire life eating only one kind of food, and apparently do so happily and healthily. In a few cases, where dogs appear to insist that their food be changed constantly to keep them eating, they have usually been habituated by an overindulgent owner to eat such a variety rather than by their own natural preferences. Even so, the reason these animals seem so reluctant to eat the same food day after day is because they don't want to make any change in their regular routine—which in this case is continuous change.

"Raw eggs make a dog's coat shiny."

Fancy. This is one of the oldest wives' tales circulating in dog feeding circles. The white of an egg is almost indigestible when raw. More important, raw egg white combines with an essential vitamin, Biotin, and makes it unavailable to the dog. In fact, scientists who want to experimentally produce a Biotin deficiency in a dog feed it raw egg whites! One of the signs of Biotin deficiency is an unhealthy condition of the skin, not a shiny one. Whole eggs can be one of the most valuable sources of protein a dog can get, but only when they are cooked. The only way a *raw* egg can make a dog's coat shiny is when it is smeared all over it.

"Bacon fat makes a dog's coat shiny."

Fact. Bacon fat will turn a dry haircoat into a shiny one—if the dog needs energy or essential fatty acids. Dry, dull haircoats are caused by many things, improper nutrition being only one. Probably the most common nutritional fault causing a dry, dull haircoat is a deficiency of total energy in the diet. The addition of bacon fat provides the extra energy the dog needs. Any fat, such as corn oil or beef tallow, would serve the same purpose. By adding the extra energy the dog needs, the haircoat's shine is restored. Often the success seen with expensive fatty acid supplements and haircoat conditioners is due to this same thing, and not to the "miracle" ingredients they contain. When fatty acids are required, bacon fat and corn oil (but not beef tallow) will also supply these.

"Dogs are able to balance their own diets."

Fancy. Dogs that are allowed to choose their own diet, from the ingredients in a balanced food, will not grow correctly. Those fed a single food, already made up from the same ingredients in balanced form, will grow normally. When offered a selection of mixed-ingredient diets, dogs will not always choose the diet that is most nourishing. Instead, they will choose the one they like the best. Dogs are very much like children in this regard. If given the choice, a child will eat ice cream three times a day rather than a balanced diet they don't like as well.

"Any dog food sold commercially is required to be nourishing for a dog."

Fancy. Simply because a dog food is put into a grocery store and sold does not mean it has been tested by its manufacturer to insure that it is adequate for a dog. In fact, it doesn't even guarantee it was made by a formula designed to be nourishing for a dog. All-meat dog foods can actually be dangerous for a dog when fed as the only diet. Some other commercial foods, while perhaps not as insidious, provide

301

little or no nourishment for the dog. These foods are made and sold by people, who either lack knowledge or concern about the dogs that are providing them a living.

"Dogs, especially adults, should not drink milk."
Fancy. Thousands of dogs drink milk every day without ill effect. While it may be true that some dogs are unable to tolerate milk, this is an individual quirk, and is not representative of all dogs. The reason for certain individuals' intolerance to milk can usually be discovered, if one wishes to take the time. For the many dogs that can tolerate milk, it is one of the better protein and calcium sources available to the dog feeder.

"Too many fats and starches in summer will cause eczema."
Fancy. The word eczema means "boiling out." Early dog feeders thought that the increase in skin diseases seen in hot weather was the result of fats and starches boiling out of the blood, through the skin, causing the disease. Some diseases of the skin do have a nutritional origin, but they have nothing to do with the feeding of fats and starches during the summer ... or during any other season, for that matter.

"Dogs tend to overeat and get fat naturally."
Fancy. This is a dog feeding myth of relatively recent origin. It has sprouted as the problem of fat pet dogs has increased. It is an excellent way for lazy pet owners to blame their dog's obesity on something besides themselves, which is where it invariably belongs. *Dogs eat to meet their caloric requirement.* This means they will eat only to replace the energy they burn up every day. Most dogs will consume little excess to store as fat. Unfortunately, the foremost concern of most dog food manufacturers is not nourishment, but palatability. Only by making a food that a dog eats ravenously can makers be assured of resales of their food. Highly palatable foods, that thwart the dog's built-in protection against becoming fat, exist because dog feeders buy them. Then, they feed these over-palatable foods in quantities far in excess of the dog's needs, simply because the dog will eat that much. If dog feeders would become more con-

302

cerned about what a food did for his dog's health, than for its palate, most dog food makers would, too!

"Candy, peanuts and chocolate make a dog sick."

Fancy. Such high-calorie, fat and carbohydrate foods are no more likely to make a dog sick than they are to make a child sick. Obviously, if either eats too much of any of these foods they are probably going to suffer the consequences. The real problem with feeding such treats to a dog is the fact that they fill a dog up, even make it fat, without providing it with adequate, nourishing food intake.

"Dogs do not need bones to chew."

Fact. Dogs fed a balanced diet can live perfectly well without any bones to eat. In fact, they may even live better without some bones, like rib, steak and chop bones. These bones, as well as those of birds, splinter and can lead to serious consequences. The calcium and phosphorus, once supplied by bones in the wild dog's diet, are now provided by ground mineral products like dicalcium phosphate and calcium carbonate, or ground bone meal. The only useful purpose bones serve today is to keep the tartar accumulations scraped away from the dog's teeth and to give the dog a little recreation.

"Onions and garlic added to a dog's food will help prevent worms."

Fancy. About the only thing onions and garlic do for a dog is to give it bad breath! Huge quantities of onions have been fed to dogs with roundworms without any effect whatsoever. The only active substance in either of these two foods that could possibly have any effect on worms is arsenic, and about all there is in either is just enough to smell.

"Purebred dogs require a special diet."

Fancy. All dogs need an adequate, balanced diet, regardless of their breed or background. The only thing that needs to vary between dogs' diets is the quantity. The quantity of food a dog eats depends on how many calories it needs. How many calories it needs is determined by its age, size and activity. The breed of a dog is a factor only to the degree that it influences the size of the dog, and in fact a 60-pound Shepherd and a 60-pound Pointer are more likely to eat the same quantity than are a 60-pound Shepherd and an 80-pound Shepherd.

"A lump of sulfur in a dog's water bowl prevents worms."

Fancy. Sulfur is totally insoluble in water. A block of wood the same shape and size as the lump of sulfur would probably do as much good as a worm preventer.

"Dogs are meat eaters."

Fact. So are you! Dog feeders eat meat, but we don't limit our diet to meat alone. And, neither do dogs, not even wild ones, if they are going to stay healthy. The fact that dogs are called "carnivores" merely means that they belong to the zoological order of animals known as "Carnivora". Some members of that same order, the binturong and kinkajou, actually eat almost nothing but fruits. Others eat about half and half, animal and plant, like the raccoons, bears and skunks. Only cats, mink and weasels limit their food exclusively to the organs and flesh of the animals they kill. The statement that dogs are meat eaters tells only half the story. Unless you know about the other half, you cannot hope to feed your dog correctly.

"Meat is a good diet for a dog."

Fancy. Meat is a good *food* for a dog . . . it is never a good diet for any animal. A dog which is forced to eat nothing but meat will die. Meat is neither balanced nor adequate for a dog. It is particularly deficient in calcium, phosphorus, copper and cobalt-minerals essential to bone growth and blood formation. Meat supplies a dog with a very high quality protein and, in proper amounts, becomes a valuable food in any dog's diet. Alone, or when added in excess of 10 to 25 percent to mixtures of balanced foods, meat will lead to multiple deficiencies. In some instances, it may even lead to the dog's death.

"Dogs normally skip a meal or two, now and then."

Fancy. No healthy dog skips a meal—now, then or ever! When a dog refuses to eat there is a definite reason for it. Always find the cause. It may be as simple as the fact that your dog was next door and mooched supper from the neighbors, and is just not hungry any more. It may be a female in heat down the block. Or, it may indicate the dog has something stuck in its mouth or throat, has a fever or even worse. Or, it may be a thousand other things. A missed meal is one of the commonest ways a dog feeder can tell that something is wrong with his dog, because 100 times out of 100 there's a reason when a meal is missed.

"Puppies always pull a bitch down during nursing."

Fancy. While this may be the thing that most often happens, it is neither normal nor necessary. It is certainly not desirable. When properly fed, a bitch should weigh about the same when she weans her pups as she did when she conceived them. The biggest single fault dog feeders make when feeding a nursing bitch is failing to provide her with enough digestible energy. If sufficient energy and balanced nutrients are provided to the nursing bitch she will not lose any weight during the nursing process.

"Dogs should be fed meat raw."

Fact. Meat is usually more digestible to a dog when it is in its raw form. The degree of digestibility lost when meat is cooked is small, however. Many forms of meat are fed to dogs in the cooked form without causing any noticeable loss to the dog. If a choice between raw and cooked can be made, the raw form is usually the more desirable. The one exception to this rule is fresh pork which, while more digestible raw, should be fed cooked to destroy any of the *Trichina* parasites present.

"Dogs should be fed all foods raw."

Fancy. While some foods in a dog's diet are more desirable in the raw form, some are likewise more desirable in the cooked form. This is particularly true of carbohydrates from grains. Starches, when cooked, are made 25 percent more available to a dog. Cooking starches also reduces digestive upsets commonly seen with raw grains.

"Too much salt causes intestinal gas in dogs."

Fancy. The quantity of salt in dog foods, at least in the amount commonly used, does nothing to affect the formation of gas in a dog's intestine. Gas is produced in the intestines of all mammals by bacteria acting on the proteins and carbohydrates in the mammal's food. Most of this gas is absorbed into the bloodstream and is breathed out through the lungs. Diets containing high levels of protein or large amounts of undigestible carbohydrates will cause so

305

much gas to be produced that it cannot all be absorbed. Some gas may then be expelled through the rectum. The high protein foods are especially obnoxious since the gases they produce have the most offensive odors. Enforced exercise may help control the gas, but does not always eliminate it.

"Dogs will eat grass even when eating a balanced diet."

Fact. Why dogs eat grass is unknown. Dogs will eat grass regardless of the nature of their diet, balanced or not. Grass-eating seems many times to be associated with an upset stomach and many times the grass appears to precipitate a siege of vomiting. It is quite possible that a blade of grass, lodged in the lower part of the throat, would cause a dog to vomit. In fact, most dogs can almost vomit at will. This latter behavior is a trait dogs have retained from ancestors who bolted large chunks of food and then vomited them back up to re-eat them in a more secluded, less dangerous place.

"Canned foods produce tartar on a dog's teeth."

Fancy: All foods produce tartar on a dog's teeth. Foods having a consistency harder than soft canned foods are better able to keep it scraped away, however. Tartar starts as a soft deposit on the teeth at the gums. This soft deposit is called plaque. Dry foods (fed dry), bones and hard biscuits will scrape most of this plaque away before it becomes hardened. Once hardened into tartar, it will be necessary to have a veterinarian scale the tartar from the teeth.

"Sugar produces an upset stomach in dogs."

Fact. Certain types of sugars will produce an intestinal upset in many dogs. The one most often guilty is sucrose (ordinary table sugar), but lactose (milk sugar) and maltose (starch sugar) have also been incriminated. Most dogs can tolerate small amounts of any of these sugars, but when the quantity in the diet becomes too high they invariably produce vomition or diarrhea. Except for the soft-moist foods, few dog foods contain sucrose. The maltose and fructose in dry foods is not high enough to be of consequence. Only lactose is fed in any great quantity to most dogs, and with a dog that cannot tolerate it, the dog feeder quickly learns not to feed it milk.

APPENDICES

Appendix A

Formulating a Homemade Diet

THE formulation of an adequate, balanced diet has always been difficult, if not impossible, for many dog feeders. The jumble of unfamiliar terms like gram, milligram, calorie, crude analysis or protein-calorie ratio; or the labor of calculating percentages, grams per pound, etc. has discouraged many a dog feeder from taking the time and effort to properly "build" a diet. As a consequence, many dog feeders have simply thrown together a concoction which they, themselves, feared was inadequate, but didn't know what else to do about it.

Diet formulation can be made easier for everyone if they have a clear understanding of what they are trying to accomplish. A little imaginary game may help illustrate the goal of diet formulation.

Pretend you have a large bowl. The object of the game is to fill your bowl with the correct number of different colored marbles. To do this you have sacks containing various combinations of colors and numbers of marbles. What each sack contains is marked on a tag in the sack. You can choose as many of any sack as you wish. But, for each sack you choose, you must dump its entire contents into the bowl. The person who fills his bowl closest to the correct number of all colors, wins.

If each sack of marbles was an ingredient, and each color of marble was a nutrient in that ingredient, and the correct number of different colored marbles was the nutrient requirements of a dog, then your bowl filled with the correct number and colors of marbles

309

would be a balanced, adequate diet, and your dog will be the winner. The first prize will be good health and a long life!

Whether it is a mixture of a dozen natural ingredients or simply a combination of two commercial dog foods, *the proper formulation of the diet is the most essential step in a dog feeder's success.* For this reason, I have developed a simplified procedure for formulating diets for a dog. This procedure is based on the marble game just described. It is not intended to make a nutritionist out of anyone, but merely to reduce the effort in diet formulation to the barest essentials that will still produce a satisfactory end product. It eliminates all references to grams, milligrams, percentages, etc., and replaces them with a *Nutrient Index Number.* The Nutrient Index Number tells you the number of a given color of marbles (quantity of that nutrient) in the sack (in the ingredient).

The number of marbles you add to your bowl not only depends on how many marbles are in a sack, but on how many of those sacks you add. The number of sacks added is represented by a *conversion constant.* The conversion constants for different quantities of ingredients, commonly used in diet formulation, are listed in Table A-I.

TABLE A-I

The conversion constants to be used for various quantities of ingredients when formulating a diet by the plan in this book.

If this quantity is used:	*Multiply nutrient index number by:*
1 pound	4.50
½ pound	2.25
¼ pound	1.13
1 ounce	0.28
½ ounce	0.14
¼ ounce	0.07

To determine how much of a nutrient you are adding to a diet when you add a certain quantity of an ingredient, multiply the Nutrient Index Number of that ingredient by the correct conversion constant for the quantity of ingredient being added.

Another simplification in the formulation procedure is the use of a hypothetical dog whose nutrient requirements have also been converted to Nutrient Index Numbers. The hypothetical dog chosen

310

was a 25-pound, adult male, whose Nutrient Index Numbers for a 24-hour period are listed in Table A-II .

TABLE A-II

Nutrient Index Numbers for the hypothetical dog for 24 hours.

Nutrient	Index Number	Nutrient	Index Number
calories	850	magnesium	125
protein	50	vitamin A	1125
fat	30	vitamin D	75
carbohydrates	80	thiamine	0.08
calcium	3000	folic acid	0.05
phosphorus	2500	riboflavin	0.50
iron	15	pyridoxine	0.25
sodium	1500	pantothenic acid	0.575
potassium	2500	niacin	2.75

In addition, the 850 calories should be divided between the three major nutrients as follows: Protein, 25% (225 cals); fat, 30% (270 cals); and carbohydrates, 45% (360 cals).

To play the game of diet formulation, choose any ingredient you wish and multiply its Nutrient Index Numbers by the conversion constant appropriate for that quantity being used. Do the same for each ingredient you use, until all have been figured. Then, total the Nutrient Index Numbers for each nutrient and compare your results with the goal in Table A-II. A hint to helping you get a good score is to keep a running total as you go along, keeping in mind that you can choose as many or as few ingredients, and as much or as little of each, as you wish. Just remember that it should all end up equal to the Nutrient Index Numbers for the hypothetical dog.

Homemade diets do not need to be elaborate—all they need to be is adequate and balanced. But, to insure that *any* diet is adequate and balanced, it must be formulated with that idea in mind.

As an example, I have taken an actual formulation of a diet and described how I made each step.

I first sketched out a little form on a ruled sheet of paper somewhat like the one in figure A-I, before all the writing was put in. Using this little chart simplifies the calculations, at least for me, anyway. Because I am such a poor mathematician, I use a chart every time. If you are more adept at math, you may be able to eliminate the chart after you've become familiar with the procedure.

TABLE A-1

INGREDIENT	AMT	CONV	CALS	PROT	FAT	CALC	PHOS	VIT. A
Hamburger	¼ lb	1.13	411	25	34	10	178	0
Hard boiled egg	2 oz	0.56	91	7	6	30	115	660
Rice (dry)	¼ lb	1.13	409	8.5	0.3	27	154	40
Raw liver	½ oz	0.14	19	2.7	0.4	1	50	2100
TOTALS	10½ oz		930	43.2	40.7	68	497	2760
Needed by Hypoth. Dog			850	50	30	3000	2500	1125
Differences			+80	−6.8	+10.7	−2932	−2003	+1635
Dicalc. Phosphate	½ oz	0.14	0	0	0	3220	2520	0
FINAL DIET	11 oz		+80	−6.8	+10.7	+288	+517	+1635

Add only enough vitamin/mineral supplement that will meet dog's MDR

Figure A-1. A handy chart for recording the data obtained while formulating a homemade diet can be sketched like this one, without the writing.

312

The initial ingredients I like to get down on my chart are those that will supply the protein. The primary protein source should be animal in nature and should supply about 50 percent of the proteins in the diet. For my example, I chose as my primary protein source, cooked hamburger. I started with $\frac{1}{2}$ pound.

STEP 1. The conversion factor for $\frac{1}{2}$ pound is 2.25 (Table A-I). I multiplied 2.25 times each of the Nutrient Index Numbers for hamburger, listed in Appendix B. The answers were recorded on the chart as they were calculated. I could quickly see that $\frac{1}{2}$ pound of hamburger supplied almost all the calories needed in the entire diet. This was far too many calories for the primary protein source to supply. Similarly, I discovered that $\frac{1}{2}$ pound of hamburger supplied almost two times the amount of fat needed by the hypothetical dog. I decided to reject the $\frac{1}{2}$ pound of hamburger and to try somewhat less.

STEP 1. (repeated) I started all over again, this time using only $\frac{1}{4}$ pound of hamburger. This quantity of hamburger was more satisfactory.

STEP 2. While the distribution of nutrients in $\frac{1}{4}$ pound of hamburger was much better, it still left the diet a little shy in protein. One of the best ingredients for adding a small amount of protein, without adding much else, is whole egg. So I tried adding a peeled, hard-boiled egg to see what it would do. A whole egg weighs about two ounces. The conversion constant for one ounce is 0.28. Consequently, the conversion constant for two ounces is 0.56 (twice that for one ounce). The addition of the egg brought the Nutrient Index Number of the protein ($25 + 7 = 32$) pretty close to the 50 that I wanted. Since it is always a good idea to leave a little room for expansion this early in the game, I decided to leave the protein alone for awhile. Remember, too, that I had to save a little room for the protein from the other ingredients I would be using to supply calories and bulk.

STEP 3. I next turned my attention to making sure that adequate calories were included in the diet. Calories in a dog's diet can be supplied by either fats or carbohydrates. Checking my chart, I could see that the diet already had about all of the fat that it needed ($34 + 6 = 40$). So, I turned to carbohydrates to furnish the additional energy I needed. For my example I chose rice. But, any of the cereal grains, or even pure corn starch, could have been used as well.

Since I already had 502 calories formulated ($411 + 91 = 502$),

313

all I needed was about 350 more. By using a little *reverse* calculation, I was able to determine the quantity of rice that would provide 350 calories. One-fourth-pound of rice will supply 409 calories. That is close enough for the type of calculations used in diet formulation of calories. Now I added the rest of the Nutrient Index Numbers for a $1/4$ pound of rice to my chart.

STEP 4. *Every* homemade diet formulated from natural ingredients should have a small amount of raw, chopped liver added to it. This usually does not need to exceed one ounce for every pound of food prepared. For my example I felt $1/2$ ounce would be ample. I checked my guess by multiplying all of liver's Index Numbers by 0.14, the conversion constant for $1/2$ ounce, and adding the answers to the subtotals on my chart.

STEP 5. Next I totaled the Nutrient Index Numbers for each nutrient to see how close I had come to meeting the hypothetical dog's requirements.

STEP 6. None of the differences in the major nutrients were large enough to be concerned about. The glaring deficiency of calcium and phosphorus had to be corrected, however, before the diet could be fed.

STEP 7. A convenient ingredient to increase and balance calcium and phosphorus, both in homemade as well as commercial diets, is dicalcium phosphate. It contains a ratio of calcium to phosphorus identical to that found in natural bone. By again using reverse calculations I determined how much dicalcium phosphate I needed to bring the amount of calcium in the diet up to the amount required by the hypothetical dog.

STEP 8. A similar step could have been taken for each and every vitamin and mineral in the diet. A far more rapid and satisfactory approach was to add a vitamin and a trace mineral supplement to the diet in the correct amounts to supply the MDR of those nutrients for a 25-pound dog (see Tables II and III, Chapter 4). The quantities of nutrients contained in all such supplements are required to be printed on the label. Using simple math and these label figures, the correct amount of any supplement can be calculated.

Once a formulation has been calculated for the hypothetical dog, it can be adjusted for any size or number of dogs. Since the hypothetical dog weighs 25 pounds, all that is needed to make an adjustment is to change the quantities of ingredients in the formulation

314

by multiples or fractions of 25. In other words, if your dog weighs 50 pounds, that's twice 25, so double the formulation. If your dog weighs 2.5 pounds, that's one-tenth of 25, so divide the formulation by 10, or, multiply the formulation by 0.1 if you're decimal oriented. Likewise, if your dog weighs 52.5 pounds, multiply the formulation by 2.1.

If you have five 5-pound dogs, that's 25 pounds worth of dogs, and you can make the formulation just as it is and divide it into five equal portions among your five dogs. If you have five 50-pound dogs, that's 250 pounds worth of dogs, or 10 times 25, so multiply the numbers in the formulation by 10 and split the results five ways.

If you are a scholar and desire the ultimate in accuracy, you can determine the exact change needed in the formulation by using the dog's caloric intake. Refer to the standard calorie chart in Table XVI, Chapter 12 and get the exact calorie needs for dogs with weights that differ from 25 pounds. Determine what percentage the calories in the formulated diet are, of the calories needed by your dog. Multiply the quantities in the formulation by that percentage figure.

For example: From Table XVI we find that a 50-pound dog needs 27 calories per pound, or 1350 calories (50 lbs $\times$ 27 cals) every day. The diet I formulated earlier contains 930 calories. 1350 calories is 145 percent of 930, so multiply the numbers of the formulation by 145 percent to make a diet for your 50-pound dog. This number is a little smaller than when multiples of 25 are used. This is because a dog requires fewer and fewer calories per pound of body weight as it becomes larger and larger in size.

315

Appendix B

Common Household Items That Can Be Used for Formulating Diets

HOMEMADE diets do not need to be elaborate. All they need to be is balanced and acceptable by the dog. Appendix B lists a number of common household foods that can be used to make highly satisfactory homemade diets. All of the foods listed have had their content converted to their Nutrient Index Number and can be used directly from the table to formulate a diet described in Appendix A.

APPENDIX B

Protein Sources

INGREDIENT	Protein	Fat	Carbohydrate	Calcium	Phosphorus	Sodium	Potassium	Vitamin A	Niacin	Riboflavin	Thiamine	Calories	REMARKS
Bacon, fried	25.0	55.0	1.0	25	255	2400	390	0	4.8	.34	.48	607	4 slices = 1 ounce
Bologna	14.8	15.9	3.6	9	112	1300	230	0	2.6	.22	.18	221	1" slice = 7 ounces
Brains	10.4	8.6	0.8	16	330	150	340	0	4.4	.26	.23	125	
Brewer's Yeast	33.2	1.1	37.9	158	1823	135	1797	0	33.3	4.10	11.00	278	4 tblsp. = 1 ounce
Buttermilk, fluid	3.5	0.1	5.1	118	93	130	140	0	0.1	.18	.04	36	1 cup = 8 ounces
Cheddar Cheese (Proc.)	23.2	29.9	2.0	673	787	1500	80	0	0	.41	.02	370	
Chicken (dk. mt.)	28.0	6.3	0	13	229	86	321	150	5.6	.23	.07	176	
Chicken (lt. mt.)	31.6	3.4	0	11	218	50	320	60	11.6	.09	.05	166	
Chuck Roast	26.0	22.0	0	11	117	51	360	0	4.1	.20	.05	309	
Cottage Cheese	19.5	0.5	2.0	96	189	290	72	20	.1	.28	.02	95	
Egg, hard-boiled	12.9	11.5	.9	54	205	122	129	1180	0.1	.28	.09	163	1 egg = 2 ounces
Frankfurter	14.0	20.0	2.0	6	49	1100	220	0	2.5	.20	.16	248	1 frank = 2 ounces

APPENDIX B

Protein Sources

INGREDIENT	Protein	Fat	Carbohydrate	Calcium	Phosphorus	Sodium	Potassium	Vitamin A	Niacin	Riboflavin	Thiamine	Calories	REMARKS
Haddock, cooked	18.7	5.5	7.0	18	182	61	304	330	2.6	.07	.04	158	
Halibut, cooked	26.2	7.8	0	14	267	134	525	640	10.5	.28	.06	182	
Ham, baked	23.0	33.0	0.4	10	166	1100	340	0	4.2	.22	.54	397	
Hamburger, braised	22.0	30.0	0	9	158	107	345	0	4.8	.21	.08	364	
Heart, beef, raw	16.9	3.7	0.7	9	203	90	160	30	7.8	.88	.58	108	
Horsemeat	19.5	12.5	0.5	10	160								
Kidney, beef, raw	15.0	8.1	0.9	9	221	210	310	1150	6.4	2.55	.37	141	
Kidney, pork	16.3	3.6	1.1	11	218	115	178	130	9.8	1.73	.58	106	
Lamb, leg of, roasted	24.0	19.0	0	10	257	70	290	0	5.1	.25	.14	274	
Liver, beef, raw	19.7	3.2	6.0	7	358	110	380	15,000	13.7	3.33	.26	136	
Liver, pork, raw	19.7	4.8	1.7	10	362	77	350	14,200	16.7	2.98	.40	134	
Milk, goat's, fluid	3.3	4.0	4.6	129	106	34	180	160	.3	.11	.04	67	1 cup = 8 ounces

318

APPENDIX B

Protein Sources

INGREDIENT	Protein	Fat	Carbohydrate	Calcium	Phosphorus	Sodium	Potassium	Vitamin A	Niacin	Riboflavin	Thiamine	Calories	REMARKS
Milk, non-fat, dry	35.6	1.0	52.0	1300	1030	528	1130	40	.9	1.78	.35	362	4 tblsp. = 1 ounce
Milk, whole, fluid	3.5	3.9	4.9	118	93	50	140	160	.1	.17	.04	68	1 cup = 8 ounces
Peanuts	26.9	44.2	23.6	74	393	460	700	0	17.2	.13	.30	559	1 cup = 5 ounces
Round Steak	27.0	13.0	0	11	224	68	400	0	5.5	.22	.08	233	
Sardines	25.7	11.0	1.2	386	586	510	560	220	4.8	.25	.02	214	
Soybeans, dried	34.9	18.1	34.8	227	586	4	190	110	2.3	.31	1.07	331	1 cup = 7 ounces
Soybean Flour	42.5	6.5	37.2	244	610	1	1700	110	2.6	.34	.82	264	1 cup = 2½ ounces
Stew Meat	25.0	21.0	0	11	124	60	355	0	4.6	.19	.05	296	
Tongue, beef	16.4	15.0	0.4	9	187	100	260	0	5.0	.29	.12	207	
Tuna Fish, drained canned	29.0	8.2	0	8	351	800	240	80	12.8	.12	.05	198	

319

APPENDIX B

Carbohydrate Sources

INGREDIENT	Protein	Fat	Carbohydrate	Calcium	Phosphorus	Sodium	Potassium	Vitamin A	Niacin	Riboflavin	Thiamine	Calories	REMARKS
Beans, kidney, can	5.7	0.4	16.4	40	124	3	264	0	.8	.05	.05	90	
Biscuits	7.4	17.0	45.8	121	175	626	117	0	1.8	.21	.21	369	1 med. biscuit = 1 ounce
Bread, white	8.5	3.2	51.8	79	92	640	180	0	2.3	.17	0.24	275	1 slice = ¾ ounce
Brewer's Yeast	33.2	1.1	37.9	158	1823	135	1797	0	33.3	4.10	11.00	278	4 tblsp = 1 ounce
Corn, canned	2.0	0.5	16.1	4	51	205	200	200	.9	.05	.03	67	
Corn Bread	6.7	4.7	36.6	139	155	628	157	130	.6	.19	0.17	219	1 muffin = 1 ounce +
Corn Flakes	8.1	0.4	85.0	11	58	660	160	0	2.1	.08	0.41	385	1 cup = 1 ounce
Farina, cooked	1.3	0.1	9.1	3	13	11	10	0	.4	.03	.04	44	1 cup = 7½ ounces
Macaroni, dry	12.8	1.4	76.5	22	165	1	160	0	6.0	.37	0.88	377	1 cup = 4 ounces
Noodles, cooked	2.2	0.6	12.8	4	35	2	44	30	1.2	.08	0.14	67	1 cup = 2 ounces
Pancakes	6.8	9.2	26.6	158	154	451	156	200	.8	.23	0.18	218	4" diam. cake = 1 ounce
Potatoes, sweet	1.8	0.7	27.9	30	49	4	530	7700	.6	.06	.09	123	

320

APPENDIX B

Carbohydrate Sources

INGREDIENT	Protein	Fat	Carbohydrate	Calcium	Phosphorus	Sodium	Potassium	Vitamin A	Niacin	Riboflavin	Thiamine	Calories	REMARKS
Potatoes, white, raw	2.1	0.1	17.1	7	53	3	407	0	1.5	.04	.10	76	
Rice, boiled, drained	2.0	0.1	24.2	10	28	374	28	0	1.0	.10	.11	109	
Rice, dried	76.	0.3	79.4	24	136	2	130	0	1.6	.03	.07	362	1 cup=6 ounces
Soybeans, dried	34.9	18.1	34.8	227	586	4	1900	110	2.3	.31	1.07	331	
Soybean Flour	42.5	6.5	37.2	244	610	1	1700	110	2.6	.34	.82	264	
Wheat Flakes	10.2	1.6	80.5	41	309	1,032	370	0	4.9	.14	.64	354	

APPENDIX B

Fat Sources

INGREDIENT	Protein	Fat	Carbohydrate	Calcium	Phosphorus	Sodium	Potassium	Vitamin A	Niacin	Riboflavin	Thiamine	Calories	REMARKS
Bacon, fried	25.0	55.0	1.0	25	255	2400	390	0	4.8	.34	.48	607	4 slices=1 ounce
Butter	0.6	81.0	0.4	20	16	980	23	3300	0.1	.15	.03	716	2 tblsp=1 ounce
Cheddar Cheese	23.2	29.9	2.0	673	787	1500	80	0	0	.41	.02	370	
Corn Oil	0	100	0	0	0	0.2	0.1	0	0	0	0	884	2 tblsp=1 ounce
Cream, half & half	3.2	11.7	4.6	108	85	46	129	480	.1	.16	.03	134	
Lard	0	100	0	0	0	0.3	0.2	0	0	0	0	902	2 tblsp=1 ounce

321

Appendix C

Definitions of Official Terms

THE terms and ingredients used in commercial dog food production are confusing to most people who are unfamiliar with them. Appendix C is an abbreviated list of definitions of terms and the ingredients used in making commercial dog foods and includes those most often seen on dog food labels.

Bran. The pericarp of the grain.

Cracklings. Residue after removal of fat from adipose tissue or skin of animals, by dry heat.

Fat. A substance composed primarily of triglycerides of fatty acids, and solid at room temperature.

Fines. Any material which will pass through a screen whose openings are immediately smaller than the specified minimum crumble size or pellet diameter.

Flakes. An ingredient rolled or cut into flat pieces, with or without prior steam conditioning.

Flour. Soft, finely-ground and bolted meal obtained from the milling of cereal grains, other seeds and products.

Germ. The embryo found in seeds and frequently separated from the bran and starch endosperm during milling.

Gluten. The tough, viscid, nitrogenous substance remaining when the flour or wheat or other grains is washed to remove the starch.

Grain. The seed from cereal plants.

Grease. Animal fats with a (melting) titer below $40\,^{\circ}\mathrm{C}$.

Grits. Coarsely ground grain from which the bran and germ have been removed, usually screened to uniform-sized particles.

Groats. Grain from which the hulls have been removed.

Hulls. Outer covering of grain or other seed.

Husks. The outer covering of kernels or seeds, especially when dry and membranous.

Lard. Rendered fat of swine.

Malt. Sprouted and steamed whole grain from which the radicle has been removed.

Meal. An ingredient which has been ground or otherwise reduced in particle size.

Middlings. A by-product of flour milling comprising several grades of granular particles containing different proportions of endosperm, bran, germ, each of which contains different levels of crude fiber.

Oil. A substance composed chiefly of triglycerides of fatty acids, and liquid at room temperature.

Pearled. Dehulled grains reduced by machine brushing into smaller smooth particles.

Polished. Having a smooth surface produced by a mechanical process, usually friction.

Pomace. Pulp from fruit.

Pulp. The solid residue remaining after extraction of juices from fruits, roots or stems.

Rolled. Having changed the shape and/or size of particles by compressing them between rollers.

Shorts. Fine particles of bran, germ, flour, or offal from the tail of the mill from commercial flour milling.

Solubles. Liquid containing dissolved substances obtained from processing animal or plant materials.

Starch. A white, granular polymer of plant origin. The principal part of seed endosperm.

Tallow. Animal fats with a (melting) titer above 40°C.

Trace minerals. Mineral nutrients required by animals in micro amounts only.

Viscera. All of the organs in the great cavity of the body, excluding contents of the intestinal tract.

Vitamins. Organic compounds that function as parts of enzymes systems essential for the transmission of energy and the regulation of metabolisms of the body.

Whey. The watery part of milk separated from the curd.

323

Official Definitions of Ingredients

The following list was abridged from the Official Publication of the Association of American Feed Control Officials. They are not in alphabetical order and may appear at random, but are listed in the same order as they appear in that publication.

Meat. The clean wholesome flesh derived from slaughtered mammals, limited to that part of the striate muscle which is skeletal or which is found in the tongue, diaphragm, heart, or esophagus. If it bears a name descriptive of its kind, it must correspond thereto.

Meat by-products. The non-rendered, clean, wholesome parts of the carcass of slaughtered mammals, such as lungs, liver, spleens, kidneys, brains, stomach, and intestines free of their contents. It does not include skin, horns, teeth, hoofs or bones.

Meat and bone meal. The finely ground, dry-rendered residue from mammal tissues exclusive of hair, hoof, horn, hide trimmings or manure and stomach contents, except as might occur unavoidably in any good factory practice.

Whale meat. The clean, dried undecomposed flesh of the whale, after a part of the oil has been removed, and not containing more than 7% salt.

Animal liver meal. The dried and ground liver from slaughtered mammals.

Animal liver and glandular meal. The dried and ground liver and other glandular tissues from slaughtered mammals.

Poultry parts. The clean, wholesome parts of dressed poultry characterized by large proportions of bone; such as necks, backs and wings.

Poultry by-products. The non-rendered clean parts of carcasses of slaughtered poultry such as heads, feet and viscera, free from fecal content and foreign matter.

Whole eviscerated chicken. The whole carcasses of chickens from which the feathers, head, feet and entrails have been removed.

Barley. At least 80% sound barley and not containing more than three percent heat damaged kernels, 6% foreign materials, 20% other grains or 10% wild oats.

Barley by-product. The entire by-product resulting from one of the processing procedures of barley products. (It is usually qualified by the processing name.)

Brewers dried grains. The dried, extracted residue of barley malt

324

alone or in mixture with other cereal grain or grain products resulting from the manufacturer of wort.

Corn distillers dried grains. The dried, coarse grains of whole stillage obtained after the removal of ethyl alcohol by distillation from the yeast fermentation of corn.

Animal fat. The fat obtained from the tissues of mammals and/or poultry in the commercial processes of rendering or extracting, and containing not less than 90% total fatty acids nor more than 2.5% unsaponifiable matter.

Vegetable fat, or oil. A product of vegetable origin obtained by extracting the oil from seeds or fruits which are commonly processed for edible purposes, and containing not less than 90% total fatty acids, nor more than 2% unsaponifiable matter or 1% insoluble matter. If the product bears a name descriptive of its kind, it must correspond thereto.

Ground corn. The entire corn kernel, ground or chopped, and containing not more than 4% foreign material.

Corn grits. The medium-sized hard flinty portions of ground corn, containing little or none of the bran or germ.

Corn flour. The fine-sized hard flinty portions of ground corn, containing little or none of the bran or germ.

Toasted corn flakes. A product obtained by running cracked corn which has been aspirated and properly tempered, over smooth flaking rolls, and subsequently dried, cooled and toasted.

Malto dextrins. The incomplete hydrolysis product of corn starch. The solids must not contain less than 13% nor more than 28% reducing sugars like dextrose.

Fish meal. The clean, dried, ground tissues of undecomposed whole fish or fish cuttings, with or without the extraction of part of the oil, and containing no more than 7% salt.

Dried skimmed milk. The residue obtained by drying defatted milk, containing no more than 8% moisture.

Dried whey. The residue obtained from drying whey. It must contain a minimum of 65% lactose.

Casein. The solid residue obtained by acid or rennet coagulation of defatted milk. It must contain a minimum of 80% crude protein.

Dried whole milk. The residue obtained by drying milk. It must contain no more than 8% moisture and at least 26% milk fat.

Steamed bone meal. The dried and ground product, sterilized by

325

cooking undecomposed bones with steam under pressure and may or may not contain the associated grease, gelatin and meat fiber.

Dried beet pulp. The dried residue from sugar beets which have been cleaned and freed from crown leaves and sand, and which have been extracted in the process of making sugar.

Dried tomato pomace. A dried mixture of tomato skins, pulp, and crushed seeds.

Dried bakery product. A mixture of bread, cookies, cake, crackers, flours and doughs which has been mechanically separated from non-edible material, artifically dried and ground.

Cane molasses. A by-product of the manufacturing or refining of sucrose from sugar cane.

Oat groats. Cleaned oats with the hulls removed.

Brewers rice. The small fragments of rice kernels that have been separated from the larger kernels of milled rice.

Soy grits and *soy flour.* The screened and graded product remaining after removal of most of the oil from selected sound, cleaned and dehulled soybeans.

Soybean meal. The product obtained by grinding the cake, chips or flakes remaining after removal of most of the oil from soybeans. (The type of meal is usually designated by the type of extraction process.)

Wheat shorts. The fine particles of wheat bran, wheat germ, wheat flour, and the offal from the "tail of the mill". It must contain not more than 7% crude fiber.

Wheat red dog. The offal from the "tail of the mill", together with some fine particles of wheat bran, wheat germ, and wheat flour. It must not contain more than 4% crude fiber.

Brewers dried yeast. The dried, non-fermentative, non-extracted yeast of the botanical classification *Saccharomyces,* resulting as the by-product from the brewing of beer or ale.

Torula dried yeast. The dried, non-fermentative yeast of botanical classification *Torulopsis* which has been separated from the medium in which it was propagated. It must contain not less than 40% crude protein.

326

Appendix D

Chemical Content of Some Ingredients of Commercial Dog Foods

THE ingredients found in commercial dog foods number into the thousands. Most dog foods, however, contain as their basic ingredients certain staple items. Appendix D is an abbreviated list of these items. It is included, not to make food technologists out of anyone, but to give those people who feed their dogs commercial foods a little better insight into what is going into those foods. These ingredients are not listed in terms of a Nutrient Index Number, but in the conventional terms of percent and grams per 100 grams.

APPENDIX D

Commercial Ingredients

INGREDIENT	Protein %	Fat %	Carbohydrate %	Ash %	Fiber %	Calcium %	Phosphorus %	Calories per 100 gm.	REMARKS
Beef	16.0	19.0	.3	.7	0	.02	.22	236	Fat low in essential fatty acids.
Beef By-products	17.9	4.9	1.0	1.5	0	.02	.40	119	Inexpensive protein source, variable quality.
Bone, green, ground	17.5	23.0	3.5	16.0	1.0	6.5	3.5	291	Preferred to bone meal.
Bone Meal, steamed	12.1	3.2	5.9	71.8	2	28.9	13.6	101	
Brewer's Dried Yeast	44.6	1.1	37.9	6.4	3	.13	1.43	399	Also rich in B-complex vitamins.
Cane Molasses	3.2	.1	63.6	8.1	0	.89	.08	312	Sugars sometimes cause digestive upset.
Casein	81.8	.5	4.4	3.3	0	.61	.99	349	Excellent animal protein source.
Cellulose	0	0	0	.1	92.0	0	0	0	Used to improve food's texture.
Chicken, whole	17.0	12.5	1.0	3.5	0	.81	.56	184	
Corn Dist. Dried Grains	27.1	9.3	41.0	2.6	12.0	.09	.37	504	
Corn Meal (Grits	8.9	3.4	72.8	1.9	2.0	.02	.16	357	
Corn Gluten Meal	42.9	2.3	39.4	2.4	4.0	.16	.40	350	

328

APPENDIX D

Commercial Ingredients

INGREDIENT	Protein %	Fat %	Carbohydrate %	Ash %	Fiber %	Calcium %	Phosphorus %	Calories per 100 gm.	REMARKS
Corn Oil	0	100	0	0	0	0	0	890	Excellent fat energy source.
Corn Starch	.3	.1	90.0	0	.05	0	0	364	Excellent carbohydrate energy source.
Corn Syrup	.3	0	64.7	8.0	0			259	Sugars sometimes cause digestive upset.
Cracked Barley	12.5	1.1	66.4	3.0	5	.09	.47	474	
Dicalcium Phosphate	0	0	0	78.1	0	27.0	19.1	0	Common inorganic mineral source.
Dried Bakery Product									
Dried Beet Pulp	9.1	.6	50.7	3.6	19	.68	.10	388	Used to improve food's texture.
Dried Skim Milk	33.0	1.5	52.0	8.2	0	1.30	1.03	362	Excellent animal protein source.
Dried Whey	17.1	1.9	67.5	9.7	0	.68	.57	339	
Eggs, whole, dried	46.0	38.0	8.0	4.0	0	.19	.77	558	Excellent animal protein source.
Fish Flour	61.3	7.7	2.4	19.6	1	5.49	2.81	324	
Grain Sorghams, ground	11.1	3.0	70.9	2.0	2.0	.05	.35	445	

APPENDIX D

Commercial Ingredients

INGREDIENT	Protein %	Fat %	Carbohydrate %	Ash %	Fiber %	Calcium %	Phosphorus %	Calories per 100 gm.	REMARKS
Horsemeat	19.5	5.5	1.5	1.0	0	.01	.15	133	
Horsemeat By-products	16.0	4.9	2.3	1.3	0	.04	.32	118	Quality highly variable
Lard	0	100	0	0	0	0	0	890	
Liver Meal	66.5	15.1	4.4	6.0	1	.50	1.25		Excellent animal protein source.
Malto-Dextrins									
Meat and Bone Meal	50.6	9.5			2				Quality of protein can vary somewhat.
Oat Groats	16.7	5.8	63.3	2.2	3	.07	.45	372	
Oat Meal	16.1	6.3	63.4	2.2	3	.07	.43	378	
Pearled Barley	11.6	1.9	67.8	2.7	5	.09	.47	335	Whole grains found in premium grade foods.
Potato Flour	5.9	.5	70.7	11.9	1			311	
Poultry By-products									Quality highly variable
Rice Grits	8.1	.8	77.3	.8	1	.03	.15	349	

330

APPENDIX D

Commercial Ingredients

INGREDIENT	Protein %	Fat %	Carbohydrate %	Ash %	Fiber %	Calcium %	Phosphorus %	Calories per 100 gm.	REMARKS
Soy Flour and Grits	52.0	.8	32.6	5.6	2	.33	.62	346	Excellent plant protein source.
Soybean Meal	45.8	.9	30.5	5.8	6	.32	.67	342	Excellent plant protein source.
Tankage	59.8	8.1	0.7	21.4	2	5.94	3.17	315	Less desirable protein supplement.
Toasted Corn Flakes	8.1	.4	85.0	2.9	.6	.01	.06	385	
Toasted Wheat Flakes	10.8	1.6	80.2	3.6	1.7	.05	.33	355	
Tomato Pomace	21.7	13.0	24.1	4.2	29	.28	.57	300	
Torula Dried Yeast	48.3	2.5	32.4	7.8	2	.57	1.68	333	
Whale Meat	78.9	6.8	1.3	4.0	1	.25	.56	382	Little used now due to scarcity of whales.
Wheat Bran	16.0	4.1	52.8	6.1	10.0	.14	1.17	312	
Wheat Red Dog	18.0	3.6	62.9	2.5	2.0	.08	.52	356	
Wheat Shorts	17.2	4.6	57.2	4.0	7.0	.10	.89	331	

331

Appendix E

Handy Figures for Dog Feeders

Common Household Measures (liquid)

1 teaspoonful (tsp)	=	4 cc	=	$\frac{1}{8}$ ounce (oz)
1 tablespoonful (tblsp)	=	15 cc	=	$\frac{1}{2}$ ounce
8 tablespoonfuls	=	4 ounces	=	$\frac{1}{2}$ cup
1 cup	=	8 ounces	=	$\frac{1}{2}$ pint (pt)
2 cups	=	16 ounces	=	1 pint
4 cups	=	32 ounces	=	1 quart (qt)
16 cups	=	128 ounces	=	1 gallon (gal)
1 dog food can	=	16 ounces	=	1 pint

Average Caloric Densities

canned dog food	=	34 calories per ounce, or 550 per pound
soft-moist dog food	=	84 calories per ounce, or 1350 per pound
dry dog food	=	94 calories per ounce, or 1500 per pound

Corn Oil Values

1 teaspoonful corn oil	=	36 calories
1 tablespoonful corn oil	=	135 calories
$\frac{1}{2}$ cup corn oil	=	1080 calories

Appendix F

Normal Growth Curves

ONE of the best measures of a food's adequacy is its ability to support normal growth. A convenient measure of normal growth is body weight. Appendix F lists graphs upon which have been recorded the normal growth (body weight) curves of the common body sizes of most dogs. In addition to their use in evaluating dog foods, these curves will prove of increasing value to any dog feeder as they become more skilled at the art.

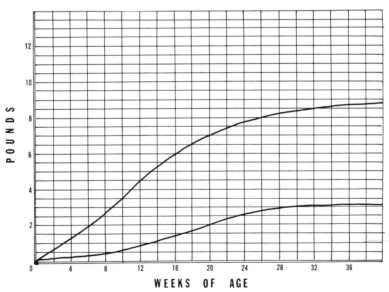

Figure F-1. A normal growth curve for dogs weighing an average of 6 pounds as an adult.

333

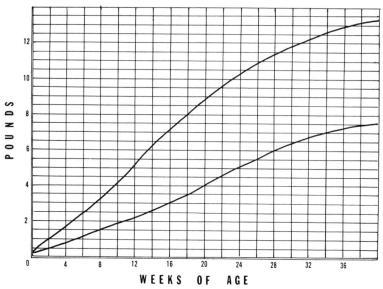

Figure F-2. A normal growth curve for dogs weighing an average of 10 pounds as an adult.

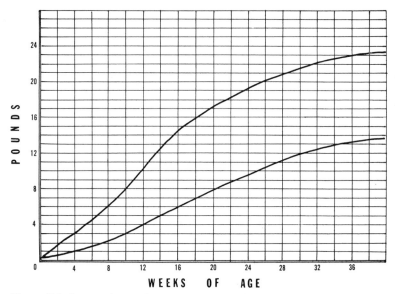

Figure F-3. A normal growth curve for dogs weighing an average of 18 pounds as an adult.

334

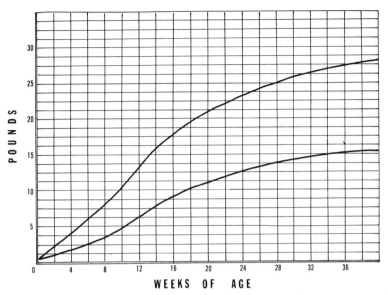

Figure F-4. A normal growth curve for dogs weighing an average of 20 pounds as an adult.

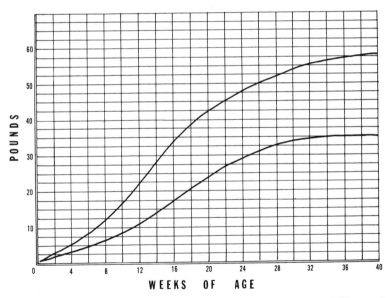

Figure F-5. A normal growth curve for dogs weighing an average of 50 pounds as an adult.

335

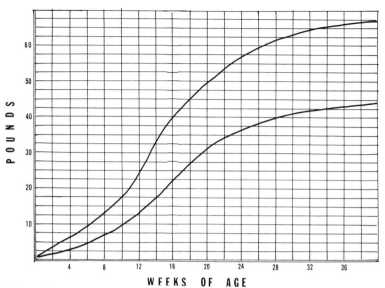

Figure F-6. A normal growth curve for dogs weighing an average of 70 pounds as an adult.

336